A HANDBOOK

ON

RETIREMENT

"Sunset to Sunrise: A Guide to a Fulfilling Retirement"

BY

M.N.ASHRAF

Preface

Hello, I'm M.N. Ashraf, a retired Mechanical Engineer who dedicated nearly 44 years to the world of power generation. Upon retiring at 66, I anticipated a well-deserved period of relaxation after decades of hard work. However, I soon found myself in an entirely unfamiliar reality. After a life structured by purpose and routine, I suddenly had no job, no responsibilities, and no clear direction. Each day stretched out endlessly from sunrise to sunset, leading to sleepless nights, frustration, and even health issues.

This experience is not uncommon among retirees. Many individuals face challenges in adjusting to the unstructured time and lack of routine that retirement brings. It's essential to recognize these feelings and seek ways to find new purpose and fulfillment in this new chapter of life.

Remember, retirement is an opportunity to redefine your life's purpose and explore new passions. Embrace this time as a chance for personal growth and discovery.

As the world grappled with the unprecedented upheaval of the COVID-19 pandemic, life as we knew it came to a standstill. The once vibrant rhythms of daily existence were replaced by an eerie stillness, casting a shadow over our collective psyche. Amidst this global crisis, I found myself not only confronting the universal challenges posed by the virus but also navigating the uncharted waters of retirement without a clear plan. The convergence of these events led to profound psychological distress, as I faced the daunting specters of boredom, uncertainty, and disillusionment in isolation.

The psychological impact of the pandemic on older adults has been significant, with increased feelings of loneliness and mental health challenges.

Reflecting on this period, I recognize the resilience required to endure such trials and the importance of seeking purpose even in the most trying times. This journey has underscored the value of adaptability and the human spirit's capacity to find meaning amidst adversity.

But one morning, while sipping tea, an idea sparked. Why not channel my years of experience into writing? Not only could it keep me engaged, but perhaps I could offer something of value to others. The thought ignited a fire in me, and with it, a sense of purpose began to return.

Of course, the next question was, *What should I write about?* What topics could be meaningful? As I reflected on my life, both professional and personal, I decided to focus on subjects that resonated deeply within me. This process gave birth to a series of books, including ***A Handbook on Gas Turbines***, ***Sands of Time: My 39 Years of Life and Work in Saudi Arabia (a memoir)***, ***Kazzab Nagar*** (written in Urdu, which translates to "Town of Liars"), ***Hand book on Retirement - Sunset to Sunrise: A Guide to a fulfilling Retirement*** and ***Wisdom Across Generations***, **"Conversations with My Great-Grandchildren"- Fiction or Fact?**

I'm thrilled to announce that my literary journey has yielded two published works, both available on Amazon in digital and print formats, with one also featured on Google Play. My third creation, *Kazzab Nagar*, is accessible exclusively in digital format on Google Play. Now, I am elated to introduce my fourth book, ***A Handbook on Retirement - Sunset to Sunrise: A Guide to a Fulfilling Retirement***. This project holds a special place in my heart, as it encapsulates my personal experiences and the practical challenges retirees often encounter. Within its pages, I offer forward-looking strategies to navigate these hurdles with foresight, empowering readers to address them gracefully before they become overwhelming.

Embarking on this writing journey has been a transformative experience, allowing me to channel my reflections and insights into works that resonate with readers. The process of crafting each book has deepened my understanding of the subjects I explore and strengthened my connection with a diverse audience. I am committed to continuing this path, sharing knowledge and stories that inspire and guide others through various stages of life.

This book isn't just about facts or tips; it reflects a personal journey—from pre-retirement through the twists and turns of post-retirement life. It tackles essential topics like financial planning, emotional and psychological preparation, health and wellness, lifestyle changes, social relationships, legacy and estate planning, and even legal considerations. My goal is to guide readers through the often overwhelming transition from a structured work life to the unknowns of retirement.

I'm confident that once you open this book, you'll be drawn into its pages, finding practical wisdom that resonates with your own journey. I've done extensive research, studying the philosophy of life, the issues that arise in our later years, and the social dynamics within families. My aim is to help others navigate those challenges when they are at their most vulnerable.

I warmly invite you to dive into this book. I believe once you begin, you won't want to put it down until the very end.

I extend my deepest gratitude to my beloved family, whose unwavering support has been the cornerstone of this endeavor. My dear wife, Monawar, has been my steadfast companion throughout this journey—her patience, encouragement, and quiet strength gave me the courage to move forward, even in moments of doubt.

To my elder son, Nadeem, and my younger son, Naseem—your generous support, both in spirit and in resources, made it possible for me to stay focused and achieve the goals I had set for myself. Your belief in my work meant more than words can express.

My dearest daughter, Dr. Nahid, has been a constant source of motivation. Her faith in this project and her inspiring words reminded me time and again of the value of perseverance and purpose.

I am also deeply thankful to my son-in-law, Dr. Fahad, and my beloved daughter-in-law, Engr. Sharmin. Their positive energy, words of encouragement—whether spoken or silent—and eager anticipation to see this book completed added an extra layer of meaning to my efforts.

To each one of you—thank you from the depths of my heart for your trust, your faith, and your encouragement. Your presence in my life has not only uplifted my work but has also made this journey one of profound joy and fulfillment.

I hold deep admiration for my innocent and curious grandchildren, Mariyam, Ibrahim & Yousuf aged between 7 and 11 years. Their wide-eyed wonder and excitement about the progress of my books, from writing to publication, fill my heart with joy. Their sweet, toddling words of encouragement, though simple, carry profound meaning and inspire me to keep going on this journey.Their vibrant imagination and creative ideas breathe new life into my work, sparking a sense of pride as they eagerly talk about following in my footsteps—embracing the art of writing to address the needs of our modern society.Thank you, my dearest young companions, for your unwavering belief in me and your loving gestures. You are not just my grandchildren but also my cherished colleagues, bringing immense pride and happiness into my life.

I am equally grateful to my esteemed colleagues and cherished friends, who not only supported me but also offered valuable advice and insights. Their thoughtful comments on the excerpts I shared helped shape this work into its final form. To all of you, my deepest thanks for being an integral part of this journey.

Disclaimer: The insights and guidance presented in ***Sunset to Sunrise: A Guide to a Fulfilling Retirement*** are intended for informational and inspirational purposes only. While every effort has been made to ensure the accuracy and relevance of the content, the author and publisher do not assume responsibility for any outcomes resulting from the application of the information provided.

Readers are encouraged to consult with qualified professionals—such as financial advisors, healthcare providers, and legal experts—before making decisions related to retirement planning, health, or other personal matters.

This book does not offer professional financial, medical, or legal advice. The author and publisher disclaim any liability for any loss or risk incurred as a consequence of the use and application, either directly or indirectly, of any information contained in this book.

The goal of this work is to inspire thoughtful reflection and meaningful discussion, fostering a sense of purpose and joy in the retirement journey.

Sincerely,

M.N.Ashraf

Introduction

The global market is flooded with books on retirement, written by renowned writers, scholars, and philosophers, but most of these focus on experiences in the Western world. These works offer valuable insights, yet they often overlook the diverse cultural, social, and religious contexts of retirement across the globe. In my book, I've attempted to address retirement from a truly global perspective—whether you're in the East or West, North or South—taking into account the unique social, cultural, and religious norms that shape how retirees are perceived and treated in different societies. I also explore what the major religions have to say about the value and role of the elderly.

How should a retired person be treated in different societies? What are the responsibilities of families, communities, and nations towards their retirees? And why is the world, despite its progress, still failing to address the pressing issues faced by the elderly with the care and honesty they deserve? In developed countries, governments are struggling to create solutions that meet the evolving needs of retirees. Meanwhile, in many developing nations, the plight of retirees is largely ignored, overshadowed by the race towards economic growth and events like hosting G20 summits. For instance, while India recently spent INR 4,100 Crore (USD 48.81 million) on the G20 summit, nearly 813.5 million of its population rely on government handouts just to survive.

The internal struggles faced by retired and elderly persons are reaching a crisis point, yet governments across the world—whether democratic, dictatorial, or monarchal—seem more focused on clinging to power than addressing these urgent issues. Retirees, who make up a significant portion of the population (nearly 10% in 2021 of the total population of the world and expected to reach 17% by 2050), are often left to fend for themselves, with little support from those in power. The world today faces unprecedented challenges: countries are divided, wars are being fought, and instead of investing in poverty reduction or education, nations are spending trillions on conflicts, such as in Gaza, Ukraine, and other parts of the world. Genocides are being carried out by powerful nations against the innocent people of impoverished and underprivileged countries.The resources that could be used to improve the lives of retirees, elderly and other vulnerable groups are instead being wasted in senseless destruction.

We have yet to learn from the mistakes of our past. Despite the haunting memories of Iraq, Afghanistan, and Vietnam, and the tragedies of two world wars that claimed over 106 million lives, the relentless cycle of violence endures, with countless more lives lost—both seen and unseen. International bodies like the UN security Council, the International Court of Justice seem paralyzed amid these crises. It's as though the world is held captive by those who choose to overlook humanity's true needs—such as the dignity and well-being of retirees, elderly & underprivileged—and instead pursue power and destruction. Ironically, in our so-called 'civilized' world, leaders speak grandly of human rights, yet they often stand among the first to violate them.

When a person retires, typically around the age of 60 or beyond, they're often compared to a car that's served its purpose, used up most of its reliable years, and is now heading towards a destination unknown—a "no man's land." Just like a car on a long, uncertain journey, your body and mind can "break down" at any moment, and without proper preparation, you may not have the means to fix it. Imagine your car's engine overheating on the highway, but you can't afford the repairs. Fuel consumption rises, the air conditioning falters, and soon, the car is no longer fit for the road.

The same applies to life after retirement. The daily challenges only grow if not addressed properly. You may have purchased or renovated your home when you were at the peak of your career, but now, with no regular and proper income, you're living off the savings and investments you made during your working years. Will those returns be enough to cover the cost of your food, medication, clothing, and the maintenance of your home, including aging air conditioning and heating systems? Can you keep up with the rising costs of electricity, gas, water, garbage collection, and garden upkeep?

The gap between the rich and poor is widening at an alarming rate across the globe, particularly in underdeveloped and developing nations. For many, even the dream of a comfortable lifestyle feels out of reach. Instead, hunger and deprivation are becoming more severe with time, driven by the unchecked expansion of a global capitalist system. The rich continue to accumulate wealth, while the poor struggle more than ever to make ends meet.

In Western nations, particularly the U.S., the situation is dire for the elderly. Homelessness among older adults is rising sharply, with many facing skyrocketing housing costs on fixed incomes. As they age, their health needs grow, but their financial resources do not. Older adults have become one of the fastest-growing groups experiencing homelessness, a heartbreaking trend that shows no signs of slowing.

The present situation of retirees and the elderly, particularly during their twilight years, paints a poignant picture. As their mental and physical abilities gradually fade, the care they so desperately need in today's advanced society often falls short. Family members, overwhelmed by fast-paced lifestyles, and communities struggling with shifting priorities, frequently delegate this responsibility to old-age homes. Unfortunately, many of these institutions, constrained by financial limitations and systemic neglect, fail to provide the adequate care and support these individuals deserve.

This growing disconnect highlights a pressing issue: the global community must urgently address the challenges of elder care with compassion and collective responsibility. Ensuring dignity, support, and quality of life for our aging population is not just a societal duty—it is a measure of our humanity.

To compound the issue, **drug**, **alcohol and Tobacco** use among the elderly is on the rise, contributing to worsening health conditions and deepening financial troubles. These factors create a vicious cycle, making it harder for older adults to break free from poverty and homelessness, while exacerbating the global divide between the wealthy and the struggling.

As you enter old age, life often brings more challenges, hardships, and illnesses than when you were younger. Picture yourself as an aging driver of a car that has given 90% of its service life. You're navigating bumpy roads, surrounded by heavy traffic. The car's tires are worn down, and you can't even replace the flat because you lack a proper spare. The brakes are unreliable, and the headlights are dimming. A single misstep could lead to disaster. And when it comes to upgrading the car, your pockets are empty.

This is the reality many elderly and retirees face—but it doesn't have to be the end of the road. In this book, you'll find practical solutions to help you drive safely and navigate through these challenges with confidence and care.

With technological advancements and modernization, life expectancy has increased, but the facilities required to sustain a good quality of life in retirement have diminished. This is especially true in the third world, where limited opportunities and harsh climatic conditions exacerbate the struggles faced by the elderly. Governments must step up to address these issues, but unfortunately, many seem more focused on short-term gains rather than ensuring the long-term wellbeing of their aging populations.

In this book, I've explored these challenges in depth, offering insights and practical solutions for retirees to navigate this critical stage of life. Whether you're about to retire or already in the midst of it, the journey is far from over—but with the right preparation and mindset, it's one that can be embraced with confidence.

This book offers thoughtful and comprehensive solutions to the many challenges retirees and elderly individuals face in life's later stages. Of course, not all problems are identical, and the ways of handling them vary from person to person, place to place, and situation to situation.

Addressing these issues requires wisdom, personal capacity, and support from family, society, and governmental institutions. It is often said that for every 100 problems, there are 101 solutions. As you explore the different chapters of this book, you'll discover a range of solutions that may bring relief to your troubled life.

This book serves as a mirror reflecting the realities of our global society today. As a retired engineer with nearly 44 years of experience in power generation, I have walked the path of success, faced the same challenges many encounter, and now strive to navigate life's complexities with wisdom. At this stage of life, I focus on understanding the issues, balancing needs, and limiting desires—drawing lessons from past mistakes while keeping my vehicle steady on life's bumpy roads.

This is not the time to lose confidence or succumb to panic. Instead, embrace contentment, set realistic goals, and cherish your health. Never let hope for a brighter future fade, for you are not a useless being but a treasure trove of wisdom. Your experience is a gift to future generations.

I invite you to explore this book, which may inspire you to find strength, purpose, and peace in this journey. Take care, stay safe, and keep contributing to a better tomorrow.

Table of Contents

"A Glimpse into Pre-Retirement: Navigating the Road Ahead"

Though we are members of a so-called civilized world, we are now passing through a crisis that has reshaped the very way we live. The relentless march of economic, industrial, and technological development has driven us toward a materialistic existence, leading to a culture of cronyism. From the earliest days of childhood, our society instills in us the lessons of wealth—how to make money, how to make more money, how to become rich, and, ultimately, how to be the richest. Parents guide their children toward the pursuit of financial success, often regardless of the cost, as though this is the only path to a fulfilling life.

This materialistic shift has birthed a life of endless struggle. The notion of rest is replaced by a constant, gnawing pressure to succeed, no matter the personal toll. We live in an age defined by competition, where survival belongs only to the fittest, to those who can outshine even the best. From infancy, we are raised on this belief. As William Shakespeare so aptly described in ***As You Like It***, we move through life's stages—infant, schoolboy, lover, soldier, judge, and finally, old man—before we retire and, in extreme old age, revert to a childlike state, dependent and frail.

The race for excellence starts early, from primary school to higher education, and extends into our careers. The motivation is always the same: to achieve better education and secure the best possible career. We are groomed for a career-oriented lifestyle that promises prospects but seldom delivers peace. The result is a life spent in perpetual exhaustion, struggling without end, as if success alone can provide meaning. Yet in this pursuit, we often lose sight of what truly matters, spending every moment striving but never finding rest for our minds, let alone our souls.

Most of us follow the same path as the rest of society, swept along by the tide of globalization. We run this race, chasing after something we deem "good" but rarely stopping to question what it is we're truly after. Our careers begin much the same way—driven by ambition, we do whatever we can to secure our place, treating career advancement as both milestone and destination. Sometimes, we succeed, while other times, we stumble, never quite reaching the summit of our aspirations. The cycle of success and failure continues throughout our lives, binding us to a rhythm of constant striving.

In the pursuit of better prospects, we find ourselves moving from city to city, country to country, shifting from one company to the next, from institutions to enterprises, sometimes even venturing into entrepreneurship. Along the way, we sacrifice much, telling ourselves it's all for career growth. Many of us rise through the ranks, becoming General Managers, Directors, even Executive Directors and Chairmen, rewarded with occasional boosts to our savings accounts.

In our relentless pursuit of career success, we pushed ourselves to the brink, enduring sleepless nights filled with stress and strain. Along the way, we unknowingly sacrificed our most precious asset—our health. The toll was heavy, manifesting in chronic conditions like diabetes, high blood pressure, heart problems, insomnia, and other severe illnesses that now loom as threats to our very existence. It's a sobering reality to admit that this downward spiral was the cost of our unending race in the quest for a career.

Yet, in the whirlwind of ambition, we become so immersed in our work that we lose sight of time, our health, and the true quality of our lives. Life moves steadily forward, and in our unending toil, we often forget that we, too, are aging. It's like being laborers working relentlessly through the day—only to look up as the sun sets and realize that time has slipped through our fingers, leaving us standing in the twilight, no longer able to continue.

And so, just as suddenly, we arrive at the inevitable point of retirement. Whether we have succeeded or fallen short in our ambitions, time declares us retired. The world no longer cares for the merits of our past; it simply informs us that our time has come. We enter the twilight of life, growing weak with age, inching closer to the stage Shakespeare described —the old man, "sans teeth, sans eyes, sans taste, sans everything," once again like a child, dependent on others.

This is the reality of our journey, a reflection of life's cycle—an unending race toward an elusive goal, punctuated by fleeting moments of success, followed by the quiet, inevitable return to dependence.

As we approach retirement, we find ourselves pausing to reflect on the long and winding journey that has shaped our lives—a relentless pursuit of dreams driven by unwavering determination and an unyielding struggle to carve out a better future. Along the way, we experienced soaring triumphs and humbling failures, celebrated victories, and endured setbacks, each moment etching its indelible mark on who we are.

Now, in the calm of retirement's embrace, looking back on those tales feels like reopening the pages of a well-worn book—stories that shaped us once but no longer define who we have become. Instead of being bound by those chapters, we begin to see them as stepping stones toward a deeper understanding of life and the possibilities that still lie ahead.

Some of us dwell on missed opportunities, feeling the weight of what could have been, while others take pride in their accomplishments, celebrating their journeys in unique ways. Yet, the truly enlightened among us are those who recognize that the past, with all its joys and regrets, is but a stepping stone. They turn their gaze forward, embracing the path that lies ahead.

These are the wise souls who choose to leave behind the baggage of yesterday, focusing instead on navigating the uncertain road ahead. They prepare for the challenges yet to come, addressing the bumps and bends of the future with grace, courage, and a renewed sense of purpose. After all, life, even in its later chapters, is a journey still worth embracing with open arms and an open heart.

1.0 Tracing the Origin of the Word 'Retire

The word "retire" has an interesting origin, tracing back to the French verb *retirer*, which means "to withdraw" or "to retreat." It combines the prefix "re-" (signifying "back" or "again") and "tirer" (meaning "to pull" or "draw"). The term entered the English language in the late 16th century, originally describing a soldier's retreat from battle. By the 17th century, it expanded to describe stepping away from an occupation or public life, eventually taking on its modern meaning—leaving one's career, typically due to age or health.

Here's how the word "retire" functions in different grammatical forms, all reflecting the central idea of ending one's working life:

1. **Verb: "Retire"** – To permanently stop working, often due to age or health concerns.
2. **Noun: "Retiree"** – A person who has left their job and entered retirement.
3. **Adjective: "Retired"** – Describing someone who has stopped working, usually after reaching a certain age.
4. **Noun: "Retirement"** – The act or process of leaving one's career, marking the transition from active work to rest or other pursuits.

This journey from a military retreat to the peaceful withdrawal from professional life gives "retirement" a rich historical context, reminding us that it's not just an end, but a conscious retreat toward new beginnings.

1.1 "Defining Retirement: Social, Cultural, and Religious Perspectives"

Retirement is the phase of life when a person permanently withdraws from their regular work or professional activities, typically after reaching a certain age or fulfilling specific career requirements depending on the individual circumstances. It is often viewed as a transition from the structured routine of employment to a period of relaxation, personal pursuits, or other forms of self-directed activities. Retirement can be seen as a time for individuals to reflect on their life's work, enjoy leisure time, focus on hobbies, spend time with family, or even engage in new ventures, volunteer work, or part-time activities.

Retirement also carries financial, social, and emotional aspects, as it often involves relying on savings, pensions, or government benefits for income. It can bring both a sense of freedom and a shift in identity, as individuals navigate the loss of the structured roles and responsibilities they held during their working years.

Different philosophical & spiritual views on the concept of retirement

The concept of retirement across Islam, Christianity, Judaism, Buddhism, Hinduism, and Sikhism shares common themes of spiritual growth, continued purpose, and social contribution, though each tradition has its unique interpretations. Here's a summary of retirement in these five religions:

1. Islam

- Work as Worship: Work is considered a form of worship and a lifelong duty, as long as one is capable.
- Spiritual Reflection and Charity: Retirement is seen as a time to increase devotion, prayer, and charity, preparing for the afterlife while continuing to contribute to family and society.
- Respect for Elders: Islam emphasizes respect for the elderly, and caring for older people is a key aspect of familial and societal duty.

2. Christianity

- Lifelong Service: Work is part of a divine calling, and there is no set retirement from serving God.
- Rest and Reflection: Retirement is viewed as a time for rest, increased spiritual devotion, volunteering, and mentoring others.
- Community Contribution: The elderly continue to serve their communities through prayer, guidance, and charitable work.

3. Judaism

- Work as a Mitzvah (a precept or commandment): Work is considered sacred, and retirement allows for more focus on spiritual growth and study.
- Honoring the Elderly: The elderly are seen as repositories of wisdom, and their role shifts towards teaching and guiding younger generations.

- Balance of Work and Rest: The Jewish rhythm of work and Shabbat (rest) extends into retirement, emphasizing reflection, Torah study, and continued societal involvement.

4. Buddhism

- Detachment from Material Life: Retirement is an opportunity to cultivate detachment from worldly attachments, focusing on inner peace and enlightenment.
- Meditation and Spiritual Practice: Older age is seen as a time for deepening one's meditation practice and preparing for nirvana (liberation from the cycle of rebirth - a place of perfect peace and happiness).
- Continued Compassionate Action: Even in retirement, Buddhists are encouraged to continue practicing compassion and mindfulness, helping others on their path.

5. Hinduism

- Stages of Life (Ashramas - a religious retreat): Retirement corresponds to Vanaprastha (the forest-dweller stage), a period of withdrawal from material pursuits to focus on spiritual growth.
- Spiritual Detachment: It is a time for deeper meditation, study of scriptures, and preparing for the final stage of life (Sannyasa - complete renunciation or purification of every thing), aimed at attaining moksha (liberation - the freedom from the eternal cycle of life, death and rebirth).
- Mentorship and Community: Retirees often become spiritual guides, sharing wisdom with the younger generation while contributing to society through service and reflection.

6. Sikhism

- Retirement aligns with the spiritual goal of living a balanced life guided by the principles of *Naam Japna* (meditation on God's name), *Kirat Karni* (honest living), and *Vand Chakna* (sharing with others). Philosophically, it is a time to shift focus from material ambitions to inner reflection and service to humanity.

- Spiritually, retirement is seen as an opportunity to deepen one's connection with the Divine through prayer, selfless service (*sewa*), and humility. Sikhs are encouraged to remain active in their faith and community, viewing this stage as preparation for merging with the eternal truth (*Waheguru*), transcending worldly attachments.

Key Themes Across Religions:

1. Continued Purpose: Retirement is not seen as an end but as a transition into deeper spiritual practice, guidance, and social contribution.
2. Spiritual Growth: Each tradition emphasizes that retirement is a time to focus on prayer, meditation, study, and connection with the divine.
3. Care and Respect for the Elderly: Elders are honored for their wisdom, and their role often shifts towards mentorship and leadership within the family and community.
4. Detachment from Material Concerns: Particularly in Buddhism and Hinduism, retirement is seen as a time to detach from worldly pursuits and focus on spiritual liberation.

Conclusion:

Retirement across Islam, Christianity, Judaism, Buddhism, Hinduism, and Sikhism is viewed as a period of reflection, spiritual growth, and continued contribution to family and society. While each religion offers unique perspectives, they all emphasize that later life is a time for deeper purpose, wisdom-sharing, and preparing for the next phase of existence, whether in this life or beyond.

Modern Ideas

The **modern** philosophy of retirement views this phase of life as an **opportunity for personal growth**, reinvention, and continuous engagement with life. It is no longer about a full stop to work, but rather a **shift toward fulfilling passions**, maintaining health and wellness, and contributing to society in new ways. Financial independence, active aging, lifelong learning, and maintaining social connections are key themes that characterize modern retirement. This phase is now seen as a **rich, dynamic period** that allows individuals to pursue purpose and meaning on their terms, with the freedom to shape their lives based on personal interests and aspirations

In the Western world, the concept of retirement is generally viewed as a significant life transition, marking the end of one's formal working career and the beginning of a new phase focused on personal pursuits, leisure, and often reflection.

"Lessons Learned: Insights from the Theories Above"

Never let panic or nervousness cloud your retirement journey. Retirement comes to us all when age and experience reach a natural point in life. This new chapter simply calls for a shift in perspective—"a chance to discover a unique, fulfilling path beyond the conventional." Don't surrender or stop contributing as long as your health allows and you feel capable. Draw from your valuable experiences and consider part-time or consulting roles you can do remotely from home. The additional income, combined with carefully planned retirement benefits, can provide welcome support during life's unexpected rainy days.

Let me share a truly inspiring story that holds a wonderful lesson for us all. It was mid-2020, the peak of the COVID-19 pandemic, and I was in San Jose, California, US, staying with my son, a software engineer. The whole world seemed to pause—workplaces were closed, social gatherings halted, and silence filled the air. During this time, my son's car battery died, and with the service life of the battery expired, replacement was the only option. But how to replace it when stepping out meant facing a world gripped by fear of the virus?

Then, we found a remarkable solution: an 85-year-old retired army officer who, even at this age, was still serving his community by offering home services. We contacted him and provided the details of the battery specifications, and within two hours, he arrived at our doorstep, wearing a face mask. He calmly replaced the battery on his own, charging only a nominal fee. What courage and dedication from a man well into his retirement!

This is the spirit of retirement—staying active, resilient, and connected to life. Let's salute these individuals who remind us that age is no barrier to purpose and dignity. For those already retired or nearing retirement, this story offers a powerful reminder: retirement is not an end but a new beginning, full of potential for those willing to embrace it.

Different views of different great authors, Scientists & Philosophers on Retirement of a person

Erik Erikson's (He was a German-American developmental psychologist and psychoanalyst, best known for his theory of **psychosocial development**) theory of retirement, embedded in his **Ego Integrity vs. Despair** stage of psychosocial development, emphasizes the emotional and psychological aspects of aging. Retirement is seen as a period of **reflection, life review, and resolution** of past experiences. The key challenge is to achieve **ego integrity**, finding meaning and satisfaction in life, while avoiding **despair**, which arises from regret or dissatisfaction. By accepting the totality of life experiences and embracing the aging process, retirees can develop wisdom, leave a meaningful legacy, and approach the end of life with peace and fulfillment. Erikson's approach provides a nuanced view of retirement.

Retirement is like a long vacation in Las Vegas. The goal is to enjoy it the fullest, but not so fully that you run out of money. —**Jonathan Clements**

As for that leisurely evening of life, I must say that I do not want it. I can conceive of no contentment of which toil is not to be the immediate parent. —**Anthony Trollope**

The only way to avoid being miserable (in retirement) is not to have enough leisure to wonder whether you are happy or not. —**George Bernard Shaw.**

For many great scientists, retirement isn't a hard stop but more of an exciting transition. Take Einstein and Hawking, for example—they viewed their work as limitless, continuing to push the boundaries of science regardless of age. Others, like **Feynman**, saw retirement as a new adventure, using the extra time to dive into fresh ways of thinking, teaching, or exploring personal passions. In essence, for these brilliant minds, retirement often opened the door to even more freedom to chase their intellectual curiosity. Most, in fact, worked tirelessly, without much concern for health or the typical retirement routine, driven by a relentless thirst for discovery.

1.2 Retirement Age

Retirement age varies globally, influenced by socioeconomic, political, and cultural conditions. Generally, wealthier countries (First World) tend to have more generous social security systems and longer life expectancies, which allow people to retire later, whereas developing nations (Third World) may have earlier retirement ages due to life expectancy, labor market needs, and weaker social security systems.

Here's a broad overview of retirement ages across different regions, based on their socioeconomic and political conditions:

First World Countries (Developed Nations)

These countries typically have well-developed social safety nets, longer life expectancies, and strong economies. As a result, retirement ages are often standardized and aligned with longer-term pension schemes.

United States:

- Standard Retirement Age: 66 to 67 years.
- Early Retirement: 62 (with reduced benefits).
- Socio-economic Factors: Longer life expectancy and an extensive social security system encourage later retirement to secure full pension benefits.

United Kingdom:

- Standard Retirement Age: 66 (gradually increasing to 68 by 2039)
- Early Retirement: Private pension access as early as 55
- Socio-economic Factors: Pension age reforms are tied to longevity and public pension sustainability.

Germany:

- Standard Retirement Age: 65, gradually increasing to 67 by 2031
- Early Retirement: Possible from 63 with reduced benefits
- Socio-economic Factors: A strong welfare system with social contributions, alongside rising life expectancy, drives the push to increase the retirement age.

France:

In France, the statutory retirement age is currently 62. However, recent reforms will gradually raise this age to 64 for individuals born in or after 1968. For those born between September 1, 1961, and December 31, 1967, the retirement age will increase incrementally by three months per generation.

Japan:

- Standard Retirement Age: 65
- Early Retirement: Some companies allow employees to retire earlier with company pensions, but a national pension is available from 65.
- Socio-economic Factors: Japan's rapidly aging population has led to reforms encouraging people to work longer.

China:

- The standard retirement age is 60 for men and 55 for women in white-collar roles, but 50 for women in blue-collar jobs. However, China's aging population has led to a push for a gradual increase in retirement ages to ensure social security sustainability.

- With an aging workforce and declining birth rate, China faces pressure to reform the retirement system to balance economic growth with social support.

Russia:

- Russia's retirement age was raised in 2019 after significant public debate: now 60 for women and 65 for men. Before this, women could retire at 55 and men at 60, but reforms aim to address funding shortfalls in Russia's pension system.
- Russia has experienced similar demographic challenges, with an aging population and increased life expectancy, leading to an urgent need for pension system adjustments.

Canada:

- In Canada, there is no mandatory retirement age, allowing individuals the flexibility to choose when to retire based on personal circumstances. However, eligibility for government pension benefits is age-specific:
- Canada Pension Plan (CPP): You can begin receiving CPP retirement benefits as early as age 60. Opting for early retirement results in reduced monthly payments. Conversely, delaying benefits up to age 70 increases the monthly amount. The standard age to start receiving CPP is 65.
  Government of Canada
- Old Age Security (OAS): This pension is available starting at age 65. In most cases, Service Canada will automatically enroll you for the OAS pension if sufficient information is available. Service Canada will inform you if you have been automatically enrolled.
  Government of Canada
- It's important to note that while these are the ages for government pensions, many Canadians choose to retire earlier or later based on personal savings, employment

situations, and lifestyle preferences. Recent data indicates that the average retirement age in Canada is around 65, with self-employed individuals tending to retire later, averaging around age 68, and public sector workers retiring earlier, around age 63.

Third World Countries (Developing Nations)

In these countries, economic pressures, lower life expectancy, and less robust social security systems often result in earlier retirement ages or more flexible retirement options.

1. **India:** The retirement age in India is one of the lowest globally (due to less life expectancy as well as unemployment, overpopulation & limited resources to offer jobs)
    - Standard Retirement Age: 58 to 65 (varies across sectors and states)
    - Government Employees: 60 years for most sectors. (High Court judge retires at 62, whereas a Supreme Court judge retires at 65)
    - Private Sector: Typically 58-60, but varies widely (Even goes to 70 or +70 depending upon the individual health, merit & ability to address the issues)
    - Socio-economic Factors: Weak pension systems and a large informal economy mean many continue working past retirement age to support themselves.

2. **Saudi Arabia:**

The retirement age varies based on the employment sector and gender broadly as follows:

Public Sector:

- Retirement Age:

    - For men and women, the official retirement age is 60.
    - This is calculated according to the Hijra calendar (Islamic calendar), which results in about 58-59 years in the Gregorian calendar.
- Early Retirement:
    - Public sector employees can retire early after completing 25 years of service, with a reduced pension.

Private Sector:

- Retirement Age:
    - The retirement age in the private sector can be 60, but some private companies may have different policies based on contracts.
- Early Retirement:
    - Private sector employees are generally eligible for early retirement if they have completed 20 years of service, though the specific terms depend on company policies and contracts.

Socio-Economic and Political Context concerning Retirement age

- Life Expectancy: With rising life expectancy (around 75 years), the Saudi government has been considering reforms to align with global trends and ensure the sustainability of its pension system.
- Economic Diversification: As part of Saudi Vision 2030, there is a focus on increasing workforce participation, particularly for women. This could lead to changes in retirement age policies in the future.
- Expatriates: Expat workers typically have different arrangements, often based on contractual agreements rather than a set retirement age. Many expatriates continue working until their contracts end or they choose to return to their home countries. Government sectors often choose to retain retired professional experts as consultants, recognizing the immense value of their experience and expertise. These professionals are typically brought back on renewable yearly contracts, allowing their contributions to continue based on

their health and performance. In many cases, their consultancy roles can extend for five years or even longer, ensuring that their knowledge is passed on and leveraged for the benefit of ongoing projects and institutional growth.

A Snapshot of the World's Aging Population

Do you know that 13% of the world's population—over 1.1 billion people—are already 60 or older? And by 2050, this number is expected to double, with nearly one in five people (22%) belonging to this age group. In India, the shift is just as dramatic, with the elderly population projected to rise from 10.5% in 2022 to 20.8% by mid-century, reshaping societies across the globe.

As of 2022, nearly 30% of Japan's population was aged 65 or older, making it the world's leading country in terms of elderly citizens. With almost one in three people in this age group, Japan stands at the forefront of a global aging trend, offering a glimpse into the future challenges and opportunities that other nations may soon face.

Key insights into how mental agility, wisdom, intellectual capacity, and physical abilities evolve across various age groups

Recent research shows that wisdom and intellectual abilities evolve throughout a person's life, and different cognitive abilities peak at different ages. While fluid intelligence (problem-solving and quick thinking) tends to peak in early adulthood, many aspects of wisdom, emotional intelligence, and crystallized intelligence (knowledge accumulated over time - Experience) improve with age. Here's a breakdown based on current research:

1. <u>Fluid Intelligence (Peaks in 20s and 30s)</u>

- What It Is: Fluid intelligence refers to the ability to think quickly, solve novel problems, and adapt to new situations.
- Peak Age: Research shows that fluid intelligence tends to peak in early adulthood, usually in the late 20s to early 30s, after which it gradually declines.

- Why It Matters: This ability is often crucial in fast-paced problem-solving, learning new tasks, and environments that require innovation.

2. **Ages 30 to 50**

- Represent a golden period in terms of productivity and capability. People in this range often have the ideal balance of experience, ambition, and energy, making them not only highly effective workers but also influential leaders and innovators. This phase is often seen as a prime time for professional growth and achieving significant milestones.

3. **Crystallized Intelligence (Peaks in 50s and Beyond)**

- What It Is: Crystallized intelligence involves accumulated knowledge, experience, language skills, and the ability to apply learned concepts. It improves with time and experience.
- Peak Age: Research indicates that crystallized intelligence continues to improve well into middle age and peaks around the 50s to 60s, and in some cases, people may maintain high levels of crystallized intelligence into their 70s.
- Why It Matters: This type of intelligence is valuable in professions that rely on deep expertise, experience, and judgment, such as teaching, counseling, or leadership roles.

4. **Wisdom and Emotional Intelligence (Improves with Age)**

- **What It Is:** Wisdom is a combination of knowledge, experience, and the ability to make sound judgments in complex social and moral situations. Emotional intelligence involves recognizing, understanding, and managing one's own and others' emotions.

- Peak Age: Studies suggest that wisdom and emotional intelligence often improve with age, particularly in the 60s and beyond. Older individuals tend to make decisions that consider long-term consequences, the perspectives of others, and empathy.
- Why It Matters: These abilities are crucial in leadership, conflict resolution, mentoring, and fostering healthy relationships. Wisdom is often tied to life experience rather than raw intellectual capacity.

5. Creativity and Innovation (Varies by Field Experience)

- What It Is: Creativity refers to the ability to generate novel and original ideas. In fields like science, mathematics, and the arts, the peak age of creativity can vary.
- Peak Age: Research shows that in highly analytical or abstract fields (e.g., physics, mathematics), creativity often peaks in the 30s or 40s. However, in fields requiring deep knowledge or synthesis (e.g., history, philosophy, writing), creativity can peak in the 50s, 60s, or later.
- Why It Matters: Creativity is not confined to youth. Many fields value both youthful innovation and the mature creativity that comes with experience.

6. Productivity and Output (Late 40s to Early 60s)

- What It Is: Productivity is a combination of output, quality of work, and ability to apply one's skills and knowledge efficiently.
- Peak Age: Research on productivity, especially in professional careers, suggests that many individuals reach their peak productivity in their late 40s to early 60s. This is when people have accumulated enough experience to make optimal use of their intellectual and practical skills.
- Why It Matters: This is often considered the most balanced stage of life, where one's intellectual abilities, life experiences, and emotional intelligence come together to produce their best work.

7. Cognitive Decline and Adaptation (Mid-60s Onward)

- What It Is: Cognitive decline refers to the gradual reduction in processing speed, memory, and some aspects of reasoning ability. However, the decline can be mitigated through mental and physical exercise, social engagement, and lifelong learning.
- Age Range: Cognitive decline typically begins in the mid-60s, but the rate and impact vary greatly from person to person. Many people continue to engage in intellectually stimulating work well into their 70s and 80s.
- Why It Matters: While processing speed might slow down, wisdom, perspective, and practical knowledge often compensate, allowing older individuals to remain highly effective in roles that rely on judgment, mentoring, and leadership.

Latest Research Findings:

- Neuroscience: Studies suggest that older brains compensate for some loss in processing speed and memory by drawing on experience and utilizing different brain regions for problem-solving, showing that wisdom and knowledge continue to grow with age.
- Experience and Reflection: Older adults often exhibit better decision-making in complex situations, where emotional and social factors are key, making them more capable of offering long-term, well-rounded insights.

Conclusion:

Different aspects of intelligence and productivity peak at different ages. While fluid intelligence may peak in the 20s and 30s, crystallized intelligence, wisdom, and emotional intelligence continue to grow into the 50s, 60s, and beyond. Therefore, the late 40s to early 60s are often considered the most productive and insightful phase of life in terms of wisdom, knowledge, and intellectual output.

Could it be a misconception or even a myth that true wisdom or intellect only blossoms after we turn 70?

The idea that wisdom or intellect comes after the age of 70 is more nuanced than a simple "yes" or "no." It is influenced by various factors such as life experience, cognitive health (the ability to think, learn,and remember clearly), and cultural perceptions which vary from individual to individual. Here's a breakdown of key points:

Wisdom and Aging:

- Wisdom is often associated with age because it involves accumulated life experience, emotional regulation, and the ability to view situations with a broad, balanced perspective. Older adults may be better at handling complex social and emotional challenges, drawing on their years of experience.
- Intellectual growth can continue well into old age. Many people over 70 maintain their cognitive abilities, engage in learning, and adapt to new situations. This intellectual engagement is often referred to as "crystallized intelligence" — the knowledge and skills gathered over a lifetime, which tend to remain strong or even improve with age.

Research on Wisdom and Aging:

- Some studies suggest that older adults, especially those in their 60s, 70s, and beyond, may show greater wisdom because they are better at perspective-taking, dealing with uncertainty, and managing emotions. This is often referred to as the "wisdom paradox" — the idea that as certain cognitive abilities (like quick processing or memory recall) decline slightly with age, deeper insight, understanding, and judgment improve.

Cognitive Decline:

- On the other hand, fluid intelligence (the ability to solve new problems quickly and reason abstractly) typically peaks earlier in

life and may decline with age. However, the decline varies greatly from person to person and can be mitigated by mental, physical, and social activity.
- Factors like good health, an active lifestyle, and mental engagement can help preserve cognitive function well into older age.

Cultural and Individual Differences:

- Cultural views on aging often influence the belief that wisdom comes with age. Some cultures hold elders in high regard for their accumulated life experience and see them as the keepers of wisdom.
- Individual differences play a huge role. Some people may continue to grow in wisdom and intellect throughout their lives, while others may experience cognitive decline earlier, depending on genetics, lifestyle, and health.

Conclusion:

While it's not universally true that wisdom or intellect only comes after the age of 70, many people continue to develop wisdom as they age, often gaining deeper understanding, better judgment, and perspective. However, maintaining cognitive health is key to sustaining intellectual capacity in old age.

Note - While many Nobel laureates are honored later in life—often between the ages of 67 and 71—some receive their accolades even at remarkable ages, like **Leonid Hurwicz**, who won at **90** for Economic Science, **Arthur Ashkin**, awarded at **96** for Physics, and **John B. Goodenough**, who made history at **97** with his Nobel in Chemistry. But what's truly inspiring is that their groundbreaking contributions were often the result of decades of relentless research, with many starting their pioneering work much earlier in their careers. These awards highlight not just a moment of brilliance, but a lifetime of innovation, perseverance, and dedication that continued well into their later years. It’s a testament to the enduring power of curiosity and the passion for discovery, showing that true achievement often spans a lifetime.

The concept of a "late" prize isn't necessarily a reflection of late-career breakthroughs but rather the culmination of years of progress. In fields like science, literature, or peace efforts, it often takes time for the full impact of a person’s work to be realized and appreciated by the broader world.

"Global Leadership Beyond 70: Exploring the Pros and Cons of Elderly Leaders and the Contrast with Retirement Norms in Other Professions"

The topic of elderly political leaders holding positions of significant power globally is an intriguing one, as it raises questions about leadership, experience, and generational differences. In recent years, a growing number of world leaders have remained in office well past the typical retirement age. This trend contrasts with retirement policies in most professions, where age limits are strictly enforced. Here's an in-depth analysis of the pros and cons of elderly leaders in politics and a comparison to the retirement norms in other sectors.

1. Elderly Leaders in Global Politics

Several of the world's most influential countries are currently led by elderly individuals:

- Donald Trump, President of the United States, was 78 when he took office in 2025, By the time he completes his term, he will be 82.
- Vladimir Putin, President of Russia, was born in 1952, making him in his 70s as of 2024. He has held power for over two decades.- 72 years
- Xi Jinping, the President of China, though slightly younger, is approaching his 70s.- 71 years
- Narendra Modi, Prime Minister of India, was born in 1950 and is in his mid-70s.- 75 years
- Pope Francis, leader of the Roman Catholic Church and a global spiritual leader, was born in 1936, making him in his late 80s.- 88 years
- Recep Tayyip Erdogan DOB - 1954 - 70 years
- UNO Secretary General - Antonio Guterres - DOB 30.04.1949 - 75 years
- Prime Minister of Israel - Benjamin Natanyahu - DOB 21.10.1949- 75 years

- King Salman Bin Abdulaziz Al Saud - King of Saudi Arabia - 89 years

These examples illustrate that leaders in their 70s and 80s are holding office in many mighty nations, shaping international policies, economies, and geopolitics.

2. Pros of Elderly Leaders in Politics

- Experience and Wisdom: One of the most significant advantages elderly leaders bring to the table is their long-standing experience. Decades of political involvement provide insights into governance, diplomacy, and international relations that younger leaders may lack.
- Stability and Continuity: Older leaders often represent stability, especially in times of political turbulence. Their established leadership styles can provide reassurance to the public and international allies.
- Historical Perspective: Leaders with a longer view of history may have a deeper understanding of global challenges. Their experience with past events (e.g., the Cold War, economic crises, wars) enables them to make informed decisions based on previous lessons.
- Resilience to Public Pressure: Elderly leaders, having already built their legacies, may feel less pressure to chase short-term popularity. This can sometimes allow them to make difficult or unpopular decisions that younger, less secure leaders may avoid.

3. Cons of Elderly Leaders in Politics

- Physical and Cognitive Decline: Age naturally brings physical and cognitive challenges, which can affect an individual's ability to respond quickly or with clarity. Fatigue, memory lapses, and slower decision-making can become obstacles to effective leadership.
- Outdated Perspectives: Older leaders may sometimes hold on to outdated worldviews or policy approaches that may not align with

the rapidly changing technological and social landscape. This can hinder innovation and adaptation to contemporary challenges, such as climate change or digital transformation.

- Lack of Representation of Younger Generations: Elderly leadership can create a disconnect between the government and younger generations, who may feel that their needs and aspirations are not adequately represented. Policies on technology, environment, and labor markets may lag behind modern expectations.
- Succession and Legacy Issues: Older leaders often raise concerns about succession, especially in nations where transitions of power are not always clear or democratic. The departure of a long-standing elderly leader can lead to power struggles, instability, or abrupt changes in governance.

4. Why Retirement Age Limits Exist in Other Professions

In contrast to politics, most professions enforce strict retirement ages. Common reasons include:

- Cognitive and Physical Decline: Many jobs, especially in sectors like manual labor, transportation, and healthcare, require physical and mental agility that naturally decreases with age. Setting retirement limits ensures that individuals do not continue to work in roles that demand peak performance when their abilities are diminished.
- Opportunity for Younger Generations: By enforcing retirement ages, institutions make room for younger professionals to rise through the ranks. This turnover brings fresh energy, new ideas, and keeps industries dynamic and evolving.
- Productivity and Efficiency: Research shows that after a certain age, many individuals' productivity declines. Retirement policies are often aimed at maintaining organizational efficiency by ensuring that individuals who may no longer be able to keep up with the demands of their role step aside for those who can.

- Health and Well-being: Retirement is also a means of allowing individuals to rest and enjoy their later years. The physical and mental demands of continuous work, especially in high-stress jobs, can take a toll on well-being. Retirement ensures that individuals do not work beyond what is sustainable for their health.

5. The Political Exception

Politics seems to be an exception to the retirement norms of other professions, largely because of the unique nature of leadership in this field:

- Leadership Skills Mature with Age: Political leadership is often seen as a role where wisdom, negotiation, and decision-making improve with time. Unlike physical labor, the core skills required in political leadership can remain strong even as an individual ages.
- Power and Influence: Politics is a realm where the accumulation of power over time can create significant influence. Leaders who have spent decades building relationships and establishing control over political systems can wield more authority than newer leaders, making it harder to enforce retirement on them.
- Public Perception: In many countries, the public may associate age with wisdom and trust, leading to the election or retention of older leaders. Societies that value tradition and continuity often favor experienced leaders who have proven their mettle over the years.
- Lack of Formal Retirement Rules: Many political systems lack formal age limits for leadership roles, allowing individuals to remain in office as long as they are elected. Unlike other jobs that have mandatory retirement ages, politics often depends on the will of the voters or the inner workings of political parties.

6. Conclusion: A Balance Needed?

While elderly leaders bring valuable experience and stability, there is a valid concern about their ability to remain effective in rapidly changing global landscapes. With rising youth activism and the need for innovation to address future challenges, there may be a growing demand for a generational shift in leadership. At the same time, balancing the wisdom of the elderly with the dynamism of the young is a challenge that every political system must navigate.

Striking a balance between honoring the invaluable contributions of elder statespeople and empowering younger generations to take the reins of leadership is crucial for sustainable governance. While most professions impose age limits, politics remains an exception, fueling a growing global debate on how long leaders should stay in power. This discourse becomes even more relevant as the average age of world leaders continues to rise.

At the same time, a troubling trend has emerged in many countries: elections marred by manipulation, where muscle power and money often determine outcomes. In nations with democratic frameworks and multi-party systems, the fragmentation of votes means leaders often secure victory with a mere 40-45% of the vote. This leaves the majority of the electorate unrepresented, yet the elected leaders and their parties often remain in power for extended periods, unchecked and unchallenged.

The consequences of such flawed systems are dire. Poor leadership breeds corruption, unemployment, and failing health and education systems. The needs of the elderly and retirees are neglected, the gap between the rich and the poor widens, and ethnic tensions simmer beneath the surface. Local issues, ranging from inadequate infrastructure to environmental neglect, go unresolved, culminating in widespread dissatisfaction and disillusionment among the population.

The question is not just about who leads but how they are chosen and how long they remain. Only by addressing these systemic flaws can nations hope to foster leadership that is truly representative, accountable, and capable of meeting the aspirations of their people.

2.0 Financial planning

Retirement is a phase in life that should ideally be carefree, comfortable, and healthy—both mentally and physically. Yet, achieving this requires careful planning and a balanced approach to savings and investment. A well-managed financial life during your working years can significantly shape the quality of your retirement, offering you the freedom to live with dignity, free from the anxiety of financial struggles.

The Key to a Comfortable Retirement: Balanced Financial Planning

A key indicator of leading a better life after retirement is how well one balances their income, savings, and investments throughout their career. It's not just about meeting today's needs but also securing tomorrow's peace of mind. Striking the right balance between what you spend now and what you save for the future can be the difference between a relaxed retirement and one filled with financial uncertainty.

Different Philosophies of Retirement Management

In many Western countries, the philosophy of retirement is deeply rooted in social insurance systems, strong governmental policies, and a focus on human rights. These systems are designed to ensure that retirees receive pensions, healthcare, and other social benefits that allow them to maintain a certain standard of living. This safety net helps many enjoy their later years without worrying about their basic needs.

However, in the developing world, the scenario is different. While some retirement policies and schemes exist, they often serve only a small fraction of the population—typically those in organized sectors or government jobs. For a vast majority, particularly those in unorganized or private employment, retirement planning is an individual responsibility, with little external support. Many spend their entire lives striving to enter the organized sectors or secure stable employment, often facing setbacks and failures along the way.

This constant struggle to improve one's social standing or income leads many to migrate within their own country or even abroad in search of better opportunities. While a few may succeed, most face disappointment and eventually reach retirement age with little financial security. The result is a life marked by frustration, hardship, and the grim reality of having no option but to endure financial instability.

The Role of Savings and Investment in a Secure Retirement

One of the most critical tools for ensuring a comfortable retirement is the disciplined management of savings and investments during one's working years. Without the expectation of a steady income in retirement, individuals must rely on the financial resources they have accumulated throughout their careers. This requires careful planning, including setting aside a substantial portion of income specifically for retirement.

But saving isn't enough; one must also invest wisely to ensure that the money grows over time. The decisions you make regarding your savings and investments should take into account various factors such as family obligations, children's education, and their financial independence. Striking a balance between your current lifestyle and your future needs is essential.

A sound retirement plan involves making sacrifices today to enjoy stability tomorrow. It's about being mindful of your financial choices, living within your means, and ensuring that your hard-earned money is working for you through smart investments.

Retirement is a Journey, Not a Destination

Ultimately, retirement is not just a matter of reaching a certain age; it's the result of decades of financial habits and decisions. Whether you are in a country with robust social safety nets or one where the burden is on the individual, the principles remain the same: managing your income wisely, saving regularly, and investing thoughtfully can ensure a more secure and enjoyable retirement.

The income theory of savings and investment in the context of a balanced lifestyle is based on the principle that individuals should manage their income in a way that balances their immediate needs with their long-term financial security. The theory highlights the need for disciplined savings, investments, and spending to ensure financial well-being without overindulging or depriving oneself. This concept may be further analyzed as follows:

1. Income Allocation

- **Necessities (Needs)**: A portion of the income should be dedicated to basic living needs, such as housing, food, healthcare, and utilities. These are non-negotiable expenses that ensure survival and quality of life.
- **Discretionary Spending (Wants)**: This includes spending on non-essential items like entertainment, vacations, dining out, and luxury goods. This portion should be limited to avoid overconsumption.
- **Savings and Investment (Security)**: A significant portion of income should be saved and invested for future needs. This helps in achieving financial security, retirement planning, and handling unexpected emergencies.

2. Balanced Lifestyle

The theory encourages a lifestyle where one's needs and requirements are met without sacrificing future security. This involves:

- **Moderation in Spending**: Avoiding overspending on luxuries while ensuring the basic needs are comfortably met.

  " For example, If your budget doesn't allow for the luxury of owning a car and hiring a driver, consider the convenience of public transport or services like Ola, Uber or Creem etc. Not only will this relieve you from the hassle of parking, navigating through congested streets, and dealing with maintenance, insurance, and other vehicle-related expenses, but it will also save you from the stress of driving in busy areas. Opting for these alternatives can make your daily commute smoother, more cost-effective, and far less stressful."

- **Future Planning**: Saving consistently for retirement, education, or unexpected events (emergencies).
- **Investment**: Growing wealth through investments to provide long-term financial stability, beyond just saving. Investments help in fighting inflation and growing wealth through asset appreciation.

3. Key Principles

- **Savings Rate**: A general recommendation is to save at least 20% of your income.
- **Emergency Fund**: Maintaining an emergency fund covering 3-6 months' worth of living expenses.
- **Contingency Financial Plan:** A contingency financial plan is your safety net, a strategy crafted to shield your finances when life throws the unexpected your way. It acts as a buffer against unforeseen challenges like losing a part-time job after retirement, sudden medical emergencies, economic downturns, or major life transitions. With a solid plan in place, you can face these financial shocks head-on, ensuring that your long-term financial goals remain intact and your peace of mind stays unshaken.

  At its core, a contingency financial plan is about preparedness and resilience. It empowers you to navigate turbulent times without compromising your quality of life or jeopardizing your future security. Here are some of the key components that make up a robust contingency financial plan:

- **Emergency Fund**:
  Set aside 3 to 6 months' worth of living expenses in a liquid, easily accessible account. This fund acts as a financial cushion during sudden income loss or emergencies.

- **Insurance Coverage**:
  Ensure you have adequate health, life, and property insurance. This helps cover major expenses like medical bills, accidents, or property damage, reducing the financial burden during crises.
- **Debt Management**:
  Avoid accumulating high-interest debt, and create a plan to pay off existing liabilities. In emergencies, minimizing debt helps prevent financial stress.
- **Diversified Income Streams**:
  If possible, create multiple sources of income (such as investments, side businesses, or rental income) to reduce reliance on a single source. This provides a safety net during job loss or economic downturns.
- **Investment Liquidity**:
  While it's important to invest for the long term, make sure some of your investments can be quickly converted into cash without significant losses, so you can access funds when needed.
- **Review and Update Regularly**:
  Periodically review your contingency plan to ensure it reflects your current financial situation, lifestyle, and potential risks.
- **Debt Management**: Avoiding high-interest debt while focusing on necessary, low-interest borrowing (e.g., for housing or education). Even I consider using proper credit cards to maintain five-star level as well as purchasing things for domestic or general use as well as debiting yourselves for purchasing expensive items on monthly installments by paying indirect heavy interest rates.
- **Compounding**: Compounding: The theory emphasizes the importance of compounding interest or returns over time, showing how early savings can grow exponentially. Beware that compounding can work both ways; while it can accelerate wealth growth through investments, it can also increase debt quickly if interest charges on loans or credit are left unpaid.

4. Investment for Balanced Growth

Investments should be diversified across various assets like stocks, bonds, real estate, or mutual funds. The objective is to achieve long-term financial growth while managing risks, ensuring that both present and future financial requirements are balanced.

In short, the income theory of savings and investment is about achieving a lifestyle that meets current needs while securing future financial well-being. It focuses on responsible income management, regular saving, smart investment, and prudent spending to create a balanced financial life.

Note: During the active service period, Well before retiring a man should plan & assess the following points to be able to handle the critical financial situations in his future life when there is no regular or routine earnings.

- Understanding Retirement Savings (pension, IRAs, etc)
- Budgeting for Retirement.
- Social Security Benefits
- Health Services & long term care
- Investment Strategies for Retirees
- Managing Debt & Expenses

2.1 Understanding Retirement Savings (pension, IRAs-Individual Retirement Account, etc)

Facilities available in India

In India, several types of pension plans are available to help individuals save for retirement and ensure financial security in their later years. These pension plans are offered by both the government and private financial institutions, providing various options based on the individual's needs and employment status. Here are the key types of pension plans available in India:

1. Employees' Provident Fund (EPF)

- What it is: The Employees' Provident Fund is a mandatory savings scheme for employees in the organized sector. Both the employer and employee contribute to the fund, and the amount grows with interest over time.
- Key Features:
    - Employers contribute 12% of the employee's salary (basic + DA) to the EPF.
    - A portion of the employer's contribution goes toward the Employees' Pension Scheme (EPS).
    - The accumulated corpus can be withdrawn upon retirement or during specific events like unemployment or illness.
    - The EPF is managed by the Employees' Provident Fund Organization (EPFO).

2. Employees' Pension Scheme (EPS)

- What it is: The Employees' Pension Scheme (EPS) is a social security pension scheme available to employees who are part of the EPF. It provides monthly pensions after retirement based on years of service and salary.

- Key Features:
    - The employer contributes 8.33% of the employee's salary (up to ₹15,000) towards EPS.
    - The pension is calculated based on the formula: Pension = (Pensionable Salary x Years of Service) / 70.
    - The pension is payable to employees after reaching the age of 58.
    - Early retirement is possible at age 50, with reduced pension benefits.
    - Benefits include pensions to the employee's spouse and children after the employee's death.

3. National Pension System (NPS)

- What it is: The National Pension System (NPS) is a voluntary, defined-contribution pension system regulated by the Pension Fund Regulatory and Development Authority (PFRDA). It is open to all Indian citizens, including private-sector employees and self-employed individuals.
- Key Features:
    - Individuals contribute to a pension account during their working years, and a portion of the accumulated corpus is used to purchase an annuity upon retirement.
    - NPS offers two types of accounts: Tier-I (mandatory retirement savings) and Tier-II (voluntary, flexible accounts).
    - Contributions grow with market-linked returns.
    - At retirement, 60% of the corpus can be withdrawn as a lump sum (tax-free), while 40% must be used to purchase an annuity to receive a regular pension.
    - There are two investment options: Auto Choice (age-based asset allocation) and Active Choice (self-selected asset allocation across equity, government bonds, and corporate debt).
    - NPS is available to government employees, private-sector employees, and the general public.

4. **Atal Pension Yojana (APY)**

- What it is: The Atal Pension Yojana (APY) is a government-backed pension scheme aimed at the unorganized sector, offering a fixed monthly pension upon retirement. The plan is regulated by PFRDA and focuses on individuals from lower-income groups.
- Key Features:
    - Available to individuals between the ages of 18 and 40.
    - Contributions are made during the working years, and upon retirement (age 60), the individual receives a fixed pension ranging from ₹1,000 to ₹5,000 per month, depending on the contribution amount.
    - The government provides a guaranteed minimum pension.
    - The spouse of the subscriber can receive the pension in case of the subscriber's death, and the nominee can receive the corpus.
    - Contributions are affordable, making the plan accessible to individuals in the informal sector.

5. **Public Provident Fund (PPF)**

- What it is: The Public Provident Fund (PPF) is a long-term savings scheme offered by the Government of India, primarily used for retirement planning. It provides a tax-free return and has a lock-in period of 15 years.
- Key Features:
    - Individuals can contribute up to ₹1.5 lakh per year.
    - The interest earned and the final corpus are tax-free.
    - The maturity period is 15 years, but partial withdrawals can be made from the 7th year onwards.
    - PPF is a low-risk, government-backed savings option.
    - It can be extended in blocks of 5 years after the initial 15-year term.

6. Superannuation Pension

- What it is: A superannuation pension is a retirement benefit employers provide to their employees. It is typically offered as part of the salary package to employees in organized sectors.
- Key Features:
    - Employers contribute a certain percentage (typically 15% of the basic salary) to the superannuation fund.
    - The fund is managed by insurance companies, and the employee gets a pension or lump-sum payment upon retirement.
    - Employees can start receiving pensions after a certain period (usually after the age of 58 or 60).
    - In case of death before retirement, the employee's family can receive the benefits.

7. Unit-Linked Pension Plans (ULPPs)

- What it is: Unit-linked pension Plans (ULPPs) are market-linked pension plans offered by insurance companies. These plans combine investment and insurance, providing a retirement corpus along with life cover.
- Key Features:
    - Part of the premium is invested in equity or debt instruments, and the remaining portion provides life insurance.
    - Returns are market-linked, meaning the value of the pension fund depends on market performance.
    - At retirement, a portion of the accumulated corpus can be withdrawn as a lump sum, and the rest is used to purchase an annuity for regular income.
    - Suitable for individuals seeking higher returns through equity investments for retirement savings.
    - Tax benefits are available under Section 80C of the Income Tax Act.

8. **Annuity Plans**

- What it is: Annuity plans are pension products provided by insurance companies where an individual invests a lump sum and receives regular payments (pension) over a specified period or for life.
- Key Features:
  - The individual buys the annuity plan by paying a lump sum amount.
  - The insurance company pays a regular pension (monthly, quarterly, or annually) after retirement.
  - Annuities can be Immediate (payments start immediately) or Deferred (payments start after a certain period).
  - Annuities are available in different types, such as Life Annuity, Joint Life Annuity, and Annuity with Return of Purchase Price.
  - Annuity income is taxable in the hands of the recipient.

Note: UAN -The Unified Account for EPFO is the Universal Account Number (UAN), which is a 12-digit number that links multiple Member IDs to a single account. The UAN is issued by the Employees' Provident Fund Organisation (EPFO). Here are some benefits of UAN which help track PF-related activities, ensure that all PF accounts are valid & genuine & reduce employer involvement. You can get your employer if you join a new establishment. You should provide your UAN so that your employer can link the new member ID to your existing UNA.

Conclusion:

India offers a variety of pension plans to cater to different segments of the population, from the organized sector and self-employed individuals to those in the unorganized sector. Choosing the right plan depends on factors such as employment status, risk appetite, and long-term financial goals. While government-backed schemes like NPS and APY provide security and stability, private plans such as ULPPs and annuity plans offer flexibility and the potential for higher returns.

Despite the array of facilities within the system, there remains a significant gap between actual financial needs and the support offered by the government or institutions. This gap is further widened by skyrocketing inflation and the unpredictability of timely financial assistance. In the Indian context, the system itself is often sluggish, marred by corruption, bribery, and lengthy delays, making it a frustrating ordeal for retirees. Instead of offering relief, these obstacles strain both the health of the services and the very purpose they are meant to serve.

Facilities available in Western world

Understanding retirement savings in the Western world involves looking at the combination of government-provided pensions, employer-sponsored retirement plans, and personal savings accounts. Each country has its unique system of providing for retirees, which typically includes state pensions and tax-advantaged savings accounts. Here's a detailed look at retirement savings systems in the US, Canada, UK, Germany, France, Japan, and other Western nations:

1. United States:

The US retirement system operates on three pillars: Social Security, employer-sponsored plans, and personal savings.

- Social Security: Funded through payroll taxes, this is the foundational income for many retirees. Benefits are based on lifetime earnings and start as early as age 62, with full retirement age ranging from 66 to 67.
- 401(k) Plans: These are tax-deferred, employer-sponsored retirement savings plans. Employees contribute part of their salary, often with employer matching, and funds grow tax-free until withdrawal.
- Individual Retirement Accounts (IRAs): Traditional IRAs allow tax-deferred savings, while Roth IRAs are funded with after-tax money but grow tax-free, and withdrawals are tax-free after age 59½.

2. Canada:

Canada's retirement system includes the Canada Pension Plan (CPP), Old Age Security (OAS), and Registered Retirement Savings Plans (RRSPs).

- CPP/QPP: Workers contribute to the Canada Pension Plan (or Québec Pension Plan) throughout their careers, and benefits depend on contributions. Retirement benefits can be claimed starting at age 60, with higher payouts for delayed claims.
- Old Age Security (OAS): OAS is a universal pension available to seniors 65 and older, subject to residency requirements. Higher earners may see a reduction in their OAS benefits through a "clawback."
- Registered Retirement Savings Plan (RRSP): An RRSP is a tax-deferred retirement savings account. Contributions are tax-deductible, and the funds grow tax-free until withdrawal.
- Tax-Free Savings Account (TFSA): While not strictly for retirement, a TFSA allows Canadians to save and invest money tax-free, with no penalties for withdrawals.

3. United Kingdom:

The UK retirement system is structured around the state pension, workplace pensions, and personal pensions.

- State Pension: The UK offers a flat-rate state pension to individuals who have made National Insurance contributions for at least 10 qualifying years. The full state pension age is currently 66, increasing over time.
- Workplace Pensions: Automatic enrollment means most employees are required to join their employer's workplace pension scheme. These are typically defined contribution (DC) schemes, where both employees and employers contribute.
- Personal Pensions (Private Pensions): These include Self-Invested Personal Pensions (SIPPs), which allow for more control over investments with tax relief on contributions.

4. Germany:

Germany has a robust public pension system, supplemented by employer-sponsored and private pensions.

- Statutory Pension Insurance (Gesetzliche Rentenversicherung, GRV): The public pension is the main source of retirement income, funded through payroll contributions by employers and employees. Benefits depend on contributions made throughout the working life.
- Riester and Rürup Pensions: These are government-subsidized private pension plans. Riester pensions are designed for employees, offering tax breaks and government subsidies. Rürup pensions are primarily for self-employed workers.
- Occupational Pensions: Many employees receive additional retirement savings through employer-sponsored pensions, often organized through pension funds or insurance companies.

5. France:

France's retirement system is primarily public, but private pensions play a growing role.

- Public Pension System: The French public pension system is based on a pay-as-you-go model, where current workers' contributions pay for retirees' benefits. Benefits are based on salary and length of contributions. The retirement age is gradually rising and is currently 62, with a full pension age at 67 for those without enough contributions.
- Complementary Pensions (ARRCO/AGIRC): These mandatory supplementary pension schemes for private-sector employees are managed by employer and employee contributions.
- Personal Retirement Savings: France has introduced tax-incentivized private savings plans, such as PER (Plan d'Épargne Retraite), which allow individuals to save for retirement with favorable tax treatment.

6. Japan:

Japan has an aging population, and its retirement system relies on a combination of public pensions and employer-sponsored plans.

- National Pension (Kokumin Nenkin): This is a basic public pension that all residents must join. Benefits are relatively modest, with payments starting at age 65. The pension is primarily funded through premiums paid by individuals.
- Employee Pension Insurance (Kosei Nenkin): This is a compulsory system for salaried workers, with higher benefits than the National Pension. Contributions are shared between employers and employees.
- Personal Retirement Savings: Japan also has tax-advantaged retirement savings accounts, such as the iDeCo (Individual-type Defined Contribution Pension Plan), which allows individuals to make tax-deductible contributions to a retirement account.

7. Other Western Countries:

- Australia: The Superannuation (Super) system is mandatory, where employers contribute a percentage of an employee's salary (currently 11%) to a retirement fund. Individuals can also make voluntary contributions, and the funds are taxed at a lower rate until retirement.
- Netherlands: The Dutch system is based on a three-pillar approach, including a state pension (AOW), workplace pensions (second pillar), and individual private savings (third pillar). The workplace pensions are particularly strong in the Netherlands, with many workers enrolled in collective defined benefit schemes.
- Sweden: The Swedish retirement system is also multi-tiered, with a guaranteed pension for low-income individuals, a public pension based on lifetime earnings, and private pension savings. Sweden's system includes a Premium Pension (PPM) where individuals can invest a portion of their pension into private funds.
- Italy: Italy's retirement system is transitioning from a pay-as-you-go model to a defined contribution system. The INPS (National

Institute for Social Security) manages public pensions, while voluntary private pension funds (such as Fondo Pensione) allow for additional retirement savings.

Conclusion:

While there are common themes among Western retirement systems—such as state pensions, employer-sponsored retirement plans, and personal tax-advantaged savings—the specifics vary widely by country. Generally, retirement planning in the Western world requires individuals to combine government pensions with employer contributions and personal savings to secure a comfortable retirement.

Each country's system also faces unique challenges, such as aging populations and the sustainability of public pensions, leading to ongoing reforms and an increasing reliance on private savings.

Tips for Maximizing Retirement Savings

- **Start Early**: The earlier you start saving, the more time your money has to grow, thanks to compound interest.
- **Contribute Consistently**: Regular contributions to retirement accounts help build savings over time.
- **Maximize Employer Matches**: If your employer offers a match on 401(k) contributions, make sure to contribute enough to get the full match—it's essentially free money.
- **Diversify Investments**: Spread your investments across different asset classes to reduce risk.
- **Review and Adjust**: Periodically review your savings strategy, especially as you near retirement, to ensure your savings will meet your goals.

Note- Understanding the various tools available for retirement savings and how they work can empower you to make the best decisions for your financial future.

2.2 Budgeting for Retirement

Budgeting for retirement is crucial to ensure that you maintain a comfortable lifestyle without financial stress. A well-thought-out retirement budget accounts for expected income, expenses, and the unpredictability of life in retirement. Here's a step-by-step guide to budgeting for retirement:

1. <u>Estimate Retirement Expenses:</u>

Start by estimating your expenses in retirement. Consider the following categories:

- **Basic Living Expenses**:
    - Housing (rent, mortgage, property taxes, utilities, maintenance)
    - Groceries and dining (Minimize or eliminate expenses on alcohol and similar habits, as they harm your health and create an additional financial burden during retirement.
    - Transportation (car payments, fuel, insurance, public transit)
    - Insurance (health, home, life)
- **Healthcare Costs**:
    - Medical insurance premiums (Medicare in the US or national health services in other countries)
    - Prescription drugs and over-the-counter medications
    - Doctor visits, dental care, and vision services
    - Routine comprehensive full-body test (must for seniors at the age of 60 or beyond)
    - Long-term care (nursing home or home health services)
- **Discretionary Spending**:
    - Travel and leisure activities
    - Hobbies and memberships (golf, social clubs, etc.)
    - Entertainment (movies, dining out, subscriptions)
- **Unexpected Costs**:
    - Home repairs (appliances, painting, plumbing, electrical)

    - Major medical emergencies or care costs not covered by insurance
    - Family support (helping children, grandchildren, or other family members)

It's often said that retirees need around **70% to 80%** of their pre-retirement income to maintain a similar lifestyle. However, this depends on your specific situation—some may need less, while others may want more for activities like travel, hobbies like painting, gardening, weekend celebrations & partying etc.

2. <u>Estimate Retirement Income:</u>

Identify all sources of income you expect to have in retirement:

- **Government Benefits**:
    - Social Security (in the US) or national pension schemes (CPP/QPP in Canada, State Pension in the UK, etc.)
    - Public pensions (if applicable)
- **Employer Pensions**:
    - Defined benefit plans (DB) if you have one
    - Defined contribution plans (401(k), RRSPs, SIPPs)
- **Personal Savings**:
    - IRAs (US), TFSAs (Canada), personal savings accounts, or investment portfolios
    - Tax-advantaged accounts like Roth IRAs (US) or iDeCo (Japan), PPF, NPS, Fixed deposits, MFs (India)
- **Part-Time Work**: If you plan to work part-time during retirement, think of it as more than just an income source—it's a smart way to enhance your financial security while staying active and engaged. This additional income can serve as a safety net, giving you greater peace of mind to handle unexpected expenses or rising costs, ensuring your retirement years are as stress-free and enjoyable as possible. Plus, it's a great way to stay connected, share your expertise, and keep a sense of purpose alive!
- **Other Income**:
    - Rental property income

- Dividends or interest from investments
- Annuities or other retirement products

Ensure that your income sources are aligned with your expected expenses. **Withdrawal rates** from savings and investments should be sustainable, with the general guideline being the **4% rule**—withdraw 4% of your retirement savings annually to avoid running out of money.

3. Account for Inflation:

Inflation erodes the value of money over time, meaning your expenses will rise as you age. You should plan for at least a **2-3% annual increase** in your cost of living. Make sure that your income sources (like Social Security, which adjusts for inflation, and investments that grow) can keep pace with inflation.

Note:- Be aware of the highest inflation rate, if you are a resident of Argentina (2.7 % on monthly basis and 236 % August 2024), Venezuela (283% Nov.23), Turkey (61.78%), and Sudan (171% in recent years). Still, India (5.48 % in Nov.2024), the US (2.7 % in Nov.2024), UK 2.3% Oct.24 & most of the Euro area 2.2% Oct.24, and Western countries are moderate for inflation.

4. Plan for Healthcare and Long-Term Care

Healthcare can be one of the biggest expenses in retirement, particularly in the later years. Consider the following:

- **Medical Insurance**: Include premiums for Medicare (in the US) or private health insurance if your country requires it. Don't forget about out-of-pocket costs for prescriptions, treatments, and regular doctor visits.
- **Long-Term Care Insurance**: Consider the potential need for long-term care and whether long-term care insurance fits your needs. Nursing homes, assisted living facilities, and in-home care can be expensive.

- **Health Savings Account (HSA)**: In the US, an HSA is a tax-advantaged account that can help cover medical expenses in retirement, but contributions must be made while you are still working.

5. Plan for Longevity:

People are living longer, which means your retirement savings need to last. Plan conservatively by budgeting for **25 to 30 years** in retirement, especially if you retire early or have a family history of longevity. Annuities or other income-generating investments can provide guaranteed income for life, reducing the risk of outliving your money.

Note: In the Abrahamic faiths, financial support for family and society has always been a cornerstone of moral responsibility. However, in recent times, this tradition is slowly fading, eroded by the rise of materialism and the influence of modern Western lifestyles that prioritize individualism over collective care. Yet, within Islamic culture and faith, these values remain more resilient, holding steadfast against the currents of change. The emphasis on charity, family ties, and mutual support continues to shine as a beacon of hope, reminding us of the importance of compassion and shared responsibility in an increasingly self-centered world.

6. Minimize Taxes in Retirement:

Understanding how your retirement income is taxed can help you retain more of your money. Consider the tax treatment of:

- **Social Security or pension income** (some countries tax these benefits)
- **Withdrawals from retirement accounts** (taxed as income in traditional accounts, but tax-free in Roth accounts)
- **Capital gains on investments** (capital gains taxes may apply depending on the country and type of account)

Using tax-advantaged accounts, such as **Roth IRAs (US)**, **TFSAs (Canada)**, and **ISAs (UK)**, Senior citizen saving scheme, National saving certificates, life insurance - in India can help you minimize taxes on withdrawals.

7. Emergency (Contingency) Fund:

Even in retirement, having an emergency fund for unexpected expenses is crucial. Set aside at least 6-12 months of living expenses in a liquid, easily accessible account (like a savings or money market account). This ensures you won't need to dip into retirement savings or investments in case of an emergency.

8. Monitor and Adjust Your Budget:

Retirement budgeting isn't a "set it and forget it" task. Review your budget regularly, especially in the early years of retirement, and adjust for changes in spending, income, or unexpected expenses.

- **Reassess Investment Returns**: Make sure your portfolio continues to perform according to your retirement needs. You might need to rebalance investments to maintain a proper risk level.
- **Track Spending**: Track your actual spending against your budget to avoid overspending. If your expenses are consistently higher than expected, consider cutting discretionary spending or downsizing.

9. Estate Planning:

Incorporate estate planning into your budget. This includes the cost of legal documents like wills and trusts, as well as potential costs related to inheritance taxes or probate fees. Planning ahead ensures that your assets are distributed according to your wishes and reduces the financial burden on your heirs.

10. Consider Downsizing:

If your housing costs are high, consider downsizing or moving to a more affordable location. Many retirees opt to sell their larger homes and move into smaller, more manageable properties, freeing up cash and reducing ongoing maintenance costs.

Warning:

In retirement, relying on credit cards or maintaining monthly installments for nonessential purchases can lead to financial instability. Fixed or limited incomes make it difficult to manage mounting interest or unexpected financial shocks, potentially depleting your savings faster than planned. Credit card debt, if not cleared promptly, can snowball due to high interest rates, impacting your ability to meet essential expenses like healthcare and housing.

Precautions:

1. Prioritize Essentials: Limit credit card usage to unavoidable or emergency expenses.
2. Set Budgets: Allocate a fixed amount for discretionary spending and avoid exceeding it.
3. Pay in Full: Settle credit card bills in full every month to avoid interest charges.
4. Avoid Installments: Refrain from financing non essential purchases through monthly installments.
5. Monitor Spending: Regularly review your credit card statements and overall financial plan.
6. Emergency Fund: Maintain a reserve fund to avoid relying on credit for unplanned expenses.
7. Low-Interest Cards: If necessary, opt for credit cards with low-interest rates and no annual fees.
8. Consult Financial Advisors: Seek advice on managing credit effectively during retirement.

By exercising financial discipline and avoiding unnecessary debts, you can safeguard your retirement savings and enjoy a stress-free retirement.

Conclusion:

Budgeting for retirement is about ensuring that your savings, income, and investments can support your lifestyle over the long term. With careful planning, realistic spending estimates, and a strategy for managing inflation, taxes, and healthcare costs, you can enjoy a financially secure retirement.

A typical Example of a Retirement Budget for US couple (living together)

Category	Monthly Cost	Annual Cost
Housing (mortgage, rent)	$1,500	$18,000
Utilities (gas, electric, etc.)	$200	$2,400
Groceries	$800	$9,600
Transportation	$300	$3,600
Healthcare (insurance, out-of-pocket)	$500	$6,000
Travel & Leisure	$400	$4,800
Miscellaneous	$300	$3,600
Total	**$4,000**	**$48,000**

Note:- This budget assumes a modest lifestyle, and your needs may vary depending on your personal circumstances and location.

Creating a retirement budget is like crafting a roadmap to a financially comfortable future. It's all about balancing your resources with your lifestyle, while factoring in a few surprises along the way. Above is an example of what a retirement budget might look like for a modest yet fulfilling retirement:

A typical Example of a Retirement Budget in India (Couple living together):

Category	Monthly Cost (INR)	Annual Cost (INR)
Housing (rent/mortgage, maintenance)	₹25,000	₹3,00,000
Utilities (electricity, water, internet)	₹4,000	₹48,000
Groceries	₹15,000	₹1,80,000
Healthcare (insurance, prescriptions)	₹10,000	₹1,20,000
Transportation (fuel, insurance, maintenance)	₹5,000	₹60,000
Leisure & Travel	₹8,000	₹96,000
Entertainment (dining out, subscriptions)	₹5,000	₹60,000
Miscellaneous (gifts, hobbies, emergencies)	₹6,000	₹72,000
Savings for Emergency Fund	₹5,000	₹60,000
Total	**₹83,000**	**₹9,96,000**

Note:- The above estimates for a retirement budget in India are based on general cost-of-living data, trends in urban and semi-urban areas, and typical expenses for a comfortable but modest lifestyle. Here's how the numbers were derived. This budget allows for a comfortable lifestyle in a mid-sized city in India. Retirees may adjust these numbers based on their location and lifestyle preferences. For instance, those living in smaller towns could save more on housing and transportation, while retirees in metro cities might need a higher allocation for living costs.

At the same time, rising inflation paints a concerning picture for the future, particularly in the developing world, such as the Indian subcontinent. Current trends suggest that caring for retirees and elderly individuals will become increasingly challenging. The escalating cost of living, coupled with limited social security systems, threatens to widen the gap, leaving many vulnerable and struggling to meet even their basic needs. This growing crisis calls for urgent attention to safeguard the dignity and well-being of the elderly in these regions.

2.3 Social Security benefits

Definition & Brief Details:

Social Security refers to government programs that provide financial assistance to individuals in times of need, such as retirement, disability, unemployment, or after the death of a family breadwinner. The structure and coverage of social security programs vary significantly between countries. Here's a brief overview of social security benefits in India and Western countries:

1. Social Security in India

In India, the concept of social security is more limited compared to Western countries. It is primarily available to formal sector workers, with much of the population relying on family support and personal savings in old age. Key components include:

Key Programs:

- Employees' Provident Fund (EPF): A retirement savings scheme for employees in the formal sector, where both employer and employee contribute to a fund that provides income after retirement.
- Employees' Pension Scheme (EPS): This provides a pension to workers after retirement, also based on contributions made during employment.
- National Pension System (NPS): A voluntary pension scheme for both public and private sector employees. Workers contribute during their employment, and the funds are invested for retirement.
- Pradhan Mantri Shram Yogi Maan-Dhan (PMSYM): A pension scheme for workers in the informal sector, providing a monthly pension after retirement at 60 years of age.
- ESIC (Employees' State Insurance Scheme): Provides health insurance and disability benefits to employees earning below a certain threshold.

- Atal Pension Yojana (APY): A government-backed pension scheme for low-income workers.

Key Features:

- Pensions: Limited to formal sector workers; most rely on personal savings.
- Healthcare: Health insurance schemes are improving but not as comprehensive as in Western countries.
- Challenges: A large informal workforce, limited retirement benefits for many, and reliance on family support.

2. Social Security in Western Countries

Western countries typically have more extensive and well-established social security systems, covering a wide range of benefits such as retirement pensions, healthcare, disability support, and unemployment insurance. Here's a look at a few key countries:

United States:

- Social Security (Retirement, Disability, and Survivors Insurance): Funded through payroll taxes, this system provides monthly income to retirees, the disabled, and families of deceased workers. Workers earn credits based on employment, and benefits are based on lifetime earnings.
- Medicare: A health insurance program for individuals aged 65 and older, and for some younger people with disabilities.
- Supplemental Security Income (SSI): Provides financial assistance to low-income individuals who are elderly or disabled.

Canada:

- Canada Pension Plan (CPP): Provides retirement, disability, and survivors' benefits. Employees and employers contribute to the fund throughout their working life.

- Old Age Security (OAS): A government-funded pension available to all citizens and residents over 65, regardless of employment history.
- Employment Insurance (EI): Provides temporary financial assistance to unemployed workers.

United Kingdom:

- State Pension: A regular payment made to people who have reached state pension age, based on their National Insurance contributions during their working life.
- National Health Service (NHS): Provides healthcare to all residents funded by taxation.
- Disability Benefits: Various allowances and payments are available to individuals who are unable to work due to disability.

Germany:

- Statutory Pension Insurance (GRV): Provides retirement pensions, disability benefits, and survivor pensions. It is mandatory for employees and funded through payroll taxes.
- Health Insurance (GKV): Public health insurance is mandatory, with contributions based on income.
- Unemployment Insurance: Provides financial support and job placement assistance to unemployed individuals.

France:

- Pension System: Funded by both employers and employees, it provides retirement income based on the number of years worked and contributions made.
- Universal Health Coverage: All residents are covered for healthcare under a government-funded system.
- Unemployment Benefits: Support for individuals who have lost their jobs.

Japan:

- National Pension (NP): A public pension system where all residents between the ages of 20-59 contribute. Benefits are provided upon retirement at age 65.
- Employees' Pension Insurance (EPI): Mandatory for employees, providing a more substantial pension than the NP.
- Healthcare: Universal health insurance system, with coverage for all residents.
- Disability Benefits: Provided for those who are unable to work due to long-term illness or injury.

Comparison: India vs. Western Countries:

- Scope: Western countries generally offer more comprehensive social security systems, covering a wider range of benefits, such as unemployment insurance and universal healthcare. In India, social security is more limited, particularly for the informal sector.
- Funding: In Western countries, social security is primarily funded through payroll taxes, while in India, it is a mix of employer contributions, government schemes, and personal savings.
- Healthcare: Most Western countries have some form of universal healthcare, whereas India's healthcare system is improving but remains largely out-of-pocket for much of the population, especially those not in formal employment.
- Retirement: Western countries provide more robust and reliable pensions, while in India, pensions are limited to those in the formal sector, with informal workers relying on voluntary schemes like the National Pension System (NPS).

Conclusion:

Social security in Western countries tends to be more comprehensive and covers a broader spectrum of the population, including retirees, the disabled, and the unemployed. In contrast, India's system is still evolving, with a significant focus on formal sector employees, though new programs are being introduced to extend coverage to informal workers (but still the system is very sluggish & retirees have to struggle much to get these facilities).

2.4 Managing Debt & Expenses

Definition of Debt and Expenses in Retirement

Managing debt and expenses in retirement refers to the strategic handling of outstanding debts and daily living costs during the retirement years to maintain financial stability. It involves developing a plan to minimize debt, control expenses, and make the most of available income sources such as pensions, retirement savings, or social security benefits. Effective management ensures that retirees can enjoy a comfortable lifestyle while avoiding financial stress.

Brief Details: Managing Debt and Expenses in Retirement

1. **Managing Debt:**
    - Debt Reduction: Retirees should aim to minimize or eliminate high-interest debts (such as credit card balances and personal loans) before or early in retirement. Paying down mortgages, car loans, and other liabilities reduces financial burdens during retirement.
    - Debt Consolidation: Retirees with multiple debts can consider consolidating loans to reduce interest rates and simplify payments. This can lower monthly payments, freeing up cash flow.
    - Refinancing: For larger debts like mortgages, refinancing to secure lower interest rates or longer repayment terms can help manage monthly payments more easily.
    - Avoid New Debt: Retirees should avoid taking on new debt unless absolutely necessary, as fixed retirement incomes may not provide the flexibility to handle additional financial obligations.

2. **Managing Expenses:**
    - Budgeting: Creating a retirement budget helps track monthly income and expenses, ensuring that living costs stay within available income. This includes planning for essential expenses (housing, food, utilities, healthcare) and discretionary spending (travel, entertainment).
    - Healthcare Costs: Healthcare is often a significant expense in retirement. Retirees should allocate a portion of their budget for medical insurance, out-of-pocket medical expenses, and emergencies. Long-term care, if needed, should also be considered.
    - Downsizing: Reducing living costs by moving to a smaller home or a region with a lower cost of living can help manage expenses effectively.
    - Discretionary Spending: Retirees should carefully manage non-essential spending (e.g., travel, hobbies) to avoid depleting savings too quickly, especially in the early years of retirement.
    - Inflation Planning: Retirees need to account for inflation in their financial plans, ensuring that their income and savings can keep up with rising living costs over time.

Key Considerations:

- Income Sources: Retirees typically rely on a fixed income from pensions, retirement savings, social security benefits, or investments. Effective debt and expense management helps stretch this income over many years.
- Emergency Fund: Maintaining a cash reserve for unexpected expenses is crucial to avoid dipping into long-term savings or taking on new debt during retirement.

Conclusion:

Properly managing debt and expenses in retirement ensures financial security and peace of mind. By reducing debt, controlling living costs, and planning for future expenses, retirees can maintain a comfortable lifestyle without the risk of running out of money.

India vs. Western Countries

Retirement is a time to enjoy the fruits of your labor, but managing debt and expenses is critical to ensuring financial security. Let's explore how managing debt and expenses in retirement differs in **India** and **Western countries**.

Managing Debt in Retirement

India:

1. **Debt in Retirement**:
    - **Cultural Context**: In India, carrying debt into retirement is less common compared to Western countries. Many Indian retirees aim to be debt-free by retirement, influenced by cultural values that emphasize living within one's means and avoiding loans, especially later in life.
    - **Common Debts**: If present, debt typically includes **home loans**, **personal loans**, or **family obligations** (e.g., children's education or weddings).
    - **Interest Rates**: Interest rates on loans can be relatively high, so paying off debts before retirement is crucial to avoid excessive interest charges. For example, home loans often carry interest rates between **8-10%** per annum.
    - **Managing Debt**: Retirees should aim to clear debts by focusing on early repayment strategies or refinancing loans for lower interest rates. Selling property or using lump-sum retirement benefits (such as **Provident Fund** or **Gratuity**) to pay off debts is also common.

2. **Credit Card Debt**:
    - Many Indian retirees avoid credit card debt, as interest rates are high (often exceeding **30% per annum**). Careful use of credit cards for necessary expenses is important, and clearing balances monthly is advised.

Note:- According to the latest survey:

Only 38% of respondents are debt-free, and alarmingly, 31% of those aged 60 and above are still dealing with EMIs (Equated Monthly Installments).

Insurance planning: A staggering 73% of respondents are either uninsured or underinsured for health, and 74% lack adequate life insurance.

Western Countries:

1. **Debt in Retirement**:
    - **Cultural Context**: In countries like the **US**, **Canada**, and the **UK**, it is more common for retirees to carry debt into retirement. Debts may include **mortgages**, **credit card debt**, and **auto loans**.
    - **Mortgages**: Many Western retirees continue to pay off their homes. However, interest rates on mortgages in Western countries tend to be lower, around **3-5%** in recent years.
    - **Refinancing and Debt Management**: Many retirees refinance their mortgages at lower rates or extend payment terms to manage monthly costs. Debt consolidation is also common to manage high-interest loans (e.g., credit cards).
2. **Credit Card Debt**:
    - Credit card debt can be a significant problem in retirement due to high interest rates (often **15-25% per annum**). Western retirees often use **debt consolidation loans** or **balance transfer credit cards** to lower interest rates and simplify payments.

Managing Expenses in Retirement

India:

1. **Living Costs**:
    - **Lower Living Costs**: In general, the cost of living in India is lower than in Western countries, particularly in smaller cities or rural areas. Retirees may spend less on **housing**, **food**, and **utilities**. For example, a modest lifestyle in a mid-tier city may require between **₹50,000 - ₹80,000 per month**.
    - **Healthcare Costs**: Healthcare is a significant expense for Indian retirees, especially for those without health insurance. Private healthcare can be expensive, but the cost is still lower than in Western countries. Health insurance is critical, and retirees should allocate part of their budget to medical emergencies.
    - **Family Support**: Many retirees in India depend on family for financial support or live with children to reduce living costs. The concept of joint families helps minimize expenses like housing and daily living costs.
2. **Budgeting for Retirement**:
    - **Pensions & Savings**: Indian retirees typically rely on government pensions, **Provident Fund** withdrawals, **National Pension System (NPS)** savings, and **Gratuity**. However, these funds may not be sufficient, so careful budgeting is necessary to stretch savings over many years.
    - **Downsizing**: Many Indian retirees downsize their homes or move to smaller cities or towns with lower living costs to manage expenses.

Western Countries:

1. **Living Costs**:
    - **Higher Living Costs**: The cost of living in Western countries, particularly in urban areas, is generally higher. Monthly retirement expenses for a couple in the **US** or **Canada** can range from **$3,500 - $6,000 USD** (approximately ₹2,80,000 - ₹4,80,000 INR), depending on the region.
    - **Healthcare Costs**:
        - **US**: Healthcare is a significant concern in the US, where **Medicare** provides some relief but does not cover all medical expenses. Many retirees purchase **Medigap** or **private insurance** to cover additional costs. Healthcare costs can consume a large portion of the retirement budget.
        - **Canada/UK**: In countries with **universal healthcare** (e.g., Canada, UK), healthcare costs are lower in retirement as the government covers most medical expenses. However, private insurance may be needed for additional services.
2. **Budgeting for Retirement**:
    - **Pensions & Social Security**: Retirees in Western countries typically rely on **Social Security** (in the US), **Canada Pension Plan (CPP)**, or **State Pension** (UK), alongside personal savings (e.g., **401(k)**, **IRAs**, or **pension funds**). These pensions provide a consistent income stream.
    - **Spending Patterns**: Western retirees often reduce their living expenses by downsizing homes, relocating to areas with lower costs, or moving to senior living communities.
    - **Travel & Leisure**: Many Western retirees allocate significant portions of their retirement income to travel and leisure activities, which can increase overall spending during the early years of retirement.

Debt and Expense Management Strategies for Retirees

1. Prioritize Debt Repayment Before Retirement:

- **India**: Try to clear off home loans, personal loans, and other debts before retiring. Use lump-sum benefits like **Provident Fund** and **Gratuity** to clear debts.
- **Western Countries**: Plan to pay down high-interest debts, such as credit cards, before retirement. Consider refinancing mortgages at lower rates.

2. Budget for Healthcare:

- **India**: Invest in **health insurance** and maintain an emergency fund for medical expenses. Healthcare is more affordable, but costs can escalate for private treatment.
- **Western Countries**: In the US, factor in **Medicare** and potential additional costs like private insurance. In countries with universal healthcare (Canada, UK), consider out-of-pocket expenses for services not covered by the government.

3. Reduce Living Costs:

- **India**: Consider downsizing to a smaller home or relocating to a city or town with lower living costs.
- **Western Countries**: Many retirees downsize or move to regions with a lower cost of living. Some choose to retire abroad in countries where their retirement savings stretch further.

4. Live Within a Fixed Income:

- **India**: Most retirees depend on savings, pensions, and **Provident Fund** withdrawals. Stick to a monthly budget and avoid large, unnecessary expenses.
- **Western Countries**: Social security and pensions provide consistent income, but be mindful of overspending, especially in

the early years of retirement. Factor in inflation and healthcare costs.

5. Minimize Discretionary Spending:

India:

- Avoid overspending on non-essential items like luxury goods or high-interest purchases (e.g., expensive electronics on EMI).
- Avoid taking on costly new projects like building or remodeling your home during this phase. Instead, focus on enjoying the space you already have. Major expenses like these can strain your finances at a time when stability is key, and the stress of managing them might outweigh the benefits. Embrace simplicity and prioritize your financial peace of mind over expensive undertakings.
- Eliminating harmful habits such as alcohol, cigarettes, or tobacco use during this time is crucial, as they not only drain your finances but also impact your health and well-being in the long run. Breaking free from these costly vices will help you save money directly and avoid the hidden costs of medical bills and reduced quality of life down the road. It's a step toward a healthier, more fulfilling retirement.
- Gambling among retirees in India is a growing concern, though it's less prevalent compared to Western countries due to cultural and social factors. However, with the rise of online gambling & betting platforms, Cards games- Teen Patti or Rummy in social gathering, Sports betting, lotteries etc may initially look thrilling & fun which will ultimately lead to a downward spiral where financial losses cause emotional distress, which in turn drives more gambling.

Western Countries:

After retirement, certain bad habits can develop as individuals adjust to a new lifestyle. In Western countries, some of the most common tendencies of retirees may fall into the following. Recognizing these tendencies and establishing a healthy routine can help retirees maintain a fulfilling and balanced lifestyle as well as financial status.

- **Excessive Spending**: Without the steady income from work, some retirees may indulge in overspending on hobbies, travel, or home improvements, leading to financial strain.
- **Increased Alcohol Consumption**: With more free time and socializing, retirees may be tempted to drink more frequently, which can negatively affect both health and finances.
- At this stage of life, having more free time and falling into the wrong social circles can often lead to the dangerous habit of consuming **drugs or tobacco**. Not only does this pose serious health risks, but it also drains a significant portion of your hard-earned savings, turning what should be a relaxing phase into a costly and harmful ordeal.
- **Over-reliance on Prescription Medications: As health issues** become more common with age, some retirees may misuse or become overdependent on medications, especially painkillers or sedatives.
- **Gambling**: For some, gambling can become a new hobby or a way to pass time, leading to potential financial problems if not controlled.
- **Unhealthy Eating**: A lack of structure can lead to poor dietary choices, such as excessive snacking, fast and processed food consumption, or overindulging in comfort foods.

Conclusion:

Managing debt and expenses during retirement is a critical aspect of securing financial well-being. In **India**, where family (mainly joint) support and cultural norms often dictate a debt-free retirement, emphasis should be on healthcare and conservative spending. In **Western countries**, where retirees may carry more debt into retirement, managing mortgages, healthcare, and living costs through smart budgeting and debt consolidation is essential. Both regions benefit from early financial planning and debt management before entering retirement.

At the same time, rising inflation paints a concerning picture for the future, particularly in the developing world, such as the Indian subcontinent. Current trends suggest that caring for retirees and elderly individuals will become increasingly challenging. The escalating cost of living, coupled with limited social security systems, threatens to widen the gap, leaving many vulnerable and struggling to meet even their basic needs. This growing crisis calls for urgent attention to safeguard the dignity and well-being of the elderly in these regions.

2.5 Investment Strategies for Retirees

Investment Strategies for Retirees in both India and Western countries (including the US and Canada) must be tailored to focus on generating consistent income, preserving capital, and minimizing risk while considering inflation and life expectancy. Below are the key elements of investment strategies for retirees, followed by country-specific details.

Core Principles of Investment Strategies for Retirees

1. **Capital Preservation**: Retirees should prioritize protecting their accumulated wealth. This means avoiding high-risk investments that could significantly erode the retirement corpus.
2. **Income Generation:** Investments should provide a steady and reliable income stream to cover living expenses, healthcare costs, and lifestyle needs during retirement.
3. **Risk Management:** Retirees typically move to a more conservative investment portfolio. However, some exposure to growth assets (stocks, etc.) is important to counter inflation and ensure long-term sustainability.
4. **Diversification:** A well-diversified portfolio across asset classes like equities, bonds, real estate, and alternative investments can help reduce risk and improve returns.
5. **Inflation Protection:** As the cost of living rises, investment strategies must account for inflation by including assets like stocks or inflation-indexed securities.
6. **Tax Efficiency:** Retirees should seek to minimize tax liabilities, whether through tax-advantaged retirement accounts or tax-efficient investment vehicles.

Investment Strategies in India

1. Senior Citizens' Savings Scheme (SCSS):

- One of the most popular investment options for retirees in India, SCSS provides regular income with government-backed security.
- Current interest rates (2024) are around 8-8.5%.
- Maturity is five years, with the option to extend.

2. Fixed Deposits (FDs):
    - Retirees often rely on FDs due to their safety and guaranteed returns.
    - Many banks offer special rates for senior citizens (0.25%-0.5% higher interest rates).
    - The downside is that returns may not outpace inflation.
3. Post Office Monthly Income Scheme (POMIS):
    - A reliable option for retirees seeking steady monthly income with minimal risk.
    - Interest rates range between 6-7%.
4. Mutual Funds:
    - Debt-Oriented Mutual Funds: Suitable for conservative investors. These funds invest in bonds and other fixed-income securities, offering more stability.
    - Balanced or Hybrid Funds: These funds provide a mix of equity and debt exposure, allowing retirees some growth potential without high risk.
    - Systematic Withdrawal Plans (SWP): Through mutual funds, retirees can set up SWPs to receive regular payouts, ensuring liquidity while maintaining a diversified portfolio.
5. Annuities:
    - Offered by life insurance companies, annuities provide a guaranteed income stream for life or for a set period.
    - Immediate Annuities: Suitable for retirees looking to start income right away.
    - However, returns on annuities can be lower than other instruments, and once invested, liquidity is limited.
6. Equities and Dividend Stocks:
    - Some retirees choose to keep a small portion in equities to beat inflation. Focusing on dividend-paying stocks ensures

some income generation while benefiting from capital appreciation.

- Blue-chip Stocks and Large-Cap Funds are usually recommended for safety.

Investment Strategies in the US and Canada

1. 401(k) / RRSP (Registered Retirement Savings Plan):
    - Retirees often rely on their 401(k) (US) or RRSP (Canada) as the cornerstone of their retirement income. These tax-advantaged accounts allow for tax-deferred growth.
    - In retirement, individuals can draw down from these accounts, typically using a Required Minimum Distribution (RMD) method to ensure sustainable withdrawals.
2. Social Security / Canada Pension Plan (CPP):
    - Social Security in the US and CPP in Canada are foundational income sources for retirees. Delaying benefits (beyond the standard age of 62-65) can increase monthly payouts.
    - Investment strategies often focus on supplementing these payouts through other savings and investments.
3. Bonds and Bond Funds:
    - Retirees in Western countries often invest in Treasury bonds or Corporate bonds for reliable income.
    - Bond ladders are a popular strategy where retirees invest in bonds with staggered maturities to manage interest rate risk and generate regular income.
4. Dividend-Paying Stocks:
    - Dividend stocks, especially blue-chip companies, are key for retirees seeking income in the US and Canada.
    - Dividend Aristocrats (companies that have increased dividends for over 25 years) are particularly attractive.
    - Stocks like these provide both income and the potential for capital appreciation, helping to fight inflation.
5. Annuities:

    - In both the US and Canada, Fixed Annuities and Variable Annuities provide guaranteed income.
    - Fixed annuities provide stability, while variable annuities allow for growth through equity market exposure, though they come with higher fees.
    - Immediate Annuities and Deferred Annuities are common for those looking for predictable lifetime income.
6. Real Estate Investment:
    - Investing in REITs (Real Estate Investment Trusts) is a popular strategy for retirees in the US and Canada, offering steady income through dividends without the hassle of managing property.
    - Some retirees may also invest in rental properties directly for a more hands-on approach to generating income.
7. Inflation-Protected Securities:
    - In the US, Treasury Inflation-Protected Securities (TIPS) are government bonds that adjust with inflation, making them a popular choice for retirees concerned about rising costs.
    - Canada offers similar instruments through Real Return Bonds (RRBs).

Key Considerations for All Retirees

1. Withdrawal Strategy:
    - A common approach is the 4% rule, which suggests withdrawing 4% of your portfolio in the first year of retirement and adjusting for inflation each year. This is widely followed in the US and Canada but can also apply in India with appropriate adjustments.
    - For a more conservative approach, retirees may consider a bucket strategy: dividing their portfolio into short-term (cash, bonds), medium-term (balanced funds), and long-term (equities, real estate) segments.
2. Healthcare Costs:

    - In the US, healthcare costs in retirement are a major concern, requiring investments to fund rising medical expenses. Health Savings Accounts (HSAs) are tax-advantaged vehicles that can help manage these costs.
    - In India, retirees may need health insurance and a medical emergency fund, as out-of-pocket expenses can be high.
3. Estate Planning:
    - Retirees should focus on passing on wealth efficiently. Trusts, wills, and beneficiary designations are important tools, especially in Western countries, where estate taxes can be high.

By focusing on a diversified, income-generating, and inflation-resistant portfolio, retirees in both India and Western countries can enjoy financial security and peace of mind throughout their retirement years.

Core Principles of Investment Strategies for Retirees - based on Islamic shariah & Sunnah

Investment strategies for retirees rooted in **Islamic Shariah and the Sunnah** emphasize a harmonious blend of ethics, responsibility, and financial security. These principles ensure that investments align with Islamic teachings while protecting one's wealth. Though navigating today's complex global financial landscape can be challenging, it is certainly not impossible. In fact, adhering to these principles offers a **pure and sustainable financial path**—one that not only strengthens personal finances but also contributes to shielding the world from the excesses of **chronic capitalism**. Here are the essential guidelines that, while demanding, offer immense value for those committed to them.

1. Avoidance of Riba (Interest)

- Riba (interest) is strictly prohibited in Islam. Any form of return on investment that involves interest, such as bonds or savings accounts in conventional banks, should be avoided. Retirees should instead seek interest-free investments like Islamic savings accounts or Sukuk (Islamic bonds), where profit-sharing is based on real assets and economic activities.

2. **Engagement in Halal Investments**

- Investments must only be in halal (permissible) businesses or industries. This excludes sectors such as:
    - Alcohol, tobacco, gambling, pornography.
    - Conventional banking and insurance that involve interest.
    - Businesses that promote unethical or harmful products.
- Retirees should focus on investments in sectors like healthcare, education, halal food, technology, and real estate.

3. Risk Sharing and Profit-Loss Sharing (PLS)

- **Islamic finance** promotes equity-based investments where profits and losses are shared between the investor and the business. This can be in the form of:
    - **Mudarabah:** A partnership where one party provides capital and the other manages the business.
    - **Musharakah**: A joint venture where both parties contribute capital and share profits and losses.
- These encourage fairness, as both the risks and rewards are shared.

4. **Diversification**

- Diversifying investments helps spread risk, which aligns with the Islamic principle of avoiding excessive risk (gharar). Retirees should diversify across different halal asset classes, such as:
    - Real estate: Investing in rental properties or Shariah-compliant real estate funds.
    - Sukuk (Islamic bonds): Bonds backed by tangible assets.
    - Islamic stocks: Stocks that are Shariah-compliant, focusing on companies with ethical business practices.

    - Gold and commodities: Historically viewed as stable, inflation-resistant assets in Islamic tradition.

5. Charitable Giving (Zakat and Sadaqah)

- Zakat is an obligatory charitable contribution, and retirees should continue to pay it, as it purifies wealth. This is typically 2.5% of annual savings and investments if above the nisab (Minimum amount of wealth a Muslim must have before they can pay Zakat) threshold.
- Sadaqah (voluntary charity) is highly encouraged, and retirees may include it in their financial plans as a means of earning ongoing rewards (sadaqah jariyah) while supporting the community.

6. Avoiding Excessive Speculation (Gharar)

- Speculation or engaging in excessively uncertain or risky investments (gharar) is forbidden. Retirees should stay away from day trading, forex trading, or any form of derivatives or futures contracts that involve uncertainty and risk akin to gambling.

7. Real Estate Investment

- Islamic finance encourages real assets as they represent tangible value. Real estate is a favored investment for retirees, as it provides:
    - A source of stable, halal income through rental.
    - Appreciation in property value over time.
    - Shariah-compliant financing options like Islamic mortgages that avoid interest.

8. Ensuring Liquidity for Daily Needs

- Retirees should keep enough liquid assets for day-to-day expenses, ensuring they don't invest everything in long-term or illiquid investments. Having a cash reserve or investing in Shariah-compliant short-term instruments ensures financial stability.

9. Estate Planning and Inheritance (Mirath)

- Islamic inheritance laws should guide retirees in planning their wealth distribution according to Shariah. Creating a will (Wasiyyah) that aligns with Islamic guidelines ensures rightful heirs receive their shares as mandated in the Qur'an.

10. Consulting with Shariah Advisors

- Retirees should seek guidance from qualified Shariah-compliant financial advisors to ensure their investments remain halal and aligned with Islamic principles. This is especially important when investing in modern financial products that may require expert scrutiny for compliance.

In summary, retirees should focus on ethical, low-risk, and halal investments, emphasizing real assets, risk-sharing models, and charitable giving, while ensuring liquidity and estate planning according to Islamic inheritance rules. These principles help maintain financial well-being in a manner that aligns with both Shariah and the Sunnah.

2.6 Health Insurance and Long Term Care

Health Insurance for Retirees

India:

In India, health insurance for retirees is still developing, with some significant challenges due to limited government-sponsored programs.

1. **Government Schemes:**
   - For retirees in India, the government offers some health insurance schemes like the Ayushman Bharat program. However, its coverage is limited, especially for the middle-class or upper-middle-class retirees who might not qualify.
   - State employees and government retirees often have access to the Central Government Health Scheme (CGHS) or similar state-run schemes, which provide lifelong health coverage.
2. **Private Insurance:**
   - Private health insurance is crucial for retirees, but premiums increase with age, and pre-existing conditions can make it harder to get coverage.
   - Specialized plans for seniors or retirees are available from companies like Star Health, Max Bupa, and HDFC Ergo, but they come with higher premiums, co-payments, and limited coverage compared to plans for younger policyholders.
3. **Challenges:**
   - Many retirees do not have access to comprehensive health insurance due to costs or limited awareness of coverage options.
   - There's a growing need for long-term care (nursing homes, assisted living) insurance, but it's relatively uncommon.

Western Countries (US, Canada, Europe)

1. **United States:**
   - Medicare is the primary health insurance for retirees aged 65 and older. It covers hospital care (Part A) and medical services (Part B), but it doesn't cover everything. Most retirees purchase Medicare Supplement (Medigap) or Medicare Advantage plans for additional coverage.
   - Medicaid: For low-income retirees or those who have exhausted their savings, Medicaid can help with long-term care costs, but only after meeting strict financial eligibility criteria.
   - Private Insurance: Some retirees maintain private insurance through their employer or purchase additional plans to cover gaps in Medicare.
2. **Canada:**
   - Canada's universal healthcare system, Medicare, covers essential healthcare services for all citizens, including retirees. Coverage includes doctor visits, hospital care, and some prescription drugs, but doesn't cover everything, such as dental care or vision.
   - Private Insurance: Retirees often buy supplemental private insurance to cover services not included in the government's plan, especially for extended health services like physiotherapy or prescription drugs.

3. **European Countries:**
   - In countries with strong welfare systems like Germany, France, and the UK, retirees enjoy government-sponsored healthcare.
   - For example, the UK's National Health Service (NHS) offers free or subsidized healthcare to all, including retirees. In countries like Germany, retirees either remain in public health insurance or switch to private insurance if they were privately insured during their working years.

Long-Term Care for Retirees

India:

Long-term care options for retirees are limited in India. While the tradition of family care for elderly members remains strong, the following trends are emerging:

- Private Care Facilities: Growing urbanization and smaller families have led to an increase in private long-term care facilities, nursing homes, and retirement communities.
- Challenges: Long-term care insurance is rare in India. Most expenses for elderly care (home nursing, assisted living) are paid out of pocket, as few insurers cover this area comprehensively.

United States:

- Medicaid: Medicaid covers long-term care for low-income retirees, but only after the individual spends down their assets. It includes nursing home care, home health services, and assisted living.
- Private Insurance: Long-term care insurance policies are available but costly, especially for older adults. These policies can help cover the high costs of nursing homes or home care, but fewer people are purchasing them due to rising premiums.
- Costs: Nursing homes and long-term care facilities in the U.S. are very expensive, and without insurance, they can quickly deplete savings.

Canada

- Long-term care in Canada is provided through a combination of public and private services.
- Public Services: Provincial health plans cover some aspects of long-term care, such as home care or basic nursing home care, but the quality and availability of services can vary widely by region.

- Private Care: Many retirees may need to supplement public care with private services, which can be costly. Long-term care insurance is available but is not as commonly used as in the U.S.

Western Europe

- Countries like Germany have mandatory long-term care insurance (LTCI), which covers home care, nursing homes, and other long-term care services. The Pflegeversicherung system helps retirees with daily care costs.
- In Scandinavian countries and the Netherlands, long-term care is funded through public taxes and provides generous coverage, though there are private options available as well.

Key Differences

- India: Relies more on out-of-pocket expenses for healthcare and long-term care, with limited government-sponsored options for retirees.
- Western Countries: Countries like the U.S., Canada, and Europe have more structured government programs (Medicare, Medicaid, universal health care), with options for private insurance. Long-term care coverage is also better established, though costs can be high in the U.S. and Canada without adequate insurance.

In all cases, planning for healthcare and long-term care during retirement is critical, especially with rising medical costs globally.

Abrahamic concept on "HEALTH INSURANCE & LONG TERM CARE" for retiree

A Challenge in the present society

The Abrahamic religions—Judaism, Christianity, and Islam— I would like to share some common ethical principles regarding care for the elderly and vulnerable. Although they differ in certain doctrines and practices, the underlying values of compassion, community responsibility, and family support are emphasized across all three. Here's an exploration of how health insurance and long-term care for retirees can be understood through these religious lenses.

The rise of nuclear families and the relentless pursuit of material success have left many struggling to balance life's demands. Financial pressures and time constraints make it increasingly difficult for individuals to focus on the needs of others, particularly the elderly. As a result, a significant percentage of retirees and senior citizens are being neglected, sparking deep concern within society about how we care for our aging population.

At the same time, spiritual and religious values are rapidly fading in today's globalized world, where the uncertainties of future lifestyles overshadow the importance of inner peace and moral grounding. This decline leaves a void in the fabric of society, as the quest for material success often eclipses the deeper meaning of life.

Islam:-

In Islamic teachings, financial and social systems are deeply intertwined with ethical and religious guidelines. When it comes to health insurance and long-term care, Islamic principles emphasize mutual aid, ethical financial practices, and family responsibility. Here's an overview of how these concepts align with Islamic values:

Islamic Concept of Health Insurance

In traditional Islamic law (Shariah), there are considerations that affect conventional health insurance, particularly regarding:

- Gharar (Uncertainty): In insurance, uncertainty is involved in the timing and amount of payout, which can conflict with Islamic principles.
- Maisir (Gambling): Insurance often involves risk-sharing where the policyholder may pay premiums without getting any benefit, which can be seen as gambling.
- Riba (Interest): Conventional insurance companies often invest premiums in interest-based financial instruments, which is forbidden in Islam.

Because of these concerns, conventional health insurance can be viewed as problematic in traditional Islamic finance. However, Islamic scholars have developed alternative models to ensure that health and financial security can still be protected under Shariah-compliant principles.

Takaful (Islamic Insurance)

The concept of Takaful (Islamic cooperative insurance) has been created as a Shariah-compliant alternative to conventional insurance. Takaful operates on the basis of mutual assistance (Ta'awun) and shared responsibility. Here's how it works:

- Risk Sharing: In Takaful, participants contribute to a fund with the intention of mutual protection, rather than profit. If a participant faces a health issue, they receive support from the shared pool.
- Cooperative Model: Takaful is based on the idea that the community supports each other, in line with the Islamic principle of social solidarity (Musharaka).
- Profit and Loss Sharing: Any surplus in the fund after claims are paid out can be distributed among the participants or reinvested. If there is a shortfall, it's either covered by additional contributions or shared among the participants.

This model allows Muslims to participate in health insurance without violating the core principles of Shariah. Many countries with significant Muslim populations, such as Malaysia and the UAE, have developed Takaful schemes that include health coverage.

Islamic Concept of Long-Term Care

In Islam, the concept of long-term care for the elderly is closely tied to family responsibility and social welfare. Several Quranic verses and Hadiths emphasize the duty of children and society to care for their elderly parents and relatives.

Family Responsibility

1. Care for Parents: Islam places great importance on respecting and caring for parents, especially in their old age. The Quran commands children to show kindness and compassion toward their parents as they grow older:
    - Quran 17:23: "Your Lord has decreed that you not worship except Him, and to parents, good treatment. Whether one or both of them reach old age [while] with you, say not to them [so much as], 'uff,' (displeasure or frustration) and do not repel them but speak to them a noble word."
    - Hadith: The Prophet Muhammad (PBUH) said: "Paradise lies at the feet of your mother" (Al-Nasa'i), underscoring the importance of serving one's parents.
2. Zakat and Charity: The Islamic welfare system encourages the support of the needy and vulnerable, including the elderly, through Zakat (obligatory almsgiving) and Sadaqah (voluntary charity). These funds can be used to support long-term care facilities or community programs for the elderly.

Islamic Welfare and Waqf (Endowment):

Waqf is an **Islamic charitable endowment** — it means **dedicating something (wealth, land, property, etc.) permanently for the sake of Allah**, to benefit people **without expecting any return**.

- Waqf (Islamic Endowment): Islamic tradition includes the creation of waqf, or charitable endowments, which can be dedicated to the care of the elderly, the sick, and the needy. Waqf properties and funds are often used to build hospitals, care facilities, or homes for the elderly & needy.
- Community and Mosque-Based Support: Historically, mosques and Islamic institutions have played a key role in supporting community members in need, including retirees and the elderly. These facilities can provide not only spiritual care but also practical long-term assistance.

Note: A Storm Around Waqf: Reform or Sabotage in India?

Recently, a bill was passed in the Indian Parliament that has sparked deep concern and unrest among the Muslim community. While the bill claims to "reform" and "improve" the Waqf system, many see it as an attempt to sabotage the very essence and sacred purpose of Islamic Waqf — a system rooted in centuries of religious, social, and charitable service.

The troubling part? These changes have been made without proper consultation or consent from the Muslim community, especially the custodians and caretakers of Waqf properties — the very people responsible for preserving its integrity and purpose.

Even more controversially, the bill proposes the involvement of members from outside the Muslim community in the management of Waqf assets. This has been widely seen as a violation of minority rights, potentially conflicting with several fundamental rights guaranteed under the Indian Constitution, including Article 26, which gives religious communities the freedom to manage their own affairs.

The fallout has been significant. Legal experts, scholars, and community leaders have raised alarms, leading to formal petitions filed in the Supreme Court of India. The Court has assured that a judicial review and constitutional judgment will follow — a step awaited with great hope and anxiety by millions.

What was presented as an administrative reform now appears to many as an attempt to dilute religious autonomy, interfere in community rights, and potentially open the gates for political exploitation of sacred institutions.

Takaful for Long-Term Care

While long-term care insurance is a relatively new concept in many Muslim-majority countries, the Takaful model is being adapted to cover elderly care services, including nursing homes and home-based care, ensuring that care is provided in a Shariah-compliant manner. However, in many Islamic societies, long-term care remains largely the responsibility of families rather than the state or private insurance.

Challenges and Opportunities

1. Cultural Expectations: In many Muslim societies, it is expected that families will care for their elderly relatives at home, which reduces the reliance on institutional long-term care. This can create tension in modern urbanized settings where family members may struggle to provide adequate care due to work commitments or financial limitations.
2. Emerging Trends: As the Muslim world modernizes and families become more nuclear, there is a growing need for Islamic long-term care facilities and services that are both culturally sensitive and Shariah-compliant. Islamic insurance products like Takaful can be expanded to cover elderly care expenses, though these products are still in their early stages.

Summary of Islamic Approach to Health Insurance and Long-Term Care:

- **Health Insurance:**
  - Conventional health insurance may conflict with Islamic principles due to issues with uncertainty (Gharar), gambling (Maisir), and interest (Riba).

    - Takaful offers a Shariah-compliant alternative for health coverage, based on cooperative risk-sharing and mutual assistance.
- **Long-Term Care:**
    - Islamic teachings place a strong emphasis on family responsibility for the elderly, with the care of aging parents seen as a religious duty.
    - Zakat, Sadaqah, and Waqf are mechanisms within the Islamic framework that can support elderly care for those without family support.
    - Takaful can be extended to cover long-term care services, although family-based care is often preferred.

Note:- Islamic principles encourage communities to provide for the health and well-being of retirees through mutual support, ethical financial practices, and family care, while emerging models like Takaful are adapting to modern healthcare needs.

Judaism:

Health Insurance and Long-Term Care in Judaism

Judaism emphasizes pikuach nefesh (Saving a life or saving a soul - the preservation of life), which mandates that a person's health and well-being are of utmost importance. Caring for the elderly and sick is considered a mitzvah (commandment), and Jewish tradition encourages proactive measures to ensure that individuals receive the care they need.

1. **Health Insurance:**
   - Tzedakah (Charity): Jewish law encourages financial responsibility and community-based welfare through tzedakah (charitable giving). This concept supports systems where communities or synagogues help fund healthcare for those in need, including retirees. Historically, Jewish communities have developed mutual aid societies to support members financially during illness.
   - Mutual Assistance: In traditional Jewish societies, community-based support mechanisms, such as gemach (free loan funds) or chevra kadisha (burial societies), often extended beyond death and assisted with health and welfare needs, including care for the sick and elderly.
2. **Long-Term Care:**
   - Family Obligation: The Torah commands honoring one's parents (Exodus 20:12), which includes caring for them in their old age. Jewish law emphasizes the moral and spiritual obligation of children to support their aging parents.
   - Charitable Institutions: Jewish communities have historically established institutions like hospitals, retirement homes, and nursing facilities to care for the elderly. Many of these are funded through donations and charitable endowments, emphasizing a communal approach to long-term care.

- Pikuach Nefesh: The value of life takes precedence over almost every other religious duty. If medical care, including long-term care, is needed to preserve life, it is obligatory.

Christianity:

Health Insurance and Long-Term Care in Christianity

Christianity emphasizes the responsibility of both individuals and the broader community to care for those in need, including the elderly and the sick. Agape (selfless love) forms the foundation of Christian ethics in this area, and the teachings of Jesus stress compassion and care for the vulnerable.

1. **Health Insurance:**
    - Church and Community Support: In early Christian communities, the church was a key provider of care, establishing hospitals, hospices, and charity organizations. Today, many Christian organizations still play a significant role in healthcare provision, often offering support to retirees through charitable donations, mutual aid societies, or church-funded programs.
    - Charitable Giving: Christian doctrine emphasizes generosity through tithing and almsgiving, which can support healthcare for the less fortunate, including retirees. This aligns with the Christian commitment to care for "the least of these" (Matthew 25:40), often leading to community-based efforts to fund health care.
2. **Long-Term Care:**
    - Biblical Commandments: Christianity teaches honoring and caring for one's parents as a commandment (Ephesians 6:2). The Fifth Commandment, common to all Abrahamic religions, stresses honoring one's father and

mother, which includes providing for their physical and emotional needs in old age.

- Institutional Care: Christian monasteries, convents, and churches have historically been at the forefront of caring for the elderly and sick. Many Christian organizations still run nursing homes, assisted living facilities, and hospices, where care is often subsidized by donations and church resources.
- Spiritual and Emotional Care: Beyond physical care, Christianity emphasizes providing spiritual comfort to the elderly, ensuring their emotional and religious needs are met through pastoral care, especially in the last stages of life.

<u>Common Themes Across Abrahamic Faiths:</u>

1. Family Responsibility: In all three Abrahamic faiths, there is a strong emphasis on the duty of children and family to care for elderly parents. This responsibility is seen as a religious obligation that fulfills commandments related to honoring one's parents.
2. Community and Charity: Each tradition emphasizes the role of the community in supporting the vulnerable. Whether through Zakat in Islam, Tzedakah in Judaism, or Christian charity, all three faiths stress the importance of communal responsibility for the health and well-being of the elderly and sick.
3. Mutual Aid and Cooperative Models: Traditional forms of mutual aid and modern forms like Takaful or charitable hospitals demonstrate a shared commitment to ensuring that everyone, including retirees, has access to healthcare, regardless of their ability to pay.
4. Institutional Care: Religious institutions across the Abrahamic faiths have historically been, and continue to be, involved in providing long-term care through hospitals, hospices, nursing homes, and elder care facilities.

Hinduism:

Health Insurance and Long-Term Care in Hinduism

In Hinduism, care for the elderly, health, and well-being is strongly rooted in the ethical and spiritual principles of **dharma** (duty), **karma** (action), and **seva** (selfless service). While the religion doesn't prescribe formal systems like health insurance or modern long-term care, its rich cultural and spiritual traditions offer a powerful framework for how individuals and communities should support and nurture the elderly, especially retirees. These values promote a holistic approach to caregiving, emphasizing the importance of family, community, and moral responsibility in ensuring the well-being of older generations.

Buddhism:

Health Insurance and Long-Term Care in Buddhism

In Buddhist philosophy, health insurance and long-term care for retirees are not just practical necessities but are deeply connected to the principles of compassion, mindfulness, and ethical living. Care for the elderly should be rooted in respect for the individual's dignity, social responsibility, and the understanding that aging is a natural part of life. While navigating modern healthcare systems may present challenges, aligning these systems with Buddhist principles encourages a more compassionate, ethical, and mindful approach to caring for retirees.

3.0 Psychological and Emotional Preparation for Retirement

Psychological and emotional preparation for retirement involves mentally adjusting to the major life changes that come with leaving the workforce. It requires preparing for shifts in daily routines, social roles, and identity, which can impact one's sense of purpose and self-worth.

The current trend in the global workforce tells a story of migration, driven by the desire for better prospects, higher opportunities, career advancement, and a safer future. In search of better wages, improved working conditions, and the hope for residency in developed nations, many leave their homes behind. People from underdeveloped and developing countries are moving to wealthier regions—such as the Gulf, the USA, Canada, and Europe—where hourly wages are higher, savings are greater, and the promise of retirement benefits looms large.

In pursuit of citizenship in developed countries and the promise of a brighter future, many risk everything by attempting the perilous "Donkey flights" journey. While a few manage to succeed, the majority face heartbreak and failure, trapped in a cycle of danger and uncertainty.

This migration story is not limited to crossing international borders. Within countries, a similar exodus occurs as individuals move from rural areas and small towns to sprawling cities, lured by the promise of a better life. Yet, for many, this pursuit of prosperity comes at a heavy cost. To save more and support their families, these individuals endure lives of immense sacrifice. Their lifestyles become increasingly burdensome, as they forego personal enjoyment to uplift their family's status and standard of living.

Tragically, these are often the prime years of their lives—the years when they should be savoring the fruits of their labor. Instead, they are overshadowed by relentless toil and unfulfilled dreams. This bittersweet reality paints a somber picture, particularly for the countless individuals from third-world countries who give their all but are unable to truly enjoy the life they work so hard to create for others.

These individuals often make the journey alone, leaving their families behind, working tirelessly to secure a brighter future for their loved ones. Their spouses and children enjoy an upgraded lifestyle: more income means access to better healthcare, higher-quality education, and the comforts of modern life. While families at home flourish, those who are away dedicate decades—sometimes 30 to 40 years—of their lives to this pursuit of financial stability and prosperity.

But then, the day arrives when the work ends. Retirement knocks at the door, and for many, it comes with the harsh reality of returning home, especially when the coveted residency permits in foreign lands remain out of reach. Here begins a new, unsettling chapter. After years of sending money home, providing for their families, and working long hours far from their loved ones, retirees return to an empty house. The once bustling family home is now silent, with only an aging spouse remaining. Their children, now grown, are likely following the same path—leaving home to seek their own fortunes abroad or in big cities, repeating the cycle their parents began.

The retired individual, now in their late 60s or 70s, finds themselves alone, grappling with the stark reality of isolation. After decades of hard work, they may need moral, financial, and physical support—yet, in many cases, no one is there to provide it. This is a bitter truth in today's global landscape, where the elderly and retirees are often left to navigate their twilight years in solitude. The shock of returning to such a reality is not just emotional but physical as well, causing profound mental stress and health challenges. For many, adjusting to this new life becomes an uphill battle.

This heartbreaking scenario is becoming all too common across the world, a byproduct of modern migration and the pursuit of better opportunities. It highlights a critical gap in how we care for our elderly and how society must address the deep emotional and physical needs of those who, after giving so much, find themselves forgotten at the end of their working years.

Key Modern Concepts:

1. **Identity Shift**: Retirement often means transitioning from a work-based identity to a more personal or hobby-based one, which can lead to a search for new meaning and purpose.
2. **Emotional Adaptation**: Retirees must manage feelings of loss, uncertainty, or isolation as they leave the structured environment of a job and potentially lose social connections.
3. **Mental Health Awareness**: Being proactive about mental health is important, as retirement can sometimes lead to stress, anxiety, or even depression due to the loss of routine and financial concerns.
4. **Positive Outlook**: Retirement is not an end but a beginning. A positive outlook, combined with the exploration of new activities, can lead to personal growth and fulfillment.

Preparing psychologically and emotionally helps retirees face this life phase with resilience and satisfaction, promoting well-being and a sense of fulfillment.

Key Religious and Spiritual Concepts:

Islamic: (2.04 billion, 25% of total world population- Mainly Indonesia, India, Pakistan, Bangladesh, Middle east, North Africa, Sub-Saharan Africa, Turkey,North America, Europe, Malaisia, Sri Lanka)

Islam's guidance for retirement is holistic, balancing spiritual growth, social responsibility, and personal peace. Key Islamic principles, such as Tawakkul (trust in Allah), Qana'ah (contentment), and preparing for the Akhirah, equip retirees with emotional stability and a deep sense of purpose. The honor and respect given to the elderly, along with the focus on continued engagement through family support and community service, create a comprehensive and well-defined framework for handling the psychological and emotional challenges of retirement. This makes the Islamic approach to retirement both practical and spiritually enriching, offering a sense of dignity, security, and fulfillment. Here is a detailed summary of **Islamic concepts for psychological and emotional preparation for retirement**, supported by **Quranic revelations, authentic Sunnah, and Hadith**:

1. Life as a Test and Continuation of Purpose

- **Qur'anic Revelation**: The Qur'an repeatedly reminds believers that life is a series of tests and each stage of life, including old age, has its purpose:
  - *"He created death and life to test you as to which of you is best in deed."* (Surah Al-Mulk 67:2)
  - *"And We bring you up in stages (through different phases of life)."* (Surah Al-Hajj 22:5)
  - This suggests that retirement is not the end of one's meaningful contributions but a period to increase devotion and introspection, leading to spiritual growth.
- **Hadith**: Prophet Muhammad (PBUH) highlighted that every action can be an act of worship if done with the right intention:
  - *"Actions are judged by their intentions, and everyone will be rewarded according to what they intended."* (Sahih Al-Bukhari 1)

2. Honor and Dignity of the Elderly

- **Qur'anic Revelation**: Islam commands respect and kindness toward the elderly, particularly parents:
  - *"And your Lord has decreed that you not worship except Him, and to parents, good treatment. Whether one or both of them reach old age while with you, say not to them [so much as], 'uff,' and do not repel them but speak to them a noble word."* (Surah Al-Isra 17:23)
  - This reinforces the high status of elderly individuals and retirees in society, ensuring they are cared for and valued.

- **Hadith**: Prophet Muhammad (PBUH) emphasized the importance of honoring the elderly:
    - *“He is not of us who does not show mercy to our young ones and esteem to our elderly.”* (Sunan Al-Tirmidhi 1919)
    - This Hadith makes it clear that a person’s moral worth is tied to how they treat the elderly, ensuring dignity for retirees.

3. <u>**Tawakkul (Trust in Allah’s Plan)**</u>

- **Qur'anic Revelation**: Believers are encouraged to place their complete trust in Allah, especially in uncertain times:
    - *"...And whoever relies upon Allah, then He is sufficient for him. Indeed, Allah will accomplish His purpose."* (Surah At-Talaq 65:3)
    - This verse reassures retirees that despite uncertainties in health or finances, Allah is the ultimate Provider, helping them maintain emotional stability through trust in His plan.
- **Hadith**: The Prophet Muhammad (PBUH) taught believers to remain calm and trust in Allah during difficult times:
    - *"If you were to rely upon Allah with the reliance He is due, you would be provided for as the birds are: they go out hungry in the morning and return full in the evening."* (Sunan Ibn Majah 4164)
    - This Hadith emphasizes the power of **Tawakkul**, easing the psychological burden retirees may feel when facing financial or health-related uncertainties.

4. <u>**Preparing for Akhirah (Hereafter)**</u>

- **Qur'anic Revelation**: Islam places significant importance on preparing for the **Akhirah (Hereafter)**, particularly in the later stages of life:
    - *"And worship your Lord until there comes to you the certainty (death)."* (Surah Al-Hijr 15:99)

    - This verse encourages retirees to use this stage of life for spiritual reflection, worship, and seeking Allah's forgiveness, shifting their focus from worldly pursuits to eternal success.
- **Hadith**: Prophet Muhammad (PBUH) reminded the believers to remain conscious of their final destination:
    - *“The wise person is the one who keeps his desires in check and works for what comes after death.”* (Sunan At-Tirmidhi 2459)
    - This guidance gives retirees a clear purpose—preparing for the Hereafter—providing psychological comfort and clarity as they age.

5. **Family Responsibility and Support**

- **Qur'anic Revelation**: The Qur'an repeatedly emphasizes the responsibility of family members, particularly children, to care for their aging parents:
    - *"We have enjoined upon man [care] for his parents. His mother carried him, [increasing her] in weakness upon weakness, and his weaning is in two years. Be grateful to Me and to your parents; to Me is the [final] destination."* (Surah Luqman 31:14)
    - This highlights that family care is a spiritual obligation, ensuring retirees are not neglected and receive emotional and physical support.
- **Hadith**: Prophet Muhammad (PBUH) placed great emphasis on treating parents with kindness in their old age:
    - *"May he be disgraced! May he be disgraced! May he be disgraced, the person whose parents, one or both, reach old age during his lifetime, and he does not enter Jannah (by serving them)."* (Sahih Muslim 2551)
    - This Hadith underscores that caring for parents is a means of entering Paradise, giving both parents and children a sense of fulfillment and purpose.

6. **Charity and Community Engagement**

- **Qur'anic Revelation**: Islam encourages continuous good deeds and community service, even in old age:
  - *"Those who spend their wealth [in Allah's way] by night and by day, secretly and publicly, they will have their reward with their Lord."* (Surah Al-Baqarah 2:274)
  - Retirees are encouraged to remain active through **Sadaqah (charity)** and other good deeds, ensuring their engagement with society and a sense of purpose beyond their working years.
- **Hadith**: Prophet Muhammad (PBUH) taught the value of ongoing charity:
  - *"When a person dies, his deeds are cut off except for three: ongoing charity, beneficial knowledge, or a righteous child who prays for him."* (Sahih Muslim 1631)
  - This Hadith encourages retirees to focus on acts that will benefit them after death, such as charity, which can bring emotional fulfillment during their retirement.

7. **Contentment (Qana'ah)**

- **Qur'anic Revelation**: Contentment with what Allah has provided is a key concept in Islam:
  - *"But seek, through that which Allah has given you, the home of the Hereafter; and [yet], do not forget your share of the world. And do good as Allah has done good to you."* (Surah Al-Qasas 28:77)
  - This verse teaches **Qana'ah** (contentment), helping retirees maintain inner peace by accepting their circumstances and focusing on spiritual growth rather than material gain.
- **Hadith**: Prophet Muhammad (PBUH) explained that true wealth lies in contentment:
  - *"Richness is not having many possessions, but richness is being content with oneself."* (Sahih Al-Bukhari 6446)

- This Hadith reassures retirees that emotional satisfaction comes not from wealth or status but from inner contentment, helping them navigate retirement with peace.

Christianity: (Approx. 2.38 billion followers, 31.1% of world total population, mainly in USA, Brazil, Mexico, Germany, UK, Russia, Philippines, China, Ireland, India)

1. **Trust in God's Plan**:
   - Christians believe in God's overarching plan for their lives, even in retirement. Verses like *"For I know the plans I have for you, declares the Lord, plans to prosper you..."* (Jeremiah 29:11) encourages retirees to trust in God's purpose for this new phase.
2. **Purpose Beyond Work**:
   - Christianity teaches that one's worth is not solely tied to work but to being created in the image of God. Retirees are encouraged to find new meaning in service, community, and deepening their relationship with God (Ephesians 2:10).
3. **Rest and Reflection**:
   - Retirement is seen as a time for rest, as God rested on the seventh day (Genesis 2:2). Retirees are encouraged to reflect on their life and grow spiritually, engaging in prayer, meditation, and scripture study.
4. **Community and Service**:
   - Christians are encouraged to serve others in retirement, embodying Jesus' teachings of love and charity (Matthew 25:40). Serving the church and community can bring emotional fulfillment and a sense of continued purpose.
5. **Hope in Eternal Life**:
   - Christian retirees are comforted by the hope of eternal life through Jesus Christ, easing the psychological and

emotional fears of aging and death (John 14:2-3). This provides peace and reassurance in the later stages of life.

Judaism: (15.7 million followers, approx. 0.2% of world population, mainly in Israel, USA, Europe & Russia)

1. **Life as a Sacred Journey:**
   - In Judaism, each stage of life is seen as part of a sacred journey. Retirement is an opportunity to embrace **reflection** and personal growth, with the belief that life continues to have value beyond work (Ecclesiastes 3:1).
2. **Kavod (Honor) for the Elderly**:
   - Jewish tradition emphasizes respect and honor for the elderly (Leviticus 19:32). This cultural and religious value ensures retirees feel dignified and supported, contributing to emotional well-being.
3. **Torah Study and Spiritual Growth**:
   - Retirement is seen as a time for deeper engagement in **Torah study** and spiritual development. Engaging with sacred texts and wisdom keeps retirees mentally and spiritually active, fostering peace and purpose (Psalm 92:12-14).
4. **Tzedakah (Charity):**
   - Jewish retirees are encouraged to give back through **Tzedakah** (charity). Acts of kindness and helping others in the community create a sense of fulfillment and reinforce social bonds (Proverbs 11:25).
5. **Continuity and Legacy**:
   - In Judaism, passing on wisdom and values to future generations is highly valued. Retirees focus on **l'dor v'dor** (from generation to generation), creating a sense of continuity, legacy, and purpose beyond their working years (Deuteronomy 4:9).

Summary:

Both **Christianity** and **Judaism** offer retirees psychological and emotional support through trust in God's plan, finding new purpose, honoring life's later stages, and focusing on community, charity, and spiritual reflection. These concepts promote peace, fulfillment, and a continued sense of meaning in retirement.

Hinduism: (one billion followers, 15.2% of world population, mainly in India, Pakistan, Bangladesh, Nepal, Sri Lanka, USA, Europe)

In **Hinduism**, psychological and emotional preparation for retirement is deeply rooted in its **philosophy of life's stages** (Ashramas), particularly the transition into **Vanaprastha** (the forest-dweller stage). This stage encourages individuals to gradually detach from material life and focus on spiritual growth, preparing for the final stage of **Sannyasa** (renunciation).

Key Concepts:

1. **Dharma (Duty):**
    - Retirement is viewed as a time to shift from **worldly responsibilities** to spiritual duties. After fulfilling family and societal obligations, one focuses on inner peace and self-realization, helping retirees mentally prepare for a life with less external activity.
2. **Detachment (Vairagya):**
    - Hindu philosophy encourages **detachment from material possessions and desires** in later life. This reduces anxiety and emotional turmoil as retirees learn to let go of past achievements, roles, and possessions, aligning with the pursuit of spiritual growth.
3. **Karma and Selfless Service (Seva):**
    - Even in retirement, the concept of **karma** and **seva** (selfless service) plays a key role. Retirees are

encouraged to contribute to society through charitable work, which fosters emotional fulfillment and purpose.

4. **Meditation and Spiritual Practices:**
   - **Meditation, yoga, and devotion (Bhakti)** become central practices in this stage, helping retirees maintain psychological balance, calmness, and emotional well-being by focusing on the **Atman (inner self)**.
5. **Acceptance and Contentment (Santosha):**
   - Hinduism emphasizes **contentment** and **acceptance of life's natural stages**. By embracing old age as part of the **cycle of life** (Samsara), retirees find peace, avoiding the fear of aging and death.

Summary:

Hindu philosophy prepares retirees for a peaceful and meaningful transition into retirement by promoting **detachment from material life, spiritual growth, selfless service**, and **inner reflection**, helping them find emotional balance and psychological well-being.

Buddhism: (Approx. 500 million, world fourth largest population, mainly in Asia pacific region, 6.6% of total population of world)

In Buddhism, psychological and emotional preparation for the elderly and retirees focuses on mindfulness, acceptance of impermanence, and spiritual growth. Key points include:

1. **Mindfulness (Satipatthana)**: Retirees are encouraged to cultivate mindfulness through meditation, staying present, and observing thoughts and emotions without attachment. This helps in maintaining mental clarity and emotional stability.
2. **Acceptance of Impermanence (Anicca)**: Buddhism teaches that everything is impermanent, including aging and death. Elders are guided to accept this reality, which reduces fear, anxiety, and emotional suffering as they age.

3. **Detachment and Letting Go (Vairagya)**: Elders are encouraged to detach from material possessions, desires, and attachments, fostering inner peace and preparing for the next phase of existence.
4. **Compassion and Loving-Kindness (Metta)**: Retirees are encouraged to practice compassion towards themselves and others, cultivating loving-kindness to promote emotional well-being and reduce feelings of isolation.
5. **Spiritual Growth (Dhamma Practice)**: Retirement is seen as a time to focus on Dhamma practice—deepening wisdom, ethical conduct, and mental discipline, working towards liberation (Nirvana).

In essence, Buddhism advises retirees to prepare psychologically and emotionally by embracing mindfulness, accepting life's impermanence, practicing detachment, and cultivating compassion and wisdom.

Jainism: (Less than 10 million, majority in India but they are available in Canada, USA, Europe & Japan also)

In Jainism, psychological and emotional preparation for the elderly and retirees centers around detachment, spiritual growth, and living a life of peace and contentment. Key elements include:

1. **Detachment and Renunciation (Aparigraha)**: As one approaches retirement and old age, Jainism encourages reducing material attachments and desires. This detachment helps individuals achieve mental peace, preparing them for the final stage of life and eventual liberation (Moksha).
2. **Spiritual Reflection and Growth**: Retirement is viewed as an ideal time to focus on spiritual practices such as meditation, self-discipline, and the study of Jain scriptures. This introspection aids in attaining a state of equanimity and inner peace.
3. **Acceptance of Aging (Anitya Bhavana)**: Jainism emphasizes the impermanence of life, helping the elderly mentally prepare for aging by accepting the transient nature of the body and material world. This acceptance reduces fear and anxiety about death.

4. **Non-violence and Compassion (Ahimsa and Karuna)**: Emotional preparation involves practicing compassion towards others and oneself. Elders are encouraged to focus on cultivating peaceful, non-violent thoughts and actions, fostering emotional resilience and harmony.
5. **Contentment and Minimalism**: The principle of contentment (Santosha) is crucial. Retirees are encouraged to live simply, minimizing worldly distractions and finding joy in spiritual fulfillment rather than material wealth.
6. **Community and Family Support**: While Jainism stresses individual spiritual growth, it also values strong community and family connections. Elders are encouraged to impart wisdom and serve as role models for younger generations, maintaining emotional bonds while preparing for detachment.

In summary, Jainism advises retirees and the elderly to prepare psychologically and emotionally by embracing detachment, deepening spiritual practices, accepting impermanence, and cultivating inner peace through non-violence and compassion.

Parsi: (Total population between 100000 to 200000 , mostly in India, Iran & North America)

In Parsi religion and tradition, the psychological and emotional preparation for the elderly and retirees is rooted in maintaining mental well-being, spiritual growth, and staying connected to community and family. Key points include:

1. **Spiritual Reflection and Inner Peace**: As retirement approaches, individuals are encouraged to focus on spirituality, seeking inner peace through reflection, prayers, and rituals like visiting the Fire Temple. This phase of life is seen as an opportunity for soul purification and aligning with Ahura Mazda (God).
2. **Emotional Resilience**: Elders are respected and honored in Parsi culture. Emotional well-being is fostered through maintaining strong family bonds, staying socially active, and

participating in community events. It is essential to stay connected with loved ones to prevent feelings of isolation.

3. **Positive Outlook on Aging**: Retirees are encouraged to view this stage as a time of wisdom and experience rather than decline. Parsis promote the idea of remaining active mentally and emotionally, by continuing to contribute to society through mentorship or charitable works (often termed "Seva").
4. **Role of Rituals and Ceremonies**: Religious ceremonies, prayers, and traditions offer comfort, helping retirees cope with life changes. Engaging in rituals fosters a sense of belonging and purpose.
5. **Psychological Balance**: Parsis believe in the duality of good and evil forces (Spenta Mainyu and Angra Mainyu), and emphasize maintaining a positive mental attitude to keep negative forces at bay. This includes practicing gratitude, optimism, and fostering contentment.

In essence, the Parsi approach to psychological and emotional preparation for retirement involves a balanced integration of spiritual practice, social connectedness, and maintaining a positive outlook on life.

Summary of all the religions on the subject

Across various world religions, psychological and emotional preparation for the elderly and retirees emphasizes spiritual growth, inner peace, and detachment from materialism. Common themes include:

1. Spiritual Reflection: Elders are encouraged to deepen their connection with the divine through prayer, meditation, and reflection, preparing for life's final stage with a sense of peace.
2. Detachment from Materialism: Most religions advise reducing worldly desires and attachments, promoting a focus on spiritual fulfillment over material wealth.

3. Acceptance and Contentment: Aging is accepted as a natural part of life. Religions teach embracing impermanence, cultivating gratitude, and finding joy in simplicity.
4. Community and Family: Strong social and family bonds provide emotional support, while elders often pass down wisdom and serve as role models.

In conclusion, world religions guide retirees to seek inner peace, spiritual growth, and emotional resilience through detachment, acceptance of aging, and maintaining meaningful relationships.

Note:- In today's world, religious teachings, principles, and philosophies face significant challenges when addressing issues like family care, retirement, and the treatment of the elderly. While these values remain important, their practical application is becoming increasingly difficult.

The traditional **joint family system**, once the backbone of caring for the elderly and maintaining religious values, is gradually eroding. While some communities continue to uphold these values, the pressures of modernization, individualism, and materialism have caused a noticeable decline. Across various societies, the decay of religious values and practices is evident, making it harder for families to adhere to spiritual teachings regarding care for retirees and the elderly.

However, **Islam** stands out in this context. A large percentage of Muslims continue to strive to uphold and practice the religious values prescribed in the Qur'an and Sunnah, particularly when it comes to honoring parents and the elderly, providing family support, and preparing for retirement. Although they too face societal pressures and modern challenges, Muslims are making conscious efforts to give practical shape to these teachings, balancing tradition with contemporary life. The commitment to maintaining Islamic values in caring for retirees offers a model of resilience in a world where such values are increasingly under threat.

This ongoing struggle to preserve religious teachings while adapting to modern challenges illustrates the resilience of faith and the importance of community support in maintaining a compassionate, value-driven approach to retirement and aging.

3.1 Adjusting to a new identity

When retirees leave the workforce, they often experience a shift in identity, as their sense of purpose and self-worth may have been closely tied to their careers. Adjusting to this new identity is a significant psychological and emotional challenge. Here's a brief overview of how retirees navigate this transition:

1. Loss of Professional Role:

- Retirement can lead to feelings of loss, as retirees no longer have the professional title or responsibilities that defined them. This can create a sense of uncertainty about their role in society and within their family.

2. Redefining Purpose:

- Retirees must find new sources of meaning and purpose outside of work. This often includes exploring hobbies, volunteer work, learning new skills, or focusing on personal development and spiritual growth.

3. Building a Social Identity:

- Work often provides a built-in social network. Retirement requires rebuilding or strengthening social connections through community involvement, family, friends, or joining groups and clubs that align with personal interests.

4. Shifting Focus to Health and Well-being:

- Retirees can take advantage of their newfound time to focus on physical and mental well-being, adopting healthier lifestyles, engaging in regular exercise, and nurturing their emotional health through mindfulness or relaxation practices.

5. Acceptance and Adaptation:

- Adjusting to a new identity involves accepting the changes retirement brings. This process requires emotional resilience and a willingness to embrace a new phase of life with flexibility and openness.

In essence, adjusting to a new identity in retirement involves redefining purpose, nurturing relationships, focusing on well-being, and embracing a new phase of life with a positive and open mindset.

3.2 Coping with loss of work structure

Coping with the loss of work structure is a major challenge for retirees as they transition from a routine-driven lifestyle to a more open, unstructured one. Here's how retirees can manage this adjustment:

1. **Creating a New Routine:**

- Establishing a daily or weekly schedule can help replace the structure once provided by work. This could include setting regular times for exercise, hobbies, social activities, or volunteer work to maintain a sense of purpose and order.

2. **Pursuing Hobbies and Passions:**

- Retirement offers the opportunity to explore personal interests that were previously limited by work commitments. Engaging in hobbies, creative activities, or travel can provide both structure and fulfillment.

3. **Volunteering or Part-Time Work:**

- Many retirees find value in volunteering or engaging in part-time work to maintain a sense of productivity. These activities offer a structured environment while contributing to personal satisfaction.
- In today's rapidly evolving world, countless new opportunities have emerged, particularly in the realm of online platforms. These avenues allow retirees to step beyond traditional boundaries and leverage their wealth of experience and wisdom in meaningful ways. Whether through consulting, freelancing, teaching, or content creation, retirees can now engage in flexible, fulfilling work that not only keeps them active but also generates additional income. This supplementary earnings stream can serve as a cushion, helping to manage unexpected expenses and emergencies while enhancing financial security and peace of mind in their golden years.

4. **Staying Socially Engaged:**

- Maintaining or building social connections through clubs, community groups, or social gatherings helps fill the void left by daily interactions with colleagues, providing emotional support and a sense of belonging.

5. **Focusing on Health and Well-being:**

- Regular physical activity, mindfulness practices, and focusing on mental health are essential. Setting aside time for exercise, relaxation, and wellness activities helps maintain structure and promotes a healthy lifestyle.

By proactively creating new routines, staying engaged, and focusing on personal growth, retirees can successfully cope with the loss of work structure and find meaning in this new phase of life.

3.3 Maintaining a Positive Mental Health

Maintaining positive mental health in retirement is essential for well-being. Here's a brief guide:

1. **Stay Active Physically**: Regular exercise, even light activities like walking or yoga, boosts mood, reduces stress, and promotes mental clarity.
2. **Engage in Social Activities**: Maintain strong connections with family, friends, or community groups to combat loneliness and improve emotional well-being.
3. **Pursue Meaningful Activities:** Engage in hobbies, volunteer work, or creative projects or timely prayers that provide a sense of purpose and satisfaction. Immerse yourself in the joy of flower and vegetable gardening—it's nature's perfect recipe for happiness and well-being. This simple yet fulfilling activity not only nurtures your health but also fills your life with vibrant colors and fresh produce, all without any additional cost. Let your garden become a sanctuary where you can unwind, stay active, and find pure contentment in watching life bloom right before your eyes.
4. **Practice Mindfulness**: Incorporate mindfulness techniques such as Yoga or deep breathing & light indoor games (which you can play without stressing much physically) to reduce anxiety and stay present.
5. **Establish a Routine**: A daily routine helps provide structure and a sense of control, which is important for mental stability.
6. **Seek New Learning Opportunities**: Keep the mind active by learning new skills, reading, watching short dramas, comedy films or taking up intellectually stimulating activities.
7. **Talk About Feelings:** Open up to trusted individuals or seek counseling if feeling overwhelmed, anxious, or depressed.
8. **Take Time for Rest and Relaxatio**n: Balance activities with enough downtime to recharge mentally and physically.

9. "Why not turn your home into a mini **adventure zone with your grandchildren**? Spend time chit-chatting and laughing together, or even better, become their first teacher! Show them how to talk, read, write, and do basic math in a fun, relaxed way. You could create magical, fictional stories with them—bring in dragons, talking animals, or even superhero versions of yourselves! Let imagination flow freely, as you share laughter and play. Not only will they learn, but those moments will be treasures you all keep for years."
10. **Grandchildren are truly a treasure** in your home, and at this stage of life, you're just as much a kid as they are! Dive into playful moments—whether it's a fun game of carom, playing cards, chess, or Ludo, or getting creative with building blocks, assembling houses, or coming up with new ideas together. Laugh, play, and enjoy every minute as you bond over these simple yet joyful activities. It's a time to relive childhood through their eyes and make lasting memories together!
11. **Grandchildren are your true friends**. They cherish your company even more than their parents do, and they care deeply about you, always noticing when you're stressed. So why not laugh, have fun, and enjoy their energy? It's not just a way to bond, but also a fantastic way to relieve mental and physical stress. After a day of playful activities with them, you'll feel happily tired and ready for a deep, restful sleep at night. It's the perfect recipe for joy and peace!

3.4 Dealing with Loneliness & Social Isolation

For a retiree, dealing with loneliness and social isolation can be challenging, but there are ways to overcome it:

1. Stay Connected: Regularly reach out to family, friends, and former colleagues through calls, visits, or video chats.
2. Join Social Groups: Participate in community clubs, senior groups, or hobby classes to meet new people and build relationships.
3. Volunteer: Helping others through volunteering provides social interaction and a sense of purpose.
4. Adopt Technology: Use social media or apps to stay in touch with loved ones and meet new friends online.
5. Stay Active: Attend local events, join exercise groups, or take walks in social settings to engage with others.
6. Set aside daily classes to teach your grandchildren, making learning a fun and interactive experience. Spice things up with IQ tests to challenge their growing minds—but be prepared! These little geniuses might surprise you with their brilliance and turn the tables by testing *your* IQ too. Get ready for some lively and brainy bonding time!
7. If you have the space, embrace the joy of gardening at home. Tending to lush green plants you've nurtured with your own hands brings unparalleled peace and relaxation to the mind. The vibrant colors of blooming flowers and their delightful fragrances fill your surroundings with natural beauty and serenity. Imagine maintaining a small fruit and vegetable garden, offering you fresh, organic produce—healthy for your body and soul. Gardening not only provides a deep sense of satisfaction and accomplishment but also serves as a gentle daily exercise, perfectly suited for this stage of life. Immerse yourself in your garden, and you'll begin to feel a magical connection—as if the vibrant green plants and colorful flowers are whispering to you, sharing their joy, and

delighting in your presence. What a heartwarming and enchanting moment to cherish!

3.5 Building a support system

Building a strong support system is essential for retirees to navigate this new phase of life. Here's how to create one:

1. Family and Friends: Stay connected with family and friends for emotional support and companionship. Regular meetups, calls, or video chats can foster these bonds.
2. Join Community Groups: Engage with local senior centers, hobby clubs, or social organizations to meet like-minded people and build new friendships.
3. Volunteer: Becoming part of volunteer groups provides a sense of purpose while expanding your social network.
4. Professional Support: Consider joining a retirement group or seeking professional advice (financial advisors, counselors) to manage life changes effectively.
5. Stay Active Online: Use social media (positive ones) or online forums to connect with fellow retirees or participate in virtual events.

4.0 Health and Wellness

For retirees, maintaining health and wellness is key to enjoying a fulfilling retirement. By focusing on these areas, retirees can maintain vitality and enjoy a healthier, more active lifestyle.

1. **Stay Physically Active**: Engage in regular exercise like walking, swimming, or yoga to improve strength, flexibility, and overall well-being.
2. **Eat a Balanced Diet**: Focus on nutritious foods—fruits, vegetables, lean proteins, and whole grains—to support energy and prevent illness. Maintaining a healthy, recommended weight at this stage of life is essential for overall well-being. Ignoring this can tip the scales either toward being overweight or underweight, both of which can open the door to a cascade of health problems. Striking the right balance now will help you stay active, energetic, and better equipped to enjoy life to the fullest.
3. **Prioritize Mental Health**: Keep the mind active with puzzles, reading, or learning new skills. Practice mindfulness or meditation to reduce stress.
4. **Regular Health Checkups**: Stay on top of routine medical visits and screenings to catch potential health issues early.
5. **Get Quality Sleep**: Aim for 7-8 hours of restful sleep each night to boost mental and physical health. At this stage of life, quality sleep becomes one of the most common challenges faced by many. To help you find the rest you deserve, several dedicated chapters in this book explore practical strategies and insights for achieving truly fulfilling and restorative sleep. Dive in and discover ways to reclaim your nights and wake up refreshed.
6. **Fasting:** Fasting is the voluntary abstention from food, drink, or both for a specified period. It has been practiced for centuries across cultures and religions, often for spiritual, physical, or mental purposes. Today, fasting is recognized not only as a

spiritual discipline but also as a powerful tool for improving overall health and promoting longevity.

There are different types of fasting, including:

1. Intermittent Fasting (IF): Cycling between periods of eating and fasting, such as the 16:8 method (16 hours fasting, 8 hours eating).
2. Prolonged Fasting: Fasting for more extended periods, typically 24 hours or more.
3. Water Fasting: Consuming only water during the fasting period.
4. Partial Fasting: Restricting certain foods or caloric intake for a specified time.
5. Religious Fasting: Spiritual fasting observed in faiths like Islam (Down to dusk abstaining from from solid, liquid food , medicines - Ramadan in specific period which is called Ramadan based on lunar months), Christianity (Lent - a period of 40 days starting in February or March of the year), Hinduism (Vrata), and Judaism (Taynis), Buddhism (Uposatha).

Health Benefits of Fasting

Fasting has a variety of scientifically supported benefits, making it a powerful practice for enhancing physical, mental, and emotional well-being:

1. Promotes Weight Loss and Fat Loss

- Fasting encourages the body to use stored fat for energy, leading to weight loss.
- It boosts metabolism and improves insulin sensitivity, helping prevent obesity-related conditions like diabetes.

2. Improves Blood Sugar Control

- By reducing insulin resistance, fasting helps regulate blood sugar levels.

- Intermittent fasting has shown promising results in managing Type 2 diabetes.

3. Enhances Heart Health

- Fasting reduces risk factors for heart disease, such as blood pressure, cholesterol, and inflammation.
- It supports better blood circulation and overall cardiovascular health.

4. Boosts Brain Function

- Fasting stimulates the production of brain-derived neurotrophic factor (BDNF), which supports brain health and cognitive function.
- It reduces oxidative stress and inflammation, lowering the risk of neurodegenerative diseases like Alzheimer's and Parkinson's.

5. Detoxifies the Body

- During fasting, the body shifts into a state called autophagy, where it cleans out damaged cells and toxins.
- This process rejuvenates cells and reduces the risk of chronic diseases.

6. Reduces Inflammation

- Fasting lowers inflammation markers, helping to alleviate symptoms of chronic inflammatory conditions like arthritis and asthma.

7. Improves Digestive Health

- Periodic fasting allows the digestive system to rest and recover, improving gut health and reducing bloating.

8. Supports Longevity and Anti-Aging

- Studies suggest that fasting can extend lifespan by reducing oxidative stress and enhancing cellular repair.
- It activates genes linked to longevity and decreases the risk of age-related diseases.

9. Enhances Mental Clarity and Focus

- Many people report improved concentration and mental sharpness during fasting, attributed to stabilized blood sugar levels and the release of ketones.

10. Prevents and Manages Chronic Diseases

- Fasting can lower the risk of diseases like cancer, type 2 diabetes, and heart disease by improving metabolic health and reducing inflammation.

11. Fasting may aid protect/cure: Fasting can protect against and potentially aid in curing cancer by

creating an environment that challenges cancer cell growth while promoting the body's natural

defense mechanisms. Here's how:

- **Triggers Autophagy:** Fasting stimulates autophagy, a process where the body removes damaged cells and cellular debris, reducing the risk of cancerous cell formation.
- **Starves Cancer Cells:** Cancer cells thrive on glucose. Fasting lowers blood sugar and insulin levels, depriving cancer cells of their primary energy source.
- **Boosts Immune Function:** Fasting strengthens the immune system by regenerating white blood cells and enhancing the body's ability to fight cancerous cells.
- **Reduces Inflammation:** Chronic inflammation contributes to cancer development. Fasting lowers inflammation, reducing cancer risk.

- **Protects Healthy Cells:** During fasting, normal cells enter a protective state, while cancer cells remain vulnerable, making treatments like chemotherapy more effective and less damaging to healthy tissue.
- **Enhances Chemotherapy Response:** Fasting sensitizes cancer cells to chemotherapy, improving its effectiveness and reducing side effects.

Note: While fasting shows promise, it should complement—not replace—conventional cancer

treatments and always be undertaken with medical supervision.

Tips for Effective Fasting

1. Stay Hydrated: Drink plenty of water to stay hydrated during fasting periods.
2. Start Gradually: Begin with shorter fasting periods and gradually increase as your body adapts.
3. Listen to Your Body: If you feel dizzy or overly fatigued, consider breaking the fast.
4. Focus on Nutrient-Dense Foods: During eating periods, consume wholesome, nutrient-rich meals to sustain energy.
5. Consult a Professional: Speak with a healthcare provider before starting prolonged or extreme fasting, especially if you have existing health conditions.

Conclusion

Fasting is not just a tool for weight loss but a holistic practice that nurtures the body, mind, and spirit. When done mindfully, it can promote a healthier, disease-free life, enhance mental clarity, and even support spiritual growth. However, balance and moderation are key, as fasting should always align with individual health needs and goals.

4.1 Importance of regular Exercise

The human body is much like an internal combustion engine—when left idle for too long, its components start to lose efficiency, becoming sluggish and prone to wear during periods of inactivity. Just as an engine needs to run regularly at a steady pace (without excessive load) to remain in peak condition, our bodies also thrive on consistent, light activity to maintain their optimal performance. Regular movement keeps the "engine" of the body well-tuned, protecting the smooth functioning of vital systems like joints, muscles, vision, and the brain. In short, keep your body in motion—because idling for too long can stall your health and slow you down when you need to perform your best.

For retirees, regular exercise is key to staying active, independent, and mentally sharp

- **Improves Physical Health**: Exercise strengthens muscles, improves flexibility, and boosts cardiovascular health, helping to prevent diseases like heart issues and diabetes.
- **Enhances Mental Well-Being**: Physical activity reduces stress, anxiety, and depression, promoting a positive mood and mental clarity.
- **Boosts Energy Levels**: Regular movement increases stamina and energy, making daily tasks easier and more enjoyable.
- **Supports Mobility and Balance**: Exercise helps improve balance and coordination, reducing the risk of falls.

Note:- A single session of moderate to vigorous physical activity provides immediate benefits for your health. In addition, regular physical activity helps prevent many chronic diseases.

Benefits:

Immediate

- Improves sleep quality.
- Reduces feelings of anxiety.

- Reduces blood pressure.

Long-term

1. **Brain Health**: Regular physical exercise improves brain health in several ways:

- Increases Blood Flow: Exercise enhances blood circulation to the brain, supplying it with more oxygen and nutrients, which supports better cognitive function and mental sharpness.
- Stimulates Neurogenesis: Physical activity promotes the growth of new brain cells (neurogenesis) and strengthens connections between neurons, especially in areas associated with learning and memory, like the hippocampus.
- Reduces Cognitive Decline: Regular exercise can slow down age-related brain shrinkage and reduce the risk of neurodegenerative diseases such as Alzheimer's and dementia.
- Enhances Neuroplasticity: Exercise boosts the brain's ability to adapt and form new neural connections, improving problem-solving skills, memory, and learning capabilities.
- Improves Mood and Reduces Stress: By regulating stress hormones like cortisol and increasing endorphins, exercise reduces anxiety and depression, both of which negatively impact brain function.

Note- In summary, regular physical exercise enhances brain health by improving cognitive function, protecting against cognitive decline, and promoting mental resilience.

2. **Heart Health:** Maintaining heart health is crucial for reducing the risk of heart disease, stroke, and type 2 diabetes. Here's a brief overview of how regular physical activity contributes to these outcomes:

- Lowers Blood Pressure: Regular exercise helps maintain healthy blood pressure levels, reducing strain on the heart and blood vessels.
- Improves Cholesterol Levels: Physical activity raises high-density lipoprotein (HDL) cholesterol (the "good" cholesterol) while

lowering low-density lipoprotein (LDL) cholesterol (the "bad" cholesterol), helping to prevent arterial plaque buildup.

- Enhances Insulin Sensitivity: Exercise improves the body's ability to use insulin effectively, reducing the risk of developing type 2 diabetes by stabilizing blood sugar levels.
- Weight Management: Regular physical activity helps maintain a healthy weight, decreasing the likelihood of obesity, which is a significant risk factor for heart disease and diabetes.
- Promotes Circulation: Exercise improves blood circulation, ensuring that the heart and organs receive adequate oxygen and nutrients, which supports overall cardiovascular health.
- Reduces Stress: Physical activity lowers stress hormones and boosts endorphins, contributing to better emotional health and lower heart disease risk.

Note - In summary, regular exercise is vital for heart health as it lowers blood pressure, improves cholesterol levels, enhances insulin sensitivity, aids in weight management, and promotes overall cardiovascular function.

3. **Cancer Prevention:** lowers risk of 8 cancers (bladder, breast, colon, endometrium, esophagus, kidney, lung, and stomach). Regular physical activity is linked to a lower risk of developing several types of cancer, including:

- Bladder Cancer: Exercise helps maintain a healthy weight and improves metabolism, reducing the risk of bladder cancer.
- Breast Cancer: Active individuals have a lower risk of breast cancer, potentially due to hormonal regulation and maintaining a healthy weight.
- Colon Cancer: Regular exercise promotes healthy digestion and reduces inflammation, which may help lower the risk of colon cancer.
- Endometrial Cancer: Physical activity helps regulate hormones and maintain a healthy weight, reducing the likelihood of endometrial cancer in women.

- Esophageal Cancer: Regular exercise may lower the risk by helping prevent obesity and gastroesophageal reflux disease (GERD), both of which are risk factors.
- Kidney Cancer: Staying active can help reduce body fat and lower blood pressure, both of which are associated with a decreased risk of kidney cancer.
- Lung Cancer: Exercise strengthens lung function and boosts the immune system, potentially reducing the risk of lung cancer.
- Stomach Cancer: Active individuals tend to have healthier lifestyles, which can help lower the risk of stomach cancer through better weight management and dietary habits.

Note -In summary, regular physical activity is associated with a reduced risk of these eight cancers by promoting healthy weight management, hormonal balance, and overall body function.

4. **Healthy Weight:** To reduce the risk of overweight in elderly and retirees, the following low-impact exercises are effective:

- Walking: Regular brisk walking improves cardiovascular health and helps burn calories.
- Swimming or Water Aerobics: These are gentle on the joints and offer a full-body workout.
- Yoga: Improves flexibility, balance, and strength while reducing stress.
- Strength Training: Light weight lifting or resistance band exercises help maintain muscle mass and boost metabolism.
- Cycling: Stationary or outdoor cycling provides cardiovascular benefits without straining joints.

Note- These exercises, combined with a balanced diet, help maintain a healthy weight.

5. **Independent Living:** For elderly individuals and retirees, maintaining independent living is a key goal, and regular physical activity plays a vital role in helping them live independently for longer. Here's how:

- **Improves Mobility and Flexibility**

Regular exercise enhances joint flexibility and muscle strength, allowing elderly individuals to move more easily and with less discomfort. Exercises like stretching, yoga, and tai chi improve range of motion, making everyday tasks like dressing, reaching, and bending easier, contributing to self-sufficiency.

- **Prevents Falls and Enhances Balance**

Falls are a leading cause of injury and loss of independence among the elderly. Strengthening muscles and improving balance through activities like walking, balance training, or strength exercises helps prevent falls. Better balance also allows for more confidence in performing daily tasks independently.

- **Increases Muscle Strength**

As people age, they lose muscle mass (a condition called sarcopenia), making daily activities like lifting, carrying, or even standing up more difficult. Resistance training, weight lifting, or bodyweight exercises help maintain and build muscle strength, enabling retirees to handle routine tasks like carrying groceries, cleaning, or getting out of a chair without assistance.

- **Enhances Cardiovascular Health**

Aerobic exercises like walking, swimming, or cycling improve heart health, stamina, and lung capacity, allowing retirees to engage in activities like walking to the store, gardening, or playing with grandchildren. This level of endurance promotes independent living by enabling seniors to remain active in their daily lives.

- **Supports Mental Health and Cognitive Function**

Physical activity is not only beneficial for physical health but also for mental well-being. Exercise boosts mood by releasing endorphins and reducing stress, anxiety, and depression, all of which can impact one's ability to live independently. Furthermore, research shows that regular exercise improves cognitive function and may help delay or prevent the onset of dementia and memory decline, allowing for more independent decision-making and self-management.

- **Promotes Better Sleep**

Quality sleep is essential for energy and overall health. Regular physical activity helps regulate sleep patterns, ensuring better rest and recovery. Good sleep helps elderly individuals remain energetic and focused, making it easier to manage day-to-day activities independently.

- **Helps Manage Chronic Conditions**

Many elderly individuals face chronic health conditions like diabetes, arthritis, or hypertension, which can limit independence. Exercise helps in managing and even improving these conditions by controlling symptoms, improving mobility, reducing pain, and increasing energy levels. This, in turn, enables retirees to continue living without the need for continuous medical intervention or assistance.

- **Fosters Social Connections and Confidence**

Group activities like walking clubs, fitness classes, or community sports provide opportunities for social interaction, reducing feelings of isolation. These connections foster a sense of confidence and belonging, encouraging retirees to engage more fully in life, contributing to their ability to live independently.

Note: By incorporating regular, appropriate exercise into their routine, elderly individuals can maintain the physical and mental strength necessary to perform daily tasks, reduce the risk of injury, and manage health conditions—enabling them to live independently longer.

6. **Bone Strength**: Regular exercise plays a key role in improving **bone strength** and **overall bone health** in the following ways:

- Increases Bone Density: Weight-bearing exercises (like walking, running, and strength training) stimulate the bones, promoting the production of bone tissue. This leads to an increase in bone density, which makes bones stronger and less likely to break.
- Prevents Bone Loss: As people age, they naturally lose bone mass. Regular exercise helps slow down this bone loss, reducing the risk of osteoporosis (a condition where bones become brittle and fragile).
- Improves Balance and Coordination: Exercises like yoga, tai chi, and resistance training enhance balance, flexibility, and muscle strength. This reduces the risk of falls, which can cause fractures, especially in older adults.
- Stimulates Bone Remodeling: Physical activity helps in the process of bone remodeling, where old bone tissue is replaced by new, stronger tissue. This constant renewal is essential for maintaining healthy bones throughout life.
- Increases Muscle Mass and Joint Support: Regular exercise strengthens the muscles around bones and joints, providing better support to bones and reducing the strain on them, leading to improved bone health.

Note: Engaging in a combination of weight-bearing and resistance exercises can help maintain bone strength and reduce the risk of bone-related issues as one ages.

7. **Balance and Coordination:** reduces risks of falls. Globally, falls are the second leading cause of unintentional injury deaths. **In the US , 78 per 100000 older adults died from unintentional falls in 2021- The death from falls was higher for men (91.4 per 100000 than for women 68.3).** Older people are more likely to fall and have serious injuries or die from a fall. Find the following main & basic reasons of falls:-
    - Impaired vision: Glaucoma, cataracts, visual acuity, the field of vision, and contrast sensitivity lead to an increased risk of falls.

- Poor or no personal aid equipment.
- Being distracted by multitasking.
- Hypotension, such as cardiac or postural causes.
- Rushing to the bathroom, especially at night.
- Foot issues: General pain when walking, calluses, long toe deformities, ulcers, and nail deformities increase balance difficulty and risk of falling.
- Medical Conditions - Certain conditions, like diabetes, heart disease & stroke.
- Medications - Taking multiple medications, especially those that help you relax or sleep.
- Local conditions - Poorly designed or maintained stairs, inadequate lighting, clutter, slippery floors & unsecured rugs, wrong shoes or slippers etc.
- Other factors - History of falls, depressions, dizziness & difficulty in walking.

Note - Though this type of accidents can not be avoided fully but be sure this unfortunate happening may be minimized by acting the following ways: If you feel you cannot do the particular job which involves risk of falling, never attempt the same.

> ➢ Make an appointment with your health care provider to review your medications & health conditions.
> ➢ Get a sight test if you are concerned about vision loss.
> ➢ Do exercises that improve your balance & strength like sit to stand exercise.

8. **Immunity:** Emerging research suggests that in elderly individuals and retirees, regular physical activity has been shown to boost immune function, a crucial aspect of maintaining health as aging can weaken the immune system. Emerging research suggests several ways exercise benefits immunity in older adults:

- Enhances Immune Cell Activity: Physical activity stimulates the production and circulation of immune cells like white blood cells (WBCs), which play a vital role in detecting and fighting infections. Exercise can enhance the responsiveness of these cells, making the immune system more efficient.
- Reduces Inflammation: Chronic low-grade inflammation is common in the elderly and is associated with several age-related diseases. Regular moderate exercise reduces inflammatory markers (like C-reactive protein) in the body, helping to lower the overall inflammatory response and reduce the risk of infections and diseases.
- Improves Circulation: Exercise increases blood flow, which helps in the efficient transportation of immune cells throughout the body. This allows immune cells to detect and respond to pathogens more quickly.
- Boosts Stress Resistance: Physical activity helps manage stress by regulating stress hormones (like cortisol). Chronic stress can weaken the immune system, but regular exercise improves the body's stress response, helping maintain a healthy immune system.
- Prevents Immune System Decline: Aging is often associated with a gradual decline in immune function, known as immunosenescence. Exercise helps slow down this process by stimulating immune function and keeping immune cells active and responsive.
- Promotes Healthy Weight: Obesity can weaken the immune system, but regular exercise helps maintain a healthy weight, which in turn supports better immune function. This is particularly important for retirees who may have a more sedentary lifestyle.
- Improves Sleep Quality: Good sleep is essential for a healthy immune system. Exercise promotes better sleep patterns, allowing the body to repair and strengthen its immune defenses during rest.

Note: For elderly individuals and retirees, engaging in moderate physical activity, like walking, swimming, or resistance training, can significantly improve immune resilience and reduce the risk of infections and illnesses.

4.2 Maintaining a Balanced Diet

Maintaining a balanced diet becomes a cornerstone of vitality for elderly individuals and retirees, offering the keys to enhanced energy, robust health, and effective management of chronic conditions. Picture yourself as an aging car & its engine—one that demands extra care and precision to keep running smoothly. Just as an engine needs the purest fuel recommended by its manufacturer, along with a well-functioning cooling and lubrication system, sturdy brakes, shock absorbers, and balanced wheels, your aging body requires the same thoughtful attention.

Your vital organs—stomach, liver, kidneys, bladder, lungs, heart, joints, bones, and brain—deserve pure, natural, and balanced nutrition to function at their best. With age, the body undergoes significant changes: metabolism slows, appetite fluctuates, and health concerns may arise. A carefully tailored diet is not just a recommendation; it is an essential part of ensuring your "engine" runs smoothly for years to come.

Here's what a balanced diet (in appropriate portion) for elderly individuals and retirees typically includes in:

1. Adequate Protein Intake

- Why: Protein is essential for maintaining muscle mass, repairing tissues, and supporting the immune system. Elderly individuals are prone to losing muscle mass (sarcopenia), so protein becomes particularly important.
- Sources: Lean meats (chicken, turkey), fish, eggs, beans, legumes, tofu, and low-fat dairy products (milk, yogurt, cheese).

2. Plenty of Fruits and Vegetables

- Why: Fruits and vegetables provide essential vitamins, minerals, fiber, and antioxidants that help prevent chronic diseases like heart disease, stroke, and certain cancers. They also help improve digestion and reduce constipation, a common issue in older adults.

- Sources: Leafy greens (spinach, kale), berries, apples, carrots, sweet potatoes, and broccoli. Opt for a variety of colorful fruits and vegetables to ensure a wide range of nutrients.
- Be mindful when buying leafy vegetables and fruits, as many of them are treated with heavy doses of pesticides and germicides to ward off insects and prevent damage to the produce. While they may look fresh and appealing, these chemicals can pose hidden risks to your health. Take precautions—wash thoroughly, soak in clean water, or opt for organic options when possible—to ensure that what nourishes you doesn't unknowingly harm you.

3. Whole Grains for Energy

- Why: Whole grains are a great source of fiber, which aids digestion and helps control blood sugar levels. They also provide sustained energy, which is important as metabolism slows with age.
- Sources: Whole wheat bread, brown rice, quinoa, oats, and barley. Replace refined grains (white bread, white rice) with whole grains to maximize nutrient intake.

4. Healthy Fats

- Why: Healthy fats support brain function, heart health, and hormone production. They also help absorb fat-soluble vitamins (A, D, E, and K).
- Sources: Olive oil, avocados, nuts, seeds, and fatty fish like salmon and mackerel (which also provide omega-3 fatty acids).

5. Calcium and Vitamin D for Bone Health

- Why: Aging leads to a natural loss of bone density, increasing the risk of osteoporosis and fractures. Calcium and vitamin D are essential for maintaining strong bones and teeth.
- Sources: Dairy products (milk, yogurt, cheese), fortified plant-based milk (almond, soy), leafy greens (broccoli, kale), and fish

like salmon. Sunlight exposure also helps the body produce vitamin D.

6. **Hydration**

- Why: Dehydration is common in the elderly due to a reduced sense of thirst, medication use, or chronic conditions. Proper hydration supports digestion, kidney function, and cognitive health.
- Sources: Water, herbal teas, and hydrating foods like cucumbers, watermelon, and soups. Avoid excessive caffeine and sugary beverages, which can lead to dehydration.

7. **Limit Sodium and Added Sugars**

- Why: High sodium intake increases the risk of high blood pressure, heart disease, and stroke, while excessive sugar contributes to obesity, diabetes, and tooth decay.
- Sources: Minimize processed foods, canned soups, salty snacks, and sugary treats. Opt for fresh or minimally processed foods, and flavor meals with herbs and spices instead of salt.

8. **Fiber for Digestive Health**

- Why: Fiber helps prevent constipation and supports digestive health, both of which are important for older adults.
- Sources: Whole grains, fruits, vegetables, beans, and legumes (pease, beans etc). Include high-fiber foods in every meal to keep the digestive system functioning well.

9. **Smaller, More Frequent Meals**

- Why: Some elderly individuals may struggle with decreased appetite or digestion. Eating smaller, more frequent meals ensures they get enough nutrients without feeling overly full or uncomfortable.

- Sources: Divide the day's intake into 4-5 smaller meals or snacks, each including a variety of food groups (proteins, carbs, fats, and fiber).

10. <u>Supplements (if necessary)</u>

- Why: Due to changing nutritional needs or health conditions, some retirees may need to take supplements, especially for calcium, vitamin D, or B12, which may be harder to get from diet alone as they age.
- Consultation: Always consult a healthcare provider before taking any supplements to ensure they are appropriate and won't interfere with medications.

Conclusion:

For elderly individuals and retirees, a balanced diet means focusing on nutrient-dense foods that provide the essential vitamins, minerals, and macronutrients needed for good health and independence. It should support bone health, muscle maintenance, digestion, immune function, and cognitive health, while limiting processed foods high in sodium, sugars, and unhealthy fats. This approach helps maintain energy levels, prevent chronic diseases, and improve overall quality of life as they age.

4.3 Preventive Health Check-ups

Preventive health check-ups are vital for retirees to maintain health and catch potential issues early. Following is a brief guide:

1. Regular Screenings: Schedule routine tests like blood pressure, cholesterol, and blood sugar checks to monitor for common health conditions.
2. Early Detection: Regular check-ups help detect illnesses like heart disease, diabetes, or cancer early, improving treatment outcomes.
3. Vaccinations: Stay up to date on vaccines, such as flu, pneumonia, and shingles, to prevent infections.
4. Dental and Vision Care: Regular dental and eye exams are important to maintain oral and visual health.

4.4 Mental & Emotional Health

Maintaining mental and emotional health is crucial for retirees to enjoy a fulfilling life. Following is a brief guide:

1. **Stay Socially Connected**: Engage with family, friends, and community groups to prevent loneliness and boost emotional well-being.
2. **Pursue Hobbies**: Keep the mind active and engaged by learning new skills, picking up hobbies, or pursuing creative projects.
3. **Practice Mindfulness**: Techniques like meditation, deep breathing, or yoga help manage stress and promote mental calmness.
4. **Seek Support**: Talk openly about emotions with loved ones or seek professional help if feeling overwhelmed or anxious.
5. **Maintain a Routine**: A daily structure helps provide purpose and stability, promoting mental balance.

4.5 Managing Chronic Illnesses

Managing chronic illnesses is important for retirees to maintain a good quality of life. Here's a brief guide:

1. **Follow Medical Advice**: Stick to prescribed medications and treatment plans, and regularly consult with healthcare providers.
2. **Monitor Symptoms**: Keep track of any changes in your health including smart full body checkup and report them to your doctor promptly.
3. **Adopt a Healthy Lifestyle**: Maintain a balanced diet, exercise regularly, and avoid smoking or alcohol or tobacco in any form to manage conditions like diabetes, hypertension, or arthritis.
4. **Stay Educated**: Learn about your condition to make informed decisions about your health.
5. **Join Support Groups**: Engage with others who have similar conditions for emotional support and practical advice.

5.0 Lifestyle Changes

Lifestyle changes for retirees are essential for maintaining health, well-being, and a sense of purpose. Here's a detailed guide:

1. **Physical Activity**: Incorporate regular exercise like walking, swimming, yoga, or light strength training. Staying physically active improves heart health, flexibility, and overall energy levels, reducing the risk of chronic diseases.
2. **Healthy Eating Habits**: Focus on a balanced diet rich in fruits, vegetables, lean proteins, and whole grains. Minimize processed foods, sugar, and salt to support healthy aging and manage weight.
3. **Mental Engagement**: Stay mentally stimulated by pursuing hobbies, learning new skills, reading, or engaging in puzzles and games. Continued mental activity keeps the brain sharp and reduces the risk of cognitive decline.
4. **Social Interaction**: Maintain strong social connections by engaging with family, friends, and community. Join clubs, participate in group activities, or volunteer to build a support network and avoid feelings of isolation.
5. **Mindfulness and Relaxation**: Practice mindfulness techniques such as meditation, deep breathing, or relaxation exercises. These help manage stress, promote mental well-being, and improve emotional health.
6. **Sleep and Rest**: Ensure a regular sleep schedule with 7-8 hours of restful sleep each night. Good sleep improves mood, mental sharpness, and physical recovery.
7. **Adapt to a New Routine**: Build a flexible but structured daily routine that balances relaxation, activity, and socializing. A consistent routine provides purpose and stability.
8. **Manage Stress**: Recognize and address stress through enjoyable activities, social connections, and relaxation practices. Keeping stress in check is essential for both mental and physical health.

Note: By making these lifestyle adjustments, retirees can maintain a healthy, active, and fulfilling life.

5.1 Structuring Daily life without a work

Structuring daily life without work can be a challenge for retirees, but it's also an opportunity to create a fulfilling routine. Here's a brief introduction:

1. Create a New Routine: Establish a daily schedule that includes a mix of activities such as exercise, hobbies, and social interactions. This adds structure and purpose to your day.
2. Set Personal Goals: Identify new goals, whether learning something new, pursuing a passion, or volunteering community involvement, to keep motivated and engaged.
3. Stay Physically Active: Include regular physical activities like walking, yoga, or gardening to maintain health and energy.
4. Plan for Social Time: Dedicate time to connect with friends, family, or community groups to maintain relationships and avoid isolation.
5. Incorporate Relaxation: Balance activity with downtime for relaxation, mindfulness, or leisure activities you enjoy.

5.2 Finding new Hobbies and Interests

Retirement is the perfect time to discover new hobbies and interests that bring joy and fulfillment. With newfound freedom, retirees can explore activities they've always wanted to try or revisit old passions.

Popular options include:

- **Creative Arts**: Painting, photography, writing (in the field of your experiences), or playing music, listening to light music or Ghazals - (a form of poetry originated in Arabic & has been adopted in Urdu/Hindi) can offer a sense of achievement and relaxation.
- **Physical Activities**: Yoga, swimming, or walking clubs keep both the body and mind healthy.
- **Intellectual Pursuits**: Learning a new language, taking online courses, or joining book clubs stimulates the mind.
- **Social Hobbies**: Volunteering, gardening groups, or community events provide social engagement and purpose and visiting religious centers.
- **Kitchen Activities:** Take the opportunity to cultivate independence in the kitchen, starting with simple yet satisfying tasks. Learn to prepare your own morning tea or coffee, whip up a healthy breakfast, or experiment with different soups and snacks and Salads. Not only will this reduce your dependency on others, but it will also bring a sense of accomplishment, creativity, and joy to your daily routine. After all, there's nothing more fulfilling than savoring something made by your own hands.

5.3 Travel and Leisure Opportunities

Retirement offers the perfect opportunity to explore the world and enjoy leisure activities at a relaxed pace. Retirees can embark on:

1. **Domestic and International Travel:** Scenic road trips, cruises, and guided tours to cultural landmarks or natural wonders with your spouse.
2. **Leisure Activities:** Enjoy outdoor pursuits like hiking, golf, or fishing, or participate in educational travel programs to learn while exploring new places.
3. **Wellness and Relaxation:** Wellness retreats, spa vacations, or relaxing beach getaways offer rejuvenation and peace.
4. **Morning Walk:** Step out with your spouse for an early morning walk and witness the magical transition as the darkness of night gracefully gives way to the golden hues of sunrise. The cool, crisp morning breeze carries with it a sense of renewal, energizing not just your body but uplifting your spirit. This serene time spent amidst nature's beauty allows you to reconnect—with yourself, your partner, and the world around you. The symphony of chirping birds, the gentle rustle of leaves, and the purity of the air work together to calm your mind, purify your soul, and set a positive tone for the day ahead. Let these peaceful moments become a cherished daily ritual, one that enhances your bond, refreshes your personality, and fills your heart with gratitude.
5. **Sunset at rooftop:** At sunset, take a moment to pause and cherish the beauty of life. Sit with your spouse in the comfort of your balcony or atop the roof, nestled into cozy armchairs with a warm cup of tea in hand. Watch as the golden hues of the setting sun merge into a tapestry of crimson, orange, and violet, painting the sky in breathtaking colors. Feel the serenity as the gentle breeze brushes your face, and the first stars timidly peek through the darkening expanse.

   As the night's quiet embrace begins to envelop the fading sunlight, reflect on the divine artistry of creation. Notice how the trees, birds, and distant landscapes seem to glow momentarily, as if bidding farewell to the day. This tranquil moment reminds us of the fleeting yet extraordinary beauty of the world, inviting us to be grateful and mindful of life's blessings.

Let the harmony of nature soothe your soul and strengthen the bond between you and your loved one, creating memories that linger like the soft glow of twilight.

5.4 Volunteering Community Involvement

Retirement is an excellent time for giving back through volunteering and community involvement. Engaging in local charities, mentoring youth, or supporting environmental causes can provide retirees with a sense of purpose and fulfillment.

1. **Local Volunteering:** Help at schools, hospitals, or food banks, offering valuable support to the community.
2. **Mentorship:** Share professional expertise or life skills by mentoring younger generations.
3. **Environmental and Global Causes:** Participate in conservation efforts or international volunteer programs

5.5 Downsizing or Relocating

Retirement often prompts the decision to downsize or relocate for a simpler, more manageable lifestyle. Downsizing can reduce home maintenance and living costs, while relocating to a retirement community, smaller home, or a location with a warmer or moderate climate can offer new opportunities for leisure and socializing.

1. **Downsizing:** Moving to a smaller home can free up time, money, and reduce upkeep.
2. **Relocating:** Many retirees opt for places that offer better weather, lower costs, or proximity to family and healthcare services.

Note: This option is specially designed for those navigating tight and challenging financial conditions during the post-retirement stage. When life demands urgent solutions and your emergency fund is running low or failing to meet the need, it's crucial to address the situation calmly and strategically, without succumbing to stress or tension.

Remember, this phase doesn't define your worth but tests your resilience and resourcefulness. With thoughtful planning and focused action, you can regain control over your finances while safeguarding your peace of mind. Let's explore practical ways to face these challenges head-on and uncover opportunities to ease your burden.

6.0 Social Relationships

In retirement, maintaining social relationships is key to emotional well-being, mental stimulation, and a fulfilling life. With more free time, retirees can nurture old bonds and build new ones, reinforcing their sense of identity and purpose.

1. **Family Relationships:**
   Staying close to children, grandchildren, and extended family not only strengthens emotional bonds but also creates opportunities for shared experiences. Storytelling, family meals, celebrating milestones together, and even helping with school pickups or homework can bring immense joy and purpose.
2. **Friendships:**
   Regular interaction with friends—whether through tea-time chats, games like cards or carom, or even digital meetups—adds laughter and lightness to life. Joining or forming groups with shared interests (books, gardening, crafts) can rekindle a sense of camaraderie and belonging.
3. **Community Involvement:**
   Actively participating in local clubs, libraries, senior centers, or volunteer organizations fosters a vibrant social life. Mentoring youth, teaching skills, or contributing to community projects not only creates new friendships but also instills a deep sense of usefulness and legacy.
4. **Faith-Based and Cultural Gatherings:**
   Joining religious or cultural events and groups offers spiritual connection and cultural continuity. These settings often provide emotional comfort, a shared value system, and intergenerational bonding.
5. **Digital Connectivity:**
   Staying in touch through video calls, messaging apps, or social platforms can be a lifeline, especially when physical meetings are not possible. Learning basic digital skills can empower retirees to stay connected across distances.

6.1 Strengthening Family Bonds

Retirement offers a golden opportunity to deepen family relationships through meaningful interactions and shared experiences. With fewer professional demands, retirees can focus on nurturing the family unit and becoming a pillar of emotional strength and wisdom.

1. **Quality Time:**
   Cherish everyday moments with your children and grandchildren. Whether it's a shared meal, a walk in the park, storytelling before bedtime, or simply relaxing together in the family room, these simple interactions lay the foundation for lifelong memories and emotional bonding.
2. **Shared Interests and Hobbies:**
   Engage in activities that both generations enjoy—such as board games, gardening, crafts, or building something together. These shared experiences not only create joy but also provide opportunities to learn from one another and appreciate each other's perspectives.
3. **Offer Support and Guidance:**
   Be emotionally available. A listening ear or a few comforting words can mean the world to younger family members. Your life experiences can serve as a compass to guide them through their own challenges, gently fostering a sense of trust and intergenerational connection.
4. **Family Traditions:**
   Preserve and pass on family traditions—be it through festive celebrations, religious customs, or storytelling about your past. You can also create new traditions such as "Grandparents' Day," weekend brunches, or themed family nights that everyone looks forward to.
5. **Create a Legacy:**
   Share family history, photo albums, or write memoirs that your children and grandchildren can treasure. Involving them in

creating a family tree or writing down cherished memories builds a bridge between the past and the future.

6. **Open Communication:**
   Encourage open dialogue in the family, where every member—young or old—feels heard and respected. This helps resolve conflicts quickly and promotes a warm, inclusive environment.

6.2 Building and Managing Friendships

Building and managing friendships during retirement and old age is crucial for maintaining emotional well-being and a sense of belonging. Following are some key aspects:

1. **Importance of Social Connections:**
    a. As people age, they may lose social contacts due to retirement, mobility issues, or the passing of friends. Establishing new friendships or deepening existing ones can help combat loneliness and feelings of isolation.
    b. Friendships provide emotional support, companionship, and opportunities for shared activities, which are essential for mental health.
2. **Types of Friendships:**
    a. **Old Friends:** Long-standing, time-tested friends are true lifelong treasures—an invaluable asset. Cherish them, love them, and always hold them in the highest respect. Lifelong friends offer deep bonds and shared history, which can be comforting. Maintaining these friendships through regular communication and meetups can be a source of great joy. In the hearts of the elderly and retirees, old memories remain vibrant and alive, woven into the fabric of their lives through years of shared experiences. New memories, however, tend to fade quickly, unable to hold the same depth or permanence. That's why old friendships are like gold—precious and irreplaceable—because they are built on a lifetime of unforgettable moments that never lose their shine.

       Friendships formed during the teenage years, especially in residential and professional colleges, often hold a unique and enduring charm. Living together in hostels creates a powerful bond, rooted in shared experiences, mutual growth, and an intimate understanding of each other's strengths and vulnerabilities. These friendships are not merely connections; they become like family, built on trust, laughter, and the countless memories created during late-night talks, shared meals, and tackling life's challenges together.

Such bonds develop a solid foundation, as these formative years are filled with unfiltered honesty and emotional openness. Teenage friends witness each other's raw, unpolished selves—whether it's the excitement of achieving a goal, the pain of failure, or the moments of doubt and self-discovery. This deep familiarity often gives these friendships a rare depth, making them a source of lifelong support and comfort.

As time passes and life unfolds, these friendships often grow stronger. Even when distance and responsibilities pull friends apart, the connection remains intact. A simple call, a message, or a chance reunion instantly reignites the old warmth and shared memories, as if no time has passed. These friendships become a constant, a reminder of a time when life was simpler, dreams were shared freely, and trust was given wholeheartedly.

Moreover, these teenage bonds teach valuable life lessons—empathy, compromise, and the importance of standing by someone during both good times and bad. They form a blueprint for future relationships, guiding individuals on how to nurture connections with honesty, loyalty, and care. For many, these friendships become a lifelong anchor, offering joy and solace even in life's most challenging moments.

In a world that often changes too quickly, the friendships of our youth stand as a timeless testament to the beauty of human connection. They remind us of who we were, who we've become, and the shared journey that has shaped us along the way.

b. **New Friendships:** Joining community groups, clubs, or participating in local activities opens up a world of opportunities for retirees to meet new people who share similar interests and passions. These connections can bring fresh perspectives, invigorate your daily routine, and create moments of joy and camaraderie. However, when it comes to old friends, the dynamic is entirely different. These are the people who know your story—the ups and downs, the strengths and vulnerabilities—making the relationship comforting, reliable, and deeply rooted in mutual trust and understanding.

   In contrast, building new friendships, while exciting, requires careful consideration. Unlike old friendships that have withstood the test of time, new relationships often lack a strong foundation of trust and shared history. They may bring unforeseen challenges or complexities, as you are still discovering each other's true nature. Misunderstandings can arise more easily, and the relationship may sometimes feel fragile, demanding patience, effort, and continuous nurturing.

   This delicate nature of new friendships requires an open yet cautious approach. While it's important to embrace new connections with optimism, it's equally vital to remain mindful of red flags or potential risks. Take the time to understand the character and intentions of new acquaintances, building trust gradually and fostering a mutual sense of respect.

   New friendships can indeed blossom into meaningful bonds with time and effort, but they demand an awareness of their fragile beginnings. By navigating these relationships thoughtfully and setting clear boundaries, you can enjoy the best of both worlds—the comfort of old friends and the excitement of new ones—while safeguarding your emotional well-being.

c. **Intergenerational Friendships:** Friendships with younger individuals, including family members or people from volunteer groups, offer fresh perspectives and energy. This unique friendship transcends generations, bridging the gap of ages with wisdom, guidance, and deep emotional connection. It is not just a bond but a relationship enriched by life experiences, where the older friend becomes a mentor, a guide, and a source of inspiration. The foundation of this friendship is built on mutual respect, where younger friends admire the maturity, knowledge, and insight of their elder counterpart, while the elder extends parental love, care, and affection to their younger companions.

   In such a friendship, the older friend often serves as a steady anchor, offering valuable advice, sharing life lessons, and helping the younger generation navigate challenges with patience and understanding. The younger friends, in turn, bring energy, fresh perspectives, and an infectious enthusiasm for life that rejuvenates and inspires their elder companion. This exchange creates a beautiful balance, where wisdom meets curiosity, and experience blends seamlessly with youthful vigor.

   The respect from the younger friends is heartfelt and genuine, rooted in their recognition of the elder's journey and the invaluable guidance they provide. At the same time, the elder's affection mirrors the unconditional love of a parent, filled with a deep desire to see their younger friends grow, succeed, and find happiness in life.

   This friendship is not bound by age but by a profound sense of care, trust, and the joy of giving and receiving. It's a relationship where wisdom flows generously, and love transcends generational boundaries, creating a bond that is both nurturing and timeless.

3. **Strategies for Building Friendships:**
   a. Participating in Social Activities: Engaging in group activities such as book clubs, religious gatherings, or volunteer work helps retirees meet like-minded people.
   b. Using Technology: Social media, video calls, and messaging apps enable retirees to stay connected with old friends or build new relationships, even if they are housebound.
   c. Pursuing Hobbies: Joining clubs or groups focused on hobbies like gardening, arts, or sports can lead to natural and fulfilling friendships.
4. **Nurturing Friendships:**
   a. Consistency: Regular meetups, calls, or messages help sustain friendships. Even small gestures, like checking in or sharing interests, can keep the relationship active.
   b. Flexibility and Understanding: Friendships in old age require flexibility due to possible health limitations or personal circumstances. Being understanding about these challenges can help keep relationships positive.
   c. Shared Experiences: Engaging in joint activities like traveling, walking, or attending events together can strengthen bonds and create lasting memories.
5. **Benefits of Friendships in Later Life:**
   a. Emotional Well-being: Friendships provide emotional security and reduce the risk of depression or anxiety.
   b. Cognitive Stimulation: Conversations and shared activities help keep the mind active, promoting cognitive health.
   c. Increased Longevity: Studies suggest that strong social connections are linked to a longer, healthier life.

Cautions: Be cautious before diving into unfamiliar waters where you can't keep swimming for long. Today's social media platforms—WhatsApp, Instagram, Facebook, and others—are overflowing with misinformation that is far from the truth. Steer clear of getting involved in political or financial media, where ill intentions often dominate. If you do, you'll soon find yourself drowning in stress, surrounded by strain, and driven to conflict with friends who have been by your side for decades. Remember, true friendship transcends religion, politics, and financial status. Don’t let fleeting emotions or divisive issues lead you down a path of hatred and hostility, where only bitterness awaits.

6.3 Engaging in Social Activities

Participating in social activities is essential for retirees to stay mentally sharp, emotionally balanced, and socially connected. Stepping out of isolation and into shared experiences helps build friendships, rekindle passions, and bring purpose to everyday life. Here's how to stay socially active:

1. **Join Clubs or Groups:**
   Explore your interests by joining book clubs, gardening circles, walking groups, fitness or yoga classes, or arts and crafts sessions. These gatherings provide not just entertainment but also meaningful companionship and intellectual stimulation.
2. **Volunteer Your Time and Skills:**
   Giving back to the community through volunteering is deeply fulfilling. Whether you're mentoring youth, teaching a language, supporting charitable events, or helping at hospitals or places of worship, your time and wisdom can make a lasting impact.
3. **Attend Local Events and Workshops:**
   Keep an eye out for community events like cultural festivals, seminars, exhibitions, or musical evenings. These occasions are not only enjoyable but also offer a great way to meet new people and feel part of something larger.
4. **Organize or Host Gatherings:**
   Invite friends or neighbors for tea, games, or storytelling sessions. Hosting doesn't have to be elaborate—it's the warmth and intention that count. Such informal meetups foster closeness and can become cherished rituals.
5. **Explore Intergenerational Activities:**
   Engage in social events that involve both the young and the old. Community picnics, school reading programs, or family sports days encourage bonding across generations and keep retirees feeling vibrant and included.
6. **Stay Connected Digitally:**
   If mobility is a challenge or loved ones live far away, use technology to join virtual meetups, watch webinars, or take part in

online group activities. Digital platforms can open doors to global friendships and learning opportunities.

6.4 Role of Retirees towards their siblings

The role of a retired and elderly father or mother toward their siblings takes on a unique depth in later years, shaped by a lifetime of shared experiences and a growing appreciation for familial bonds. As they step into this stage of life, their role often shifts to that of a mentor, confidant, and emotional anchor, fostering unity, support, and wisdom within the sibling relationship. Here are some ways elderly parents can play a meaningful role toward their siblings:

1. Being a Source of Emotional Support

Retired parents often become pillars of emotional stability for their siblings, offering comfort during times of loss, illness, or personal struggles. Their life experience and perspective allow them to provide thoughtful guidance and a listening ear, ensuring that their siblings feel valued and cared for.

- Example: A retired elder may frequently check on their siblings' health, ensuring they are emotionally and physically well, especially if they live alone or face personal challenges.

2. Preserving Family Unity

Elderly parents often become the glue that holds extended families together. They encourage regular communication among siblings and their respective families, organize gatherings, and help resolve disputes to maintain harmony.

- Example: Hosting a family reunion or acting as a mediator during misunderstandings, reminding everyone of the shared love and memories that bind them together.
- Amid the hustle and bustle of life, arranging an annual gathering with all siblings during long holidays or special occasions becomes a cherished tradition that nourishes the soul. These moments of togetherness are best celebrated during festivals that resonate deeply with our hearts and faiths—be it the joyous spirit of Christmas and New Year, the heartfelt prayers of Eid al-Fitr

and Eid al-Adha, the solemn reflection of Good Friday, or the vibrant lights of Diwali and Dussehra. From the soulful rituals of Rosh Hashanah and Yom Kippur to the serene mindfulness of Magha Puja Day and Guru Nanak Jayanti - each occasion offers a unique tapestry of love, faith, and unity. These annual reunions are more than just events; they are a celebration of shared memories, unbreakable bonds, and the beautiful diversity that enriches our lives.

3. Sharing Wisdom and Life Lessons

With age comes wisdom, and retired individuals are often eager to share their insights with siblings. Whether it's about managing health, navigating retirement, or dealing with life's challenges, their advice is often cherished.

- Example: Advising a younger sibling on preparing for retirement or suggesting ways to maintain a healthy lifestyle.

4. Providing Practical Assistance

Even in retirement, elderly parents often play a proactive role in helping their siblings with everyday tasks or challenges. This can include helping manage finances, offering transportation, or simply being there when their siblings need support.

- Example: Accompanying a sibling to medical appointments or helping them organize personal affairs.

5. Strengthening Bonds Through Shared Memories

As people age, reminiscing about the past becomes a comforting and joyful activity. Elderly parents can strengthen their bond with siblings by sharing old stories, revisiting childhood memories, and keeping family traditions alive.

- Example: Discussing childhood events over a cup of tea or recreating old family recipes during gatherings.

6. Encouraging Spiritual Growth

For many retirees, spirituality becomes a significant focus. They can inspire and support their siblings in exploring spiritual growth, engaging in community service, or simply finding peace and purpose in their later years.

- Example: Encouraging siblings to join them in prayers, meditation, or visiting places of worship together.

7. Being a Role Model of Graceful Aging

By embracing retirement and old age with dignity, retirees can inspire their siblings to do the same. Their approach to health, relationships, and finding purpose in retirement can motivate siblings to lead a fulfilling life.

- Example: Taking up hobbies, volunteering, or staying socially active, showing siblings how to remain vibrant in later years.

8. Offering Unconditional Love and Patience

As siblings age together, differences from the past often fade, and a new depth of connection emerges. Elderly parents can nurture this bond with patience, forgiveness, and unconditional love, valuing the unique relationship they share.

- Example: Reconnecting with an estranged sibling and mending old wounds, focusing on the importance of family over past disagreements.

In essence, the role of a retired and elderly father or mother toward their siblings is one of care, connection, and legacy. They serve as a living testament to the strength of family ties, bringing warmth, wisdom, and unity to relationships that have stood the test of time. By embracing this role with love and purpose, they not only enrich their siblings' lives but also find deep fulfillment in their own.

6.5 Role of Grandparenting

Grandparenting is a role that fills the hearts of retirees with unparalleled joy and purpose, offering a chance to embrace a deeply fulfilling chapter of life. It provides an opportunity to share wisdom, nurture emotional bonds, and create a legacy of love that transcends generations. This relationship between grandparents and grandchildren is one of the most beautiful and heartwarming connections, built on unconditional love, mutual admiration, and shared wonder.

For grandparents, their grandchildren represent a precious second chance to relive the innocence and magic of childhood—this time, through the sparkling eyes and boundless energy of the little ones they cherish. Every laugh, every hug, and every playful moment becomes a treasure. This bond is not merely familial; it is an emotional sanctuary, a relationship that grows stronger with every shared story, every heartfelt lesson, and every moment of pure togetherness.

The presence of grandchildren in a grandparent's life is transformative. They are more than just the next generation; they embody continuity, carrying forward family traditions, values, and cherished memories. As mentors, grandparents pass down wisdom and life lessons with patience and love, offering guidance that resonates across a lifetime. In return, grandchildren inject vibrancy and youthfulness into their grandparents' lives, their curiosity and innocence acting as a refreshing breeze that rejuvenates the soul.

The emotional depth of this bond is profound. To a grandchild, grandparents are often a safe haven—a place of unconditional love and acceptance. They listen with empathy, respond with encouragement, and stand as unwavering pillars of support. For grandparents, the joy of witnessing a grandchild's milestones—whether it's their first steps, their first words, or their blossoming personalities—is incomparable. Moments spent together, whether playing a simple game or enjoying a quiet cup of tea, are etched into memory as golden threads in the fabric of family life.

Imagine the tender joy of a two-year-old grandchild toddling eagerly towards you, hoping to share a sip of tea from your cup, only to stumble and fall mid-journey. In that instant, your heart aches as you rush barefoot to lift them, soothing their tears with gentle pats and whispered reassurances. Such moments, filled with raw emotion, encapsulate the essence of grandparenting—a blend of love, care, and unforgettable memories.

Grandchildren also bring a sense of companionship that is deeply reassuring. Their innocent observations and concern for their grandparents' well-being—whether it's a simple hug when they notice stress or an earnest question to lighten a heavy heart—create a bond of mutual care. These interactions often alleviate loneliness, filling retirees' lives with laughter, love, and renewed purpose.

Often, it is in the eyes of our grandchildren that we find the purest reflection of love—unfiltered, unconditional, and untouched by the complexities that sometimes creep into our relationships with our own children. Grandchildren's maximum requirements from grandparents are colorful toys & a few pieces of toffees. While time and responsibilities may create distance with our grown-up children, grandchildren arrive like fresh morning dew—trusting, open-hearted, and full of innocent wonder.

They love without questioning, trust without doubting, and embrace you without expecting anything in return—except your love. They carry no grudges, no misunderstandings, no selfishness—just wide eyes filled with curiosity and a heart eager to connect. It feels as though two souls, one seasoned by life and the other just beginning the journey, are dancing in perfect harmony—synchronized in joy, peace, and silent understanding.

In their playful laughter and tiny hands, they offer us a second chance at joy, a peaceful companionship that seeks nothing but your presence. Their mission is simple: to enjoy life and let you enjoy it too—peacefully, calmly, and comfortably—asking for nothing but your time, your stories, your smile.

Perhaps, this is what true companionship looks like—love in its rawest, most beautiful form: free of conditions, free of demands, and full of soul.

Grandparents often serve as a bridge between the past and the future, preserving family traditions while connecting with the ever-evolving world of their grandchildren. This is especially true for maternal grandparents, whose bonds with grandchildren are often particularly strong due to the closeness of maternal ties.

The precious bond between generations is gradually eroding, largely due to the rise of nuclear families and the migration of younger generations seeking better job opportunities and higher wages in distant locations. This often leaves elderly parents behind in their native places, creating an emotional void. The fast-paced lifestyle of the younger generation, coupled with an increasingly materialistic outlook on life, has further distanced families emotionally.

Unfortunately, this cultural shift has severely impacted the cherished role of grandparenting, particularly in Western societies. Grandparents and grandchildren often lose meaningful contact with one another, weakening the threads of intergenerational love and wisdom. Such disconnection is, in essence, a subtle violation of human values, undermining the very soul of the grandparent-grandchild relationship.

The loss is profound for both sides. Grandparents miss the joy and vitality brought by their grandchildren, while children are deprived of the warmth, wisdom, and unconditional love that only grandparents can offer. This unique bond, rich with shared stories, life lessons, and affection, is irreplaceable. Its absence often leaves both generations with a sense of incompleteness—diminishing the happiness of the elderly and depriving children of moral grounding and emotional stability.

Rebuilding this connection is vital for preserving not just familial harmony but the essential human values that make life meaningful and enriching.

Grandparents' Roles in Their Grandchildren's Lives

1. **Mentorship:** Imparting wisdom, values, and family traditions helps grandchildren navigate life with guidance and strength.
2. **Emotional Support:** Providing unwavering love, care, and encouragement creates a nurturing environment for growth.
3. **Shared Activities:** Participating in games, storytelling, and creative pursuits fosters fun, learning, and deeper connections.

In essence, the bond between grandparents and grandchildren is a celebration of life's most tender and meaningful moments—a connection that brightens their days and warms their hearts in ways words can scarcely capture. This relationship is a testament to the enduring power of love and the beauty of shared experiences, enriching lives on both sides of the generational divide.

6.6 Managing Marital Relationship

Spousal relationship - The bond between spouses, which can be legally recognized as a marriage, civil, or domestic.

Marriage is often described as a union made in heaven, formally recognized on earth by a Registrar, Qadi, Rabbi, Priest, Pandit, Monk, or Guru. It represents a unique and sacred bond—moral, spiritual, and built on deep trust—standing as one of the most respected commitments two individuals can make. Together, they embark on a journey of harmony, mutual respect, and shared purpose.

Spousal relationship in elderly individuals and retirees refers to the deep emotional, physical, and social partnership between spouses, where they provide mutual support, companionship, and care as they navigate the challenges of aging, health issues, and life transitions together. This bond grows in importance, offering stability and resilience in their later years.

In elderly individuals and retirees, the role and relationship of spouses become even more crucial than in earlier stages of life. As people age and retire, they face various challenges such as declining health, reduced social interactions, financial insecurity, and emotional changes. In this context, the bond between spouses can provide immense emotional support, companionship, and stability. Here are some key aspects of spousal relationship in the lives of elderly individuals and retirees:

- **Emotional Support and Companionship**

  In retirement, spouses often become the primary source of emotional support. With children grown and careers concluded, couples spend more time together, which can deepen their emotional connection. They share memories, face the realities of aging together, and provide a comforting presence, reducing feelings of loneliness and isolation, which are common among the elderly.

- **Physical Care and Health Management**

  As health issues become more prevalent with age, spouses often take on caregiving roles. They help manage each other's medical needs, provide physical assistance, and remind each other about medications, treatments, and health appointments. This mutual care can greatly enhance the quality of life, as the support of a trusted partner can make the health management process less overwhelming.

- **Social and Mental Well-being**

  Spouses help maintain social connections, especially when one partner might find it difficult to engage in social activities due to physical limitations or cognitive decline. Regular conversations, shared activities, and hobbies can keep both partners mentally stimulated. In this way, spouses play a role in protecting each other from mental health challenges like depression or cognitive decline.

- **Financial Stability and Decision-Making**

  Financial security often becomes a major concern in retirement. Spouses work together to manage household expenses, savings, and investments. Their partnership in making financial decisions is crucial for ensuring a stable retirement. They also discuss important legal and financial matters such as wills, pensions, and inheritance planning, contributing to their long-term financial well-being.

- **Resilience in Facing Life Transitions**

  Retirees undergo significant life transitions, from adjusting to a new daily routine to coping with the loss of friends and family members. Having a spouse by one's side during these transitions can provide emotional stability and resilience. They encourage each other to adapt to new circumstances, find purpose in life after retirement, and navigate major life changes.

- **Strengthening the Bond of Partnership**

With more time spent together, the elderly often find new dimensions in their relationship. They may develop new routines or hobbies, travel, or explore new interests. The shared experience of aging and retirement can strengthen their bond, as they rely on each other for both physical and emotional support in ways that may have been less pronounced earlier in life.

- **Coping with the Loss of a Spouse**

One of the most profound challenges for elderly individuals is the potential loss of a spouse. The death of a spouse can have devastating effects on the surviving partner's mental and emotional well-being. Grief, loneliness, and the need to adapt to a new life without their partner can be overwhelming. For many, the bond with a spouse helps prepare them for this loss, and the memories of their shared life become a source of comfort and strength.

In such a scenario, the focus of the surviving partner must shift toward looking ahead, embracing the future with resilience and hope. The past, though filled with cherished memories, should remain as a treasure rather than a weight. Haunting reflections of loss can be gently replaced with the promise of a meaningful life—one where living independently yet surrounded by the love of siblings and the joy of grandchildren becomes a source of strength and renewal.

Celebrating the lives of those who have departed by honoring their memory through impactful acts—such as establishing schools, supporting charitable organizations, and uplifting underprivileged communities—infuses this journey with purpose. These noble endeavors not only pay tribute to the departed but also bring light to the lives of others, creating a legacy of compassion and hope amidst the sorrow.

- **Legacy and Shared Memories**

  As couples reflect on their lives together, they often find solace in shared memories and the legacy they've built—whether through raising children, building a home, or contributing to society. This sense of shared history can offer fulfillment in old age, reinforcing the idea that they've walked through life's journey together, leaving behind a meaningful legacy.

  In summary, spousal relationships in elderly individuals and retirees plays a central role in providing emotional, physical, and social support. It is a partnership that grows in significance with time, as both partners rely on each other to navigate the challenges and joys of aging. Spousal relationship becomes a cornerstone of resilience and well-being during this stage of life, highlighting the profound importance of the marital bond in later years.

In retirement, maintaining a strong marital relationship is vital for emotional well-being and companionship. Here are some key strategies:

1. **Open Communication:** Regularly share thoughts, feelings, and concerns to strengthen understanding and trust.
2. **Quality Time Together:** Engage in shared activities, date nights, or hobbies to nurture connection and enjoyment.
3. **Support Each Other:** Be attentive to each other's needs and aspirations, offering encouragement and assistance.
4. **Adapt to Change:** Embrace the changes that retirement brings and work together to create a fulfilling life together.
5. **No Ego: Ego can have a negative impact on relationships by causing conflicts, misunderstandings & a lack of empathy.** In

the elderly stage, the spouse relationship becomes healthier and more balanced, as both partners stand on equal footing in every aspect of life. Mutual respect, care, and value are shared equally, fostering a deeper, more harmonious connection that strengthens their bond as they age together.

7.0 Legacy and Estate Planning

Introduction

Legacy and estate planning are crucial components of financial management, particularly for retirees. This process ensures that your assets are distributed according to your wishes after your passing while also providing peace of mind for you and your loved ones. Here's a detailed overview of the key elements and steps involved in legacy and estate planning.

7.1 Understanding Legacy and Estate Planning

- **Legacy Planning**: Focuses on how you want to be remembered, including charitable contributions, family heirlooms, and personal values you wish to pass down.
- **Estate Planning**: Involves the legal and financial strategies for managing your assets during your lifetime and distributing them after your death.

7.2 Key Components of Estate Planning

- **Will**: A legal document that outlines how your assets will be distributed upon your death. It also names guardians for minor children.
- **Trust**: A legal entity that holds your assets for the benefit of designated beneficiaries. Trusts can help avoid probate, reduce taxes, and protect assets from creditors.
- **Durable Power of Attorney**: This document designates someone to make financial decisions on your behalf if you become incapacitated.
- **Health Care Proxy**: A document that allows you to appoint someone to make medical decisions for you if you are unable to do so.
- **Beneficiary Designations**: Ensure that assets like retirement accounts and life insurance policies are transferred directly to designated beneficiaries.

7.3 Steps to Effective Estate Planning

Step 1: Assess Your Assets

- Make a list of all your assets, including real estate, bank accounts, investments, retirement accounts, and personal property. Determine their value and any associated debts.

Step 2: Define Your Goals

- Decide how you want your assets distributed. Consider the needs of your family, potential tax implications, and any charitable wishes.

Step 3: Choose the Right Documents

- Depending on your goals, decide which legal documents you need. Consulting with an estate planning attorney can help you determine the best options for your situation.

Step 4: Consider Tax Implications

- Be aware of potential estate taxes and other tax implications. Strategies like gifting assets during your lifetime can help reduce the taxable value of your estate.

Step 5: Communicate Your Plans

- Discuss your estate planning decisions with family members and relevant parties. Clear communication can help prevent misunderstandings and conflicts after your death.

Step 6: Review and Update Regularly

- Life circumstances change, so it's essential to review and update your estate plan regularly—after major life events like marriage, divorce, births, or deaths.

7.4 Legacy Planning Considerations

- **Charitable Contributions**: Consider establishing a foundation or making bequests to charities that are important to you.

- **Personal Values and Memories**: Write down your values, lessons learned, and wishes for your heirs to pass on your legacy beyond material assets.

- **Family Heirlooms**: Decide how to distribute cherished items and communicate their significance to your heirs.

7.5 Working with Professionals

- **Estate Planning Attorney**: Essential for creating legally binding documents and providing guidance on the complexities of estate law.

- **Financial Advisor**: Can help assess your financial situation and develop a strategy for effective estate and tax planning.

- **Tax Professional**: Valuable for understanding the tax implications of your estate plan and ensuring compliance with tax laws.

7.6 Common Pitfalls to Avoid

- **Procrastination**: Delaying estate planning can lead to complications and increased stress for your loved ones.

- **Ignoring Digital Assets**: Don't forget to include online accounts, digital currencies, and social media (Social media platforms often have personal data, photos, and messages. Estate planning can dictate whether these accounts should be memorialized, deleted, or transferred to a trusted person) in your estate plan.

- **Failure to Update**: Regularly review and update your plan to reflect any changes in your life or the law.

Conclusion:

Legacy and estate planning are essential for retirees looking to ensure their wishes are fulfilled and their loved ones are taken care of after their passing. By taking proactive steps, working with professionals, and maintaining open communication with family members, you can create a plan that provides peace of mind and preserves your legacy for future generations.

8.0 Legal Considerations

Legal Considerations for Retirees: Key Concepts and Strategies

As retirees transition into a new phase of life, various legal considerations become increasingly important. From estate planning to healthcare directives, ensuring that all legal aspects are properly managed can protect your assets, provide for your loved ones, and safeguard your personal welfare. Below are the critical legal concepts retirees should be aware of:

1. Estate Planning

Estate planning allows retirees to dictate how their assets will be managed and distributed after their death. Key elements include:

- **Last Will and Testament**: A legal document that details how you want your property distributed after death and can name guardians for any dependents. Without a will, the state determines asset distribution, which may not align with your wishes.
- **Trusts**: Trusts can help avoid probate (the legal process of distributing a deceased person's estate) and provide flexibility in managing assets. There are various types of trusts:
    - **Revocable Living Trust**: Allows control of your assets during your lifetime and specifies distribution after death while avoiding probate.
    - **Irrevocable Trust**: Often used to reduce estate taxes or protect assets from creditors, as assets in this trust are no longer under your direct control.
- **Probate**: The legal process where the court oversees the distribution of your estate if you only have a will. This process can be lengthy and costly, and avoiding it through trusts may simplify matters for your heirs.

2. Power of Attorney

A Power of Attorney (POA) allows another person to act on your behalf in financial or legal matters, especially if you become incapacitated. There are different types:

- **Durable Power of Attorney**: This document remains effective even if you become mentally or physically incapacitated. It grants your designated agent the power to handle financial transactions such as managing investments, paying bills, or selling property.
- **Limited Power of Attorney**: Grants someone the authority to handle specific matters (e.g., selling a house) for a limited period.

It's essential to choose a trustworthy agent, as they will have control over critical aspects of your financial well-being.

3. Healthcare Directives and Medical Power of Attorney

As a retiree, it's important to have legal tools in place to guide your medical care in case you're unable to make decisions yourself. Two key documents are:

- **Health Care Proxy/Medical Power of Attorney**: Allows you to appoint a trusted individual to make healthcare decisions on your behalf if you're incapacitated.
- **Living Will/Advance Directive**: Specifies your preferences for medical treatment in scenarios where you cannot communicate, such as life-sustaining treatments, resuscitation, and organ donation. This document can relieve loved ones of the burden of making these decisions under stress.

4. Guardianship

In cases where you or your spouse becomes mentally or physically incapacitated, the court may appoint a legal guardian to manage your affairs if you haven't already appointed someone via a power of attorney. Planning ahead can help avoid court intervention.

- **Conservatorship**: A conservator may be appointed by a court to manage your financial affairs if you are unable to do so due to incapacity.

5. Long-Term Care Planning

Legal preparation for long-term care, such as nursing home care or in-home health services, is essential as medical needs often increase with age. Some legal considerations include:

- **Long-Term Care Insurance**: Protects against the high costs of extended care by covering services like nursing home care, in-home assistance, and hospice care.
- **Medicaid Planning**: If you plan to rely on Medicaid, you may need to structure your assets properly to meet eligibility requirements. Medicaid has strict asset and income limits, and improper planning could result in losing your assets to cover healthcare costs. Some retirees establish irrevocable trusts to shelter assets from being counted by Medicaid.

6. Tax Planning

Tax considerations are essential for preserving wealth and minimizing tax liability in retirement. Important aspects include:

- **Estate and Inheritance Taxes**: Federal estate taxes apply only to estates over a certain value (which changes yearly), but some states also impose estate or inheritance taxes. Planning can help reduce the taxable value of your estate.
- **Capital Gains Tax**: Selling assets such as property or investments after retirement could trigger capital gains taxes. Proper planning, like transferring assets via trusts or using tax-exempt retirement accounts, can reduce this burden.

7. Beneficiary Designations

Assets like life insurance policies, retirement accounts (e.g., IRAs or 401(k)s), and bank accounts often pass directly to beneficiaries outside of a will. Keeping beneficiary designations updated is crucial, especially after major life events like the death of a spouse, marriage, or divorce.

- **Transfer on Death (TOD)** and **Payable on Death (POD)** accounts can help avoid probate by directly transferring assets to named beneficiaries.

8. Digital Assets

In today's digital age, retirees often have significant online accounts and assets that require attention in estate planning. Legal considerations for digital assets include:

- **Passwords and Access**: Include instructions in your estate plan for accessing online financial accounts, emails, social media, and other digital assets.
- **Digital Executor**: Some states allow you to name a digital executor, a person responsible for managing your digital assets after death.

9. Elder Abuse and Legal Protections

Retirees are sometimes vulnerable to elder abuse, including financial exploitation. To protect yourself:

- **Fraud Prevention**: Work with trusted advisors and consider appointing someone to monitor your accounts. You can also authorize a financial institution to notify a trusted contact if suspicious activity occurs.
- **Guardianship and Conservatorship Protections**: Ensure that your legal documents are up to date, so only trusted individuals can act on your behalf if you become incapacitated.

10. Funeral and Burial Arrangements

Planning for end-of-life arrangements can alleviate the emotional and financial burden on your family. Consider legal arrangements such as:

- **Prepaid Funeral Contracts**: These contracts lock in the costs of funeral services and can help spare your loved ones from making tough decisions during emotional times.
- **Burial Instructions**: You may include your burial or cremation preferences in your will or separate document, ensuring that your wishes are respected.

Conclusion

For retirees, legal considerations encompass everything from protecting your assets and healthcare to ensuring your loved ones are cared for after your passing. By addressing these issues through proper estate planning, healthcare directives, and legal documents, you can ensure your wishes are honored and provide peace of mind for yourself and your family. Consulting with professionals, such as estate planning attorneys and financial advisors, is a key step in tailoring these legal considerations to your unique needs.

9.0 Personal Reflections and Life Review

A Retiree's Guide to Meaningful Reflection

Retirement offers a unique opportunity for introspection, allowing retirees to take a step back from the demands of work and daily responsibilities to reflect on the entirety of their lives. This "life review" process is a chance to evaluate past experiences, relationships, accomplishments, and challenges with an eye toward understanding, closure, and legacy. Here's a detailed guide for retirees looking to embark on this deeply personal journey.

1. What is Life Review?

Life review is the process of reflecting on and reviewing one's past experiences, achievements, regrets, and lessons learned throughout life. This often happens naturally in later years as retirees find themselves with more time and a desire to make sense of the lives they've lived.

This process often involves:

- **Revisiting key life events**: Significant moments like career achievements, personal milestones, family relationships, and major challenges.
- **Evaluating life choices**: Understanding the motivations behind important decisions and considering how they shaped your present life.
- **Finding meaning**: Looking at how experiences, both positive and negative, contributed to your personal growth and the values you now hold.
- **Creating closure**: Resolving lingering regrets, unfinished business, or unresolved emotional issues.

Life review can be a formal or informal process, and many retirees undertake it to foster a sense of fulfillment, purpose, and legacy.

2. Benefits of Personal Reflection and Life Review

- **Emotional Well-Being**: Reflection allows retirees to process unresolved emotions, leading to emotional healing and a greater sense of peace. Understanding past decisions, failures, and triumphs can bring closure and contentment.
- **Sense of Accomplishment**: Recognizing accomplishments—whether in career, family life, or personal growth—can foster a strong sense of self-worth and satisfaction.
- **Clarifying Life Lessons**: Life review often helps retirees understand the wisdom they've gained and how they want to share it with future generations.
- **Strengthening Relationships**: Reflecting on important relationships can lead to forgiveness, deeper connection, and expressions of gratitude toward loved ones.
- **Legacy Building**: Life review helps retirees define their legacy, whether it's passing down family stories, values, or tangible assets. This can help preserve memories and ensure future generations remember their contributions.

3. Steps to Begin a Life Review Process

Step 1: Reflect on Significant Life Stages

- **Childhood and Adolescence**: Reflect on your early family life, schooling, friendships, and early influences. Consider what values or beliefs were formed during this time and how they shaped your adult life.

- **Adulthood and Career**: Review your professional life, career achievements, and major challenges. How did your career choices shape your life and personal identity? Consider reflecting on moments of pride, as well as failures or setbacks that taught valuable lessons.
- **Family Life**: Reflect on your roles as a spouse, parent, grandparent, and sibling. How have your relationships evolved over time? What are you most proud of in your family life, and what would you do differently?
- **Later Years**: Consider your recent life, including retirement and the transition from work. How have you adapted to the changes? What new experiences have you embraced?

Step 2: Consider Major Themes

- **Achievements and Regrets**: Reflect on your greatest accomplishments, as well as any regrets you may have. What were your major life goals, and to what extent were they achieved?
- **Challenges and Resilience**: Revisit difficult times in your life, such as personal losses, health issues, or career struggles. What strategies did you use to overcome these challenges? How did they shape your character and values?
- **Relationships and Love**: Focus on your relationships with family, friends, and colleagues. What relationships have been the most meaningful to you? How have you expressed love and care **throughout your life? Are there any relationships in need of healing or closure?**

Step 3: Document Your Reflections

- **Journaling**: Writing down your reflections is a powerful tool for organizing thoughts and emotions. You might choose to write about specific events, people, or periods of your life.
- **Creating a Memoir**: Some retirees opt to write memoirs or autobiographies as a way of documenting their lives for future generations. This can be a structured way to preserve memories, stories, and insights.

- **Oral Histories**: If writing isn't your style, consider recording your reflections in audio or video format. This is a meaningful way to capture your voice, stories, and personality for your family.

Step 4: Reconciliation and Closure

- **Forgiveness**: Life review often involves processing unresolved conflicts or regrets. This may involve forgiving others or seeking forgiveness, whether in person or in your own heart.
- **Acceptance**: Accepting past mistakes, missed opportunities, or life's unpredictability can bring emotional relief and peace.
- **Gratitude**: Focus on the positive experiences in your life. What are you most thankful for? Who are the people, moments, or experiences that brought you joy, support, and meaning?

4. Tools and Techniques for Life Review

- **Reminiscence Therapy**: A therapeutic technique often used with older adults, reminiscence therapy involves discussing past experiences to promote self-understanding and emotional well-being. This can be done individually or in group settings.
- **Guided Autobiography**: Involves structured writing or discussion based on specific life themes. Topics may include family, work, spirituality, and turning points. This process is usually guided by prompts or a facilitator.
- **Creating a Legacy Project**: Retirees may choose to create a tangible legacy, such as writing a family history, organizing photo albums, compiling scrapbooks, or creating digital archives for future generations.

5. Key Areas of Focus During Personal Reflection

a. Life Lessons and Values

- What core values guided you throughout your life?
- What lessons would you like to pass on to future generations? Consider lessons on work ethic, love, friendship, integrity, or spirituality.

b. Purpose and Legacy

- How do you define your purpose now, in your retired life? What contributions do you continue to make, and how do they enrich your sense of self?
- What kind of legacy do you want to leave behind? This might include financial legacy planning, but also the emotional and intellectual legacy of your values, stories, and wisdom.

c. Spiritual and Existential Reflection

- Many retirees take the opportunity to reflect on deeper existential or spiritual questions: What is the meaning of life? How do you feel about mortality? What are your beliefs about what comes after death?
- Whether through religion, spirituality, or personal philosophy, reflecting on these questions can bring a sense of peace and acceptance about life's finite nature.

6. Sharing Your Life Review with Others

- **Family Gatherings and Conversations**: Share your reflections with family members or loved ones in a meaningful way. Conversations about your life, values, and experiences can deepen family bonds and create intergenerational understanding.
- **Ethical Wills**: An ethical will is a non-legal document where you pass on your spiritual values, personal insights, blessings, and life lessons to your loved ones. It's a personal way to express what truly matters to you.

Conclusion

Personal reflections and life review offer retirees a chance to look back on their lives with pride, understanding, and emotional resolution. This process fosters a sense of completeness and can contribute to a deeper sense of purpose in the present. By taking time for thoughtful reflection, retirees can shape how they are remembered and strengthen their connection to both the past and the future. Whether through writing, storytelling, or quiet reflection, this practice offers emotional rewards and a profound sense of fulfillment.

10.0 Conclusion

A Man's Retirement Journey

Retirement is not merely the end of a career; it's the beginning of a new chapter filled with possibilities, reflection, and transformation. After years of hard work, responsibility, and personal growth, retirement provides a man with the unique opportunity to redefine his life in ways that align with his values, dreams, and relationships. Here's a detailed look at the emotional, psychological, and practical aspects that culminate in the conclusion of a man's retirement journey.

1. Looking Back: Reflecting on Achievements

The conclusion of a man's retirement often begins with a reflection on his working life. It's a time to celebrate achievements and contributions—whether in a professional career, business, or personal endeavors. These reflections may encompass:

- **Career Accomplishments**: The years of dedication, hard work, and skill-building that led to promotions, leadership roles, or notable projects. This reflection might evoke pride in the work done and the legacy left behind in the workplace.
- **Personal Milestones**: Retirement is also a time to acknowledge the personal milestones achieved alongside the professional ones—whether raising a family, building lasting friendships, or being involved in community service.
- **Lessons Learned**: The culmination of decades of experiences, both successes and failures, brings invaluable wisdom. Reflecting on these lessons helps a retiree realize how those experiences shaped his character and the person he has become today.

2. Closure and Emotional Reconciliation

Retirement is a significant life transition, and the conclusion of this journey often involves finding emotional closure, both with the past and with the changes that retirement brings.

- **Letting Go of the Past**: A man retiring from a long career may need to emotionally detach from his former identity as a worker or leader. This can be challenging, but it is essential for embracing new roles and finding fulfillment outside the professional sphere.
- **Accepting Unfulfilled Goals**: No life is without unmet goals or dreams. The conclusion of retirement may involve accepting that certain career ambitions or personal aspirations didn't materialize. This acceptance allows for peace with the past and opens the door to new opportunities.
- **Healing Relationships**: With more time for reflection, retirees often seek to reconcile strained relationships, whether with family, friends, or colleagues. Mending these bonds can bring emotional healing and a sense of completion.

3. Transitioning to a New Identity

A man's retirement marks the transition from the role of a provider, worker, or business leader to new identities that may include being a mentor, volunteer, caregiver, or simply a man pursuing his passions. The key to a fulfilling retirement lies in embracing this transition.

- **Reimagining Purpose**: The end of a professional career doesn't mean the end of purpose. Many retirees find immense satisfaction in new endeavors, such as teaching, volunteering, or pursuing creative outlets. These activities offer new meaning and a way to contribute to society outside the traditional workforce.
- **Embracing Leisure and Hobbies**: For the first time in years, retirees often have the time to dive deep into hobbies they may have set aside during their working years. Whether it's golfing,

gardening, painting, or learning a new skill, retirement opens the door to personal fulfillment through leisure.

- **Family Roles**: Retirement often reshapes a man's role within his family. He may find himself with more time to spend with children, grandchildren, or even elderly parents. This increased involvement allows him to nurture relationships that may have taken a backseat during his working years.

4. Navigating Emotional and Psychological Changes

The psychological impact of retirement can vary. For many, the absence of a structured workday and professional identity leads to feelings of anxiety, loss of direction, or even depression. Concluding this phase requires adjusting to these emotional changes and finding a new balance.

- **Managing Loneliness**: Work often provides social interaction and a sense of community. The absence of these daily connections can lead to loneliness, especially for men who may not naturally seek out social engagements. Building or reconnecting with social networks is crucial during retirement.
- **Adapting to Unstructured Time**: Retirement offers the freedom of an unstructured schedule, which can be liberating for some but overwhelming for others. Finding a balance between relaxation and activity is key to maintaining mental well-being.
- **Maintaining Physical and Mental Health**: A man's retirement is an ideal time to focus on his health. Regular exercise, proper nutrition, and engaging in mentally stimulating activities like reading or problem-solving games can enhance the quality of life in retirement.

5. Legacy and Life Review

As retirement progresses, many men reflect on the legacy they are leaving behind, both professionally and personally. The conclusion of retirement often involves a thoughtful assessment of one's life, focusing on how they will be remembered and the values they hope to pass on to future generations.

- **Personal Legacy**: For some, legacy is about the wealth or assets they leave behind, but for others, it is about the intangible—memories, life lessons, values, and family traditions. This can also include creating a memoir, passing down stories to children and grandchildren, or writing letters to loved ones.
- **Charitable Contributions**: Retirement often motivates individuals to give back, whether financially through donations or personally by volunteering. Many retirees find deep satisfaction in contributing to causes they care about, thereby leaving a legacy of generosity.
- **Mentorship and Guidance**: Some retirees take on roles as mentors, offering guidance to the younger generation based on their life experience and career wisdom. This allows them to stay connected to their field of expertise or community and pass on valuable insights.

6. Final Reflections: Finding Peace and Contentment

The conclusion of a man's retirement is not just about reviewing the past but also about looking forward with contentment. This stage of life can be one of the most rewarding if embraced with the right mindset.

- **Gratitude**: The end of the retirement journey is often marked by a deep sense of gratitude—gratitude for the career that provided, for the family and friends who supported, and for the opportunity to rest, reflect, and enjoy life's simpler pleasures.
- **Embracing Simplicity**: As retirement concludes, there is often a greater appreciation for the simple things in life: the peace of a morning walk, the joy of time spent with loved ones, and the satisfaction of being present in the moment.
- **Looking Toward the Future**: Retirement doesn't mark the end of life's adventure but the start of a new one. Whether it's traveling, learning, or simply enjoying the fruits of past labor, there is always

something to look forward to. Concluding retirement with a forward-thinking mindset keeps life fulfilling and meaningful.

Conclusion:

For a man, retirement is a time to reflect, reconcile, and reinvent. The journey of retirement culminates in a deep understanding of oneself, a sense of closure on the professional chapter of life, and an openness to new roles, experiences, and opportunities. It's a phase of life filled with reflection, renewed purpose, and ultimately, contentment. The conclusion of a man's retirement is not an end but a beginning—a celebration of the past and an embrace of the future.

11.0 Do's

The following essential Do's are vital for elderly individuals and retirees to follow closely. By embracing these principles, they can nurture a positive lifestyle and sustain both physical and mental well-being throughout the golden years of life.

Disclaimer: The information provided here regarding health issues and diseases affecting elderly individuals is intended for informational purposes only. The author does not assume responsibility for any specific health conditions or treatments. For personalized advice, diagnosis, and treatment, always consult a qualified doctor, physician, or healthcare professional. It's essential to seek guidance from healthcare centers tailored to your individual needs and medical concerns.

11.1 Early to Bed & Early to Rise

" Before we dive deep into the main topic, let's first take a fascinating little detour — **What exactly is sleep? What secret magic does the body perform while we snooze? And why is this nightly shutdown so incredibly important for our body, mind, and soul?** Let's unwrap the mystery of sleep step by step!"

What is Sleep? – A Simple Definition:

Sleep is a natural, reversible state of rest where your body and mind slow down, allowing you to recover energy, repair cells, and process everything you've experienced while awake. During sleep, you're less aware of your surroundings, but your brain and body are still very active — doing behind-the-scenes work like:

- Storing memories
- Repairing tissues
- Releasing hormones
- Strengthening your immune system

How Does Sleep Happen in the Body?

Sleep doesn't just "happen" — it's a beautifully coordinated process involving the brain, hormones, body temperature, and even light and darkness.

1. The Biological Clock (Circadian Rhythm)

Your body has a natural 24-hour clock, called the circadian rhythm, which tells you when to feel sleepy and when to wake up. It's mostly controlled by a part of the brain called the suprachiasmatic nucleus (SCN), located in the hypothalamus.

- This clock responds to light and darkness.

- When it gets dark, your brain starts producing a hormone called **melatonin**, which makes you sleepy.

2. Brain Activity Changes

Your brain goes through different sleep stages:

Stage	Description
Stage 1 (Light Sleep)	You're dozing off, easy to wake up.
Stage 2	Your body temperature drops, heart rate slows, and brain waves become slower.
Stage 3 (Deep Sleep)	Physical repair happens, the body builds bones and muscles, and the immune system strengthens.
REM (Rapid Eye Movement)	Brain is very active, you dream, and emotions and memories are processed.

You cycle through these stages multiple times each night.

3. Body Repair & Hormones

While you sleep:

- Growth hormone is released (helps with healing and growth)
- Muscles relax
- Blood pressure and body temperature drop
- The brain flushes out toxins (like a cleaning crew!)

Why is Sleep Important?

- Helps store and organize memories

- Boosts learning and focus
- Repairs damaged cells and tissues
- Strengthens the immune system
- Keeps your mood and emotions balanced
- Regulates hunger and metabolism

In Short:

"Sleep is like charging your phone – except you're the phone. No sleep = low battery life, poor performance, and system crashes!"

Early to bed & early to rise, makes a man healthy, wealthy & wise:

It is a very famous phrase well known since 1735 given by Benjamin Franklin in his book “Poor Richard's Almanack. Meaning & message of the idiom is very clear & self explanatory.

Older individuals, defined as those aged 60 and over, require 7 to 8 hours of shut-eye per night to maintain their physical and mental health. This quantity of slumber allows their bodies to recover and rejuvenate, while also improving cognitive performance and mood control.

For optimal health and well-being, the ideal timing for early sleeping and waking up generally aligns with the body's **circadian rhythm**. Here’s a guideline for timing:

Early Sleeping

- **Best bedtime**: Between **9:00 PM and 10:30 PM**.

Sleeping between **9:00 PM and 10:30 PM** aligns with the body’s natural circadian rhythm, offering numerous **medical benefits** for both the body and mind. Here's how it positively impacts your well-being:

1. Better Sleep Quality

- **Deep sleep**: This time period allows the body to enter deeper stages of sleep (slow-wave sleep) earlier in the night, which is crucial for **physical repair** and growth. Your muscles, tissues, and immune system regenerate during this stage.
- **Hormone regulation**: Early sleep helps regulate the production of **melatonin**, which promotes restful sleep and helps to regulate your biological clock. It also balances other important hormones like cortisol (stress hormone) and growth hormone.

2. Improved Physical Health

- **Heart health**: Early and quality sleep reduces the risk of cardiovascular diseases by lowering blood pressure and regulating heart function. It also helps reduce inflammation in the body, which is linked to heart disease.
- **Boosted immune system**: During deep sleep, the immune system produces cytokines, which fight off infection and inflammation. Early bedtime ensures you reach this vital phase.
- **Weight management**: Early sleepers tend to have better control over appetite hormones, such as **ghrelin** and **leptin**, which helps prevent late-night snacking and promotes healthier eating habits.

3. Enhanced Mental Health

- **Reduced stress and anxiety**: Going to bed early lowers levels of the stress hormone **cortisol**, leading to a calmer and more relaxed mind. It helps manage anxiety and stress, improving emotional well-being.
- **Better memory and cognitive function**: Early sleep provides ample time for the brain to consolidate memories and process information from the day. It enhances **learning, problem-solving skills, and creativity**.
- **Mood stability**: Sufficient sleep, especially at the right time, stabilizes **neurotransmitters** like serotonin and dopamine, which are essential for maintaining a positive mood and mental clarity.

4. Increased Energy and Productivity

- **Morning alertness**: Waking up early after a good night's sleep leads to higher energy levels and improved focus, making you more productive throughout the day.
- **Balanced circadian rhythm**: Aligning sleep with the natural light-dark cycle enhances your body's ability to regulate energy levels, ensuring you feel awake and alert during the day and restful at night.

5. Improved Mental Resilience

- **Emotional regulation**: Quality sleep improves your ability to handle stress and respond calmly to challenging situations. It also reduces the risk of mood disorders like depression and anxiety.

By going to bed between 9:00 PM and 10:30 PM, you allow your body and mind to enter the most restorative stages of sleep, leading to significant improvements in your **physical health, mental clarity, emotional balance, and overall well-being**.

Early Waking Up

Waking up between **5:00 AM and 6:30 AM** is highly beneficial for elderly individuals and retirees, offering both physical and mental health advantages. Here's why this wake-up time is ideal:

1. Alignment with the Circadian Rhythm

- The body's **internal clock** (circadian rhythm) naturally prompts early waking as we age. Waking up at this time aligns with natural light patterns, boosting alertness and energy.

- Exposure to **morning sunlight** helps regulate sleep-wake cycles, improving sleep quality at night and keeping the body's internal clock in balance.

2. Enhanced Physical Health

- **Improved metabolism**: Waking up early helps regulate the body's metabolism, supporting digestion and overall physical health.
- **Better appetite regulation**: Early risers tend to have healthier eating habits, starting the day with a nutritious breakfast and maintaining consistent meal times throughout the day.
- **Time for exercise**: Early mornings provide a calm environment for gentle exercises like **yoga, walking, or stretching**, which are particularly beneficial for seniors to maintain flexibility, strength, and cardiovascular health.

3. Mental Health and Emotional Well-being

- **Reduced stress**: Early risers often experience less rush and stress, as they have ample time to plan their day, reflect, or engage in relaxing activities like meditation or prayer.
- **Improved mood**: Natural light exposure in the early morning increases levels of **serotonin**, a mood-boosting neurotransmitter, reducing the risk of depression and anxiety.
- **Mental clarity**: Early waking promotes mental sharpness and allows for peaceful time to read, write, or engage in hobbies, keeping the mind active and engaged.

4. Boosted Productivity and Routine

- **Structured day**: Waking up early gives retirees and elderly individuals a head start on daily tasks, allowing for more **time management** and purposeful activities. This sense of structure brings a feeling of accomplishment and satisfaction.
- **Time for hobbies and interests**: The quiet morning hours provide an excellent opportunity to focus on hobbies, reading, writing, or

learning new things—enhancing lifelong learning and mental stimulation.

5. Social Benefits

- **More time for family or community**: Waking up early gives retirees time to connect with family, engage in morning routines with grandchildren, or participate in community activities.
- **Engagement with nature**: Early morning walks allow time to enjoy the peace of nature, fresh air, and a sense of calm, which contributes to mental and emotional well-being.

6. Improved Sleep Patterns

- Waking up between 5:00 AM and 6:30 AM encourages **consistent sleep schedules**, ensuring that the individual gets tired earlier in the evening and maintains a regular bedtime. This balance promotes **better sleep quality**.

7. Spiritual and Reflective Time

- For many, early mornings offer a precious window for reflection, meditation, or prayer—activities that nurture inner peace and instill a profound sense of purpose, especially during the retirement phase when life slows down to allow deeper self-discovery.
- In **Islam**, this rhythm of spiritual connection is beautifully woven into the day through five prayers: the serene dawn prayer (Fajr), the tranquil noon prayer (Dhuhr), the reflective afternoon prayer (Asr), the peaceful prayer after sunset (Maghrib), and the serene night prayer (Isha). Each moment invites mindfulness, grounding, and a renewed sense of devotion, providing a perfect framework for spiritual fulfillment in any stage of life.

Note: There is nothing in Shari`ah to suggest that a Muslim has to sleep at a certain time and wake up at a certain time, and Islam does not tell the Muslim to sleep a certain number of hours. That depends on people's ages and natures, and how much rest their bodies need, and it also depends on the nature of their work. One who works at night will sleep more during the day and one who works during the day will sleep more at night. Sleep during the winter is different from sleep during the summer and so on.

The natural average length of sleep is between 5 and 8 hours every day. If someone sleeps less than that because he is able to put up with that, or someone sleeps more than that because his body needs that, there is nothing wrong with that. What matters is that Islam obliges the Muslim to observe the times of prayer, at which time he should be awake so that he can perform the act of worship in the proper manner and with energy. If his body needs rest and sleep, he should not resist that.

- **Ancient Hindu scriptures** recommend us to sleep between 9 PM to 3:30 AM. The sleep required for our body (for the cell regeneration) in a number of hours is proportional to the physical tiredness of that day.
- **In the Buddhist scriptures**, the Buddha once explained the influence and retribution of "excessive and insufficient" sleep, and taught all living beings to practice diligently and stop the three poisons of greed, hatred, and ignorance. Naturally, when we get proper sleep, our practice will be effective as well.
- **Christianity**: For one, the Bible doesn't say how much sleep we should get. Seven to nine hours may be a medical recommendation, but there's no scriptural prescription for the number of hours we should spend in bed. Still, rest should characterize God's people. Sleep as Spiritual Discipline. In the Psalms, David shows that peaceful sleep is an act of trust and a sign of humility.
- **Judaism:** According to Jewish sources, sleep is important for health and worship, and there are several Jewish perspectives on sleep. Religious Jews often say they should sleep around eight hours per night, but wake up early for prayer.
- **Sikhism and Human Sleep: A Spiritual View:**
  Sikhism sees sleep as a natural part of human life, gifted by Waheguru (God) to restore the body and mind. Like eating, breathing, and walking, sleep is necessary for health and

balance. It's a time when the body rests and the soul, in a way, reconnects with divine peace.

Conclusion:

For elderly individuals and retirees, waking up between 5:00 AM and 6:30 AM encourages **physical vitality, mental sharpness, emotional balance**, and a more structured and productive day. This routine aligns with their natural body clock, promotes healthy habits, and offers the opportunity for meaningful activities and peaceful reflection, contributing to overall well-being in the later years of life.

Modern Concept of Sleep

The modern concept of sleep emphasizes its critical role in rejuvenating the body's vital organs and maintaining overall health. From a medical standpoint, the timing and duration of sleep are tailored to align with the body's natural circadian rhythm, which regulates biological processes over a 24-hour cycle. Here's how sleep contributes to the restoration of key body systems:

1. Brain and Nervous System

- Cognitive Function and Memory: Sleep, particularly during the deep (slow-wave) and REM (rapid eye movement) phases, allows the brain to consolidate memories, process information, and enhance learning.
- Neurotoxin Clearance: During sleep, the brain's glymphatic system becomes active, removing waste products such as beta-amyloid, which is linked to neurodegenerative diseases.

2. Cardiovascular System

- Heart and Blood Vessels: Adequate sleep helps lower blood pressure and regulate heart rate, reducing the risk of heart disease and stroke.
- Repair and Recovery: The body's cardiovascular system undergoes repair, with reduced stress hormone levels promoting arterial health.

3. Endocrine System

- Hormone Regulation: Sleep plays a vital role in balancing hormones such as cortisol (stress hormone), insulin (blood sugar regulation), and growth hormone (cell repair and growth).

4. Immune System

- Immune Response Enhancement: Sleep strengthens the immune system by facilitating the production of cytokines, proteins essential for combating infections and inflammation.

5. Digestive and Metabolic Systems

- Metabolism Regulation: Proper sleep ensures the efficient functioning of metabolism, preventing disruptions that can lead to obesity, diabetes, and other metabolic disorders.
- Gut Health: The digestive system benefits from the body's reduced activity, allowing for nutrient absorption and detoxification.

6. Musculoskeletal System

- Tissue Repair and Growth: During deep sleep, the body repairs damaged tissues, builds muscle, and strengthens bones.

Optimal Sleep Timing and Duration

- Timing: Aligning sleep with natural circadian rhythms—typically sleeping between 10 p.m. and 6 a.m.—is crucial for maximizing the body's regenerative processes.
- Duration: Adults generally require 7-9 hours of uninterrupted sleep per night, while children and teenagers may need more.

Incorporating consistent sleep patterns and ensuring a restful environment can significantly enhance the body's ability to rejuvenate and maintain optimal function.

Note: In the ideal cycle of sleep aligned with the body's circadian rhythm, the recommended time to go to bed and wake up depends on the need for 7–9 hours of quality sleep for most adults. Here's a breakdown:

Recommended Sleep and Wake Times:

- Go to Bed: Between 9:30 PM and 10:30 PM
    - This timing allows the body to naturally wind down and enter the first stages of sleep before midnight, maximizing the duration of restorative deep sleep.
- Wake Up: Between 5:30 AM and 6:30 AM
    - This aligns with the body's natural wakefulness phase as sunlight increases and the body transitions out of sleep.

Why Is This Timing Optimal?

1. Pre-Midnight Deep Sleep: Sleep before midnight is particularly restorative, with higher amounts of slow-wave (deep) sleep that rejuvenates the body and brain.
2. Alignment with Melatonin Levels: The hormone melatonin, which promotes sleep, peaks during the early night hours (around 9–10 PM). Delaying bedtime can disrupt this natural signal.
3. Early Morning Energy: Waking up early aligns with the body's cortisol surge (highest in the morning), which supports alertness and energy for the day ahead.

Factors Influencing Bedtime and Wake Time

- Individual Variations: Some people are naturally "night owls" or "early birds" due to genetic factors, so slight adjustments may be necessary.
- Age: Teenagers and young adults may have a delayed sleep phase, while older adults tend to sleep earlier.
- Lifestyle: Shift work, stress, and electronic device usage can affect bedtime and wake times.

Note: Sticking to a consistent sleep schedule, even on weekends, helps maintain the body's natural rhythm, promoting better overall health and energy levels.

Conclusion:

For elderly individuals and retirees, waking up between 5:00 AM and 6:30 AM encourages **physical vitality, mental sharpness, emotional balance**, and a more structured and productive day. This routine aligns with their natural body clock, promotes healthy habits, and offers the opportunity for meaningful activities and peaceful reflection, contributing to overall well-being in the later years of life.

11.2 Day Time Napping in Elderly & Retirees

Daytime napping for elderly individuals and retirees can be both beneficial and detrimental, depending on various factors such as duration, timing, and overall nighttime sleep quality. Here's a breakdown of the potential benefits and drawbacks:

Benefits of Napping for the Elderly and Retirees

1. **Improved Cognitive Function**
   - A short nap (less than 30 minutes) can help boost alertness, memory, and focus. It gives the brain a chance to rest and recharge, particularly for those who may not have had sufficient sleep the night before.
2. **Enhanced Mood and Emotional Health**
   - Napping can improve mood, reduce irritability, and decrease feelings of stress. It helps the brain relax, offering a sense of refreshment, which is important for maintaining emotional balance.
3. **Increased Energy Levels**
   - A well-timed nap can reduce daytime fatigue and provide a burst of energy, making it easier to stay active and engaged in activities like walking, hobbies, or spending time with family.
4. **Cardiovascular Health**
   - Studies have shown that a moderate nap can lower blood pressure and improve heart health, especially in people who experience midday fatigue.
5. **Better Physical Health**
   - A short nap can promote physical recovery, especially for retirees who may experience tiredness or muscle fatigue. It helps the body recuperate and rejuvenate.
   - A study found that short, less frequent naps may be the most helpful and can lead to an 84% decrease in the chances of developing Alzheimer,s.

Conclusion:

For elderly individuals and retirees, only a **short, well-timed nap** can be beneficial, improving cognitive function, mood, and energy levels. However, **napping too long or too late** in the day can disrupt nighttime sleep and reduce overall sleep quality. Keeping naps under 30 minutes and avoiding them in the late afternoon is key to reaping the benefits while minimizing any negative effects.

11.3 Don't worry - Falling sick once or twice in a year is good for health

Yes, experiencing mild sickness once or twice a year can actually be beneficial for your health. It may sound surprising, but this natural process plays a vital role in strengthening your immune system. Each time your body encounters a new virus or pathogen, it goes into action—mobilizing its internal defense forces, known as the immune system. Like a well-trained army, it responds by producing antibodies, learning how to recognize and neutralize the invader more effectively in the future.

Think of it as a *drill or rehearsal* for your body's security forces—similar to how a nation's army conducts exercises or how a city's firefighters carry out mock drills. These exercises ensure preparedness, keep systems sharp, and update protocols based on new threats. In the same way, mild illnesses help your immune system stay alert and adaptive, better equipping your body to face more serious health challenges that may come later.

So, occasional sickness isn't just a nuisance—it's nature's way of keeping your internal defense team fit, aware, and ready.

The mild illnesses that can occur once or twice a year and might help strengthen the immune system include:

1. **Common Cold** – A viral infection that typically affects the upper respiratory tract, causing symptoms like a runny nose, sore throat, and mild fever.
2. **Seasonal Flu** – Another viral infection with symptoms such as body aches, fever, fatigue, and cough, which usually resolves with rest and proper care.
3. **Seasonal Allergies** – Symptoms like sneezing, runny nose, or itchy eyes triggered by pollen or other environmental factors.
4. **Minor Respiratory Infections** – Infections like mild bronchitis or sinusitis, which often clear up on their own with basic home care.

11.4 Good, attractive & comfortable dresses

Good, attractive, and comfortable dresses for elderly and retirees should focus on providing comfort, ease of movement, and style appropriate for their lifestyle. Stylish and well-chosen attire for the elderly not only enhances their appearance but also brings a refreshing sense of confidence, making them feel vibrant, youthful, and full of life. Here are some suggestions:

1. Loose-Fitting Clothing

- **Cotton and Linen Fabrics**: Soft, breathable, and natural fabrics like cotton and linen help regulate body temperature and are gentle on the skin.
- **Elastic Waistbands**: Pants or skirts with elastic waistbands provide comfort without restricting movement.

2. Easy to Wear and Remove

- **Front-Button Shirts**: Shirts with buttons or zippers in the front are easier to put on and take off, especially for those with mobility or dexterity issues.

3. Soft and Stretchable Fabrics

- **Jersey Knit or Stretch Fabric**: Fabrics with a bit of stretch allow for more freedom of movement while still looking polished.
- **Sweaters and Cardigans**: Light, cozy sweaters made from wool blends or cashmere are perfect for layering, adding comfort without bulk.

4. Adaptive Clothing

- **Adaptive Footwear**: Shoes with cushioned soles, slip-resistant grips, and extra room for orthopedic inserts are ideal.

- **Clothing with Adjustable Features**: Adaptive clothing that has adjustable straps or Velcro offers customization for fit and is great for people with limited mobility.

5. Stylish and Practical

- **Patterns and Colors**: Vibrant, yet subtle patterns or solid colors like pastels or earth tones can make clothing more attractive without being too bold.
- **Layering Options**: Light jackets, shawls, or scarves not only add style but also provide warmth and flexibility for different temperatures.

6. Seasonal Choices

- **Summer**: Lightweight fabrics like cotton and breathable sandals or slip-on shoes.
- **Winter**: Layered clothing such as cardigans, pullovers, and fleece-lined pants with comfortable boots.

These outfits can provide a balance of comfort and style, making retirees feel relaxed and confident in their daily activities.

11.5 A Humble and Heartfelt Advice to All Elderly & Retirees

Embrace the Golden Years with Wisdom and Serenity

You are the custodians of your body, mind, and soul. God has entrusted you with this precious life, and it is your responsibility to protect, nourish, and cherish it. You've worked tirelessly from childhood through adulthood, overcoming challenges and building a career, a family, and a comfortable life. Now, you stand at the threshold of retirement—a time for you to savor the fruits of your labor. This period is not just about rest; it's about living with grace, wisdom, and contentment.

The Two Pillars of a Fulfilling Retirement

1. Good Health & Peace of Mind: Your Greatest Assets

Health is the foundation of happiness. Without good health, even the most luxurious lifestyle can feel hollow. Maintaining your physical and mental well-being will allow you to truly enjoy the freedom and relaxation retirement offers.

- **Why Health Matters:**
  A healthy body and mind keep you active, engaged, and joyful. Without it, even the best financial security can't bring true comfort. Poor health can consume your energy, time, and money, leaving you drained.
- **Physical Health:**
  Take care of your body by staying physically active, even if it's just through light exercise like walking or stretching. Regular movement keeps your joints supple and your heart strong.
- **Mental Health:**
  Stay mentally sharp by engaging in activities that stimulate your mind—read books, solve puzzles, or take up new hobbies. Remember, a peaceful and positive mindset will make every day brighter.

- **Social Engagement:**
  Keep in touch with friends, family, and the community. Social interaction is a powerful tool for maintaining emotional health. Don't isolate yourself—spend time with loved ones, make new friends, and maintain a strong bond with your spouse.
- **Train the Next Generation:**
  Impart your wisdom to your children and grandchildren. Teach them to respect and care for you, not only in times of need but also as a natural part of family love and duty. Guide them with your experience, so they cherish and support you in your later years.
- **Rest Well:**
  Prioritize quality sleep. Good rest rejuvenates both the body and mind. Develop a calming bedtime routine, and make your sleep environment comfortable and peaceful.

2. Financial Stability: Plan Wisely for a Comfortable Future

Financial security is the backbone of a peaceful retirement. You've worked hard to save and invest—now, it's time to ensure that your money supports the life you want to live.

- **Sufficient Reserves:**
  Before retiring, ensure you have enough savings set aside for emergencies. Life is unpredictable, and having a financial cushion will protect you from unexpected expenses.
- **Invest for Returns:**
  Make smart investments that generate consistent returns during retirement. Whether it's property, stocks, or other savings plans, make sure your money works for you, providing a steady income in your golden years.
- **Mindful Spending:**
  While it's tempting to indulge in extravagance, remember to spend wisely. Differentiate between needs and wants—focus on what truly enhances your life. Avoid emotional spending, which can drain your resources unnecessarily.

- **Spend on What Matters:**
  Don't hesitate to spend money where it truly counts—your health, comfort, and happiness. Experiences, memories, and well-being are worth every penny.

Steer Clear of Politics: Protect Your Peace of Mind

The world is in a state of political and social turmoil. Countries are struggling, and leaders are often embroiled in conflicts and power struggles. While it's important to stay informed, this is not the time to immerse yourself in political chaos.

Why Avoid Politics?

- The standards of politics and the integrity of politicians have significantly declined, with moral values taking a backseat. Many politicians now treat their roles as mere tools to cling to power, secure positions, and amass wealth, often sidelining the genuine needs of the people they are meant to serve. Meanwhile, the innocent masses are left bearing the brunt—enduring unnecessary stress, divisions, and tensions with little to gain in return. It is crucial, therefore, to remain vigilant and avoid getting caught up in the chaos of such self-serving agendas. Protect your peace, and focus on what truly matters in life.
  Engaging too much in political debates and news can rob you of your peace of mind and disrupt your sleep. The stress and anxiety caused by the world's problems are unnecessary burdens in your retirement. The global landscape is beyond our control, and worrying about it will only drain your mental energy.
- Choose Peace Over Conflict:
  Focus on peace, unity, and brotherhood. Engage in conversations about kindness and compassion, not division or hatred. Promote harmony in your own life, and lead by example, showing the younger generation the value of peace.

- **Respect Human Rights:**
  Remember that all human beings are born free and equal, as emphasized by the Universal Declaration of Human Rights and most of the religious teachings. Regardless of race, gender, or religion, everyone deserves respect and dignity. Let this principle guide your interactions and thoughts.

Limit Time on Social Media: Protect Your Sanity

Social media today is often flooded with misinformation, baseless propaganda, and negativity. Don't let it consume you. Too much exposure can lead to stress, confusion, and even anger. Instead of getting lost in the virtual world, use technology sparingly and focus on real-life experiences.

- **Engage in Real Conversations:**
  Spend more time with loved ones, enjoying meaningful face-to-face conversations. Social media may connect us globally, but true happiness comes from the people closest to us.
- **Follow a Balanced Path:**
  Stay connected online in a balanced, healthy way. Focus on positivity, avoid harmful content, and spend your time on uplifting activities.

Embrace Peace and Brotherhood

Every religion on Earth—whether it's Islam, Hinduism, Buddhism, Sikhism, Christianity, or Judaism—carries the same timeless message at its heart: peace, compassion, and the well-being of all. These are not just spiritual ideals; they are guiding values meant to shape how we live and treat one another.

Echoing this universal truth, the *United Nations' Universal Declaration of Human Rights* reminds us that every human being, regardless of race, gender, faith, or background, is born equal—with dignity, respect, and the right to live a life of freedom and fairness.

As you step into your golden years of retirement, let these principles become your inner compass. Speak for peace when others choose conflict. Stand for justice when faced with inequality. And let your words and actions reflect the deep respect you hold for every soul.

Because at the end of the day, it's not wealth or status that defines us—but the love we spread, the peace we promote, and the respect we show to others.

Final Thoughts: Make Your Retirement Count

Retirement is not just the end of your working life; it's the beginning of a new, fulfilling chapter. Take care of your health, secure your finances, stay away from unnecessary stress, and focus on what truly matters—family, friends, and peace of mind. This is your time to live freely, enjoy every moment, and leave a lasting legacy of wisdom, love, and tranquility.

Embrace your golden years with zest, transforming them into a radiant chapter of your life. As George Burns wisely said, "You can't help getting older, but you don't have to get old."

By maintaining a youthful spirit and engaging in activities that bring joy and fulfillment, you can ensure these years are truly golden.

11.6 Humor, happiness and Laughter

Humor and happiness play pivotal roles in enhancing the quality of life for the elderly and retirees, offering a multitude of physical and emotional health benefits. Engaging in regular laughter and maintaining a joyful disposition can significantly impact overall well-being, particularly concerning chronic conditions such as high blood pressure, diabetes, and sleep disorders.

Physical Health Benefits:

- **Cardiovascular Health:** Laughter has been shown to lower blood pressure and heart rate, contributing to improved cardiovascular function. By reducing the production of stress hormones like cortisol and epinephrine, laughter helps relax blood vessels, thereby decreasing the risk of heart-related issues.
- **Diabetes Management:** Incorporating humor therapy can be beneficial for individuals with type 2 diabetes. Studies indicate that laughter therapy may delay cardiovascular complications associated with diabetes, highlighting its potential as a complementary approach to traditional treatments.
- **Immune System Enhancement:** Engaging in laughter boosts the immune system by increasing natural killer (NK) cell activity, which plays a crucial role in combating infections and diseases. This enhancement is particularly valuable for seniors, as a robust immune system aids in maintaining health and preventing illnesses.

Emotional and Mental Health Benefits:

- **Stress and Anxiety Reduction:** Laughter serves as a natural stress reliever, reducing anxiety and promoting relaxation. By lowering stress hormone levels, it helps mitigate the physical effects of stress, contributing to better mental health and emotional balance.
- **Combating Depression:** Regular engagement in humorous activities can alleviate feelings of depression and loneliness

among retirees. Laughter therapy has been found to decrease pain and perceptions of loneliness, while significantly increasing happiness and life satisfaction.

- **Improved Sleep Quality:** Humor and laughter have positive effects on sleep patterns, helping to alleviate sleep disorders common among the elderly. By promoting relaxation and reducing stress, laughter contributes to better sleep quality and overall restfulness.

Social Benefits:

- **Enhanced Social Connections:** Sharing laughter strengthens social bonds and fosters a sense of community. For retirees, engaging in group activities centered around humor can lead to increased social interaction, reducing feelings of isolation and enhancing overall life satisfaction.

Incorporating humor into daily routines—through activities like watching comedies, participating in laughter yoga, or sharing jokes with friends—can serve as a powerful, non-pharmacological strategy to improve health outcomes for the elderly. By embracing the joy of laughter, retirees can experience a more vibrant, healthy, and fulfilling life.

12.0 "Things to Avoid"

The following essential "Don'ts" (things to avoid) are not just helpful guidelines—they are lifelines for elderly individuals and retirees striving to live with dignity, vitality, and peace of mind. As we enter the golden years of life, our bodies become more delicate, and our minds more reflective. This stage is not an end, but a precious chapter that deserves to be lived with grace and intention.

By consciously avoiding certain harmful habits, attitudes, and choices, we protect ourselves from unnecessary stress, physical strain, and emotional turbulence. **These 'Don'ts' serve as gentle reminders—helping us let go of what no longer serves us and making space for what truly matters: good health, meaningful relationships, spiritual contentment, and inner peace.**

Embracing these principles is not about restriction—it's about liberation. It's about living smarter, not harder. When we eliminate the negatives, we naturally make room for more joy, more connection, and a deeper sense of well-being in our later years.

Disclaimer: The information provided here regarding health issues and diseases affecting elderly individuals is intended for informational purposes only. The author does not assume responsibility for any specific health conditions or treatments. For personalized advice, diagnosis, and treatment, always consult a qualified doctor, physician, or healthcare professional. It's essential to seek guidance from healthcare centers tailored to your individual needs and medical concerns.

12.1 "Avoid Excessive Sleeping"

How Much Sleep Is Ideal for the Elderly & Retirees & Negative effects of oversleeping?

The **National Sleep Foundation** recommends that elderly individuals, typically aged 65 and older, should aim for **7 to 8 hours** of sleep per night. This amount supports both **physical and mental well-being** without causing the negative effects associated with too little or too much sleep.

However, individual needs can vary slightly:

- Some elderly individuals may feel well-rested with **6 to 7 hours** of sleep.
- Others may benefit from slightly longer sleep durations of **up to 9 hours** depending on health conditions, diets or lifestyle.

Harmful Effects of Oversleeping for the Elderly

While it's important for retirees and the elderly to get enough rest, **oversleeping** (more than 9 hours regularly) can have negative effects on their physical and mental health. Here's how, it affects:

1. Increased Risk of Cognitive Decline

- Studies show that **excessive sleep** is linked to a greater risk of **cognitive impairment** and **memory problems** in older adults. It may affect brain function and lead to issues such as slower thinking and decreased attention span.
- Oversleeping can also increase the risk of **dementia** or **Alzheimer's disease**, especially when combined with poor nighttime sleep quality.

2. Higher Risk of Depression

- **Oversleeping** has been associated with a higher risk of **depression** and **anxiety**. Sleep disturbances and excessive sleep can worsen mood disorders, leading to a cycle of low energy, decreased motivation, and feelings of isolation.

3. Increased Risk of Cardiovascular Issues

- Too much sleep is linked to a higher risk of **heart disease** and **stroke**. Studies have shown that individuals who sleep more than 9 hours per night have a higher likelihood of developing **hypertension (high blood pressure)**, which strains the cardiovascular system.
- **Oversleeping** can also contribute to metabolic issues, like **type 2 diabetes**, which is more common in older adults.

4. Decreased Physical Activity

- When elderly individuals oversleep, they often become **less active** during the day. Reduced physical activity can lead to **muscle loss**, reduced strength, and an increased risk of **falls** or **injuries**.
- **Sedentary lifestyle** can contribute to weight gain, and it might worsen conditions like **arthritis** or **osteoporosis**.

5. Weakened Immune System

- Oversleeping can actually weaken the immune system, making retirees and elderly individuals more prone to infections, **inflammation**, and slower recovery times from illness or injury.

6. Worsened Sleep Quality

- Sleeping too much during the day can disrupt the body's **circadian rhythm**, leading to **fragmented nighttime sleep**. This can result in **poor sleep quality** overall, causing **fatigue** and **daytime drowsiness** despite longer sleep durations.
- Excessive daytime napping can make it harder to fall asleep at night, creating an unhealthy sleep-wake cycle.

Why Oversleeping Happens in the Elderly

Oversleeping is often linked to underlying health issues, including:

- **Sleep disorders**: Such as sleep apnea or restless leg syndrome.
- **Chronic illnesses**: Such as heart disease, diabetes, or arthritis, which cause fatigue.
- **Depression or anxiety**: Mental health issues can affect sleep patterns, leading to oversleeping.
- **Medications**: Certain medications may cause drowsiness or fatigue, leading to longer sleep durations.

Conclusion

For the elderly and retirees, **7 to 8 hours of sleep** per night is ideal for maintaining physical health, mental sharpness, and overall well-being. **Oversleeping**, particularly more than 9 hours regularly, can lead to cognitive decline, depression, cardiovascular issues, and other health risks. It's important for seniors to maintain a balanced sleep schedule and address any underlying health issues that may cause excessive sleep.

Note:-

By addressing the following factors, oversleeping can be managed to improve overall health and well-being.

1. **Medical Check-up**: See a doctor to rule out conditions like sleep apnea, depression, or medication side effects that may cause oversleeping.
2. **Consistent Sleep Schedule**: Stick to a routine by going to bed and waking up at the same time every day. Limit naps to 20-30 minutes.
3. **Improve Sleep Environment**: Ensure a quiet, cool, and dark bedroom to promote restful sleep and reduce the need for excessive sleep.
4. **Increase Activity**: Engage in light exercise like walking or stretching to boost energy and reduce daytime drowsiness.

5. **Balanced Diet**: Eat healthy foods and stay hydrated, but avoid heavy meals and caffeine late in the day.
6. **Mental and Social Engagement**: Stay mentally active and socially connected through hobbies, socializing, or volunteering to prevent boredom and excessive sleep.
7. **Limit Sedatives**: Avoid alcohol and sedative medications that can disrupt sleep and lead to oversleeping.

12.2 "Limit Prolonged Daytime Napping"

Potential Drawbacks of Napping for the Elderly

1. **Disruption of Nighttime Sleep**
   - **Long or late naps** can interfere with **nighttime sleep** by making it harder to fall asleep at night or causing frequent awakenings during the night. This can lead to poor sleep quality overall, which is especially problematic for older adults who may already experience fragmented sleep.
2. **Increased Sleep Inertia**
   - Naps longer than 30-60 minutes can lead to **sleep inertia**, which is the groggy, disoriented feeling you get after waking up from deep sleep. This can make it harder to feel refreshed after waking and may reduce productivity for the rest of the day.
3. **Potential Sign of Underlying Health Issues**
   - Excessive daytime napping might be a symptom of **sleep disorders** like sleep apnea or **underlying health conditions** (e.g., depression, cardiovascular issues). Frequent naps could indicate that the person isn't getting quality sleep at night.

Ideal Nap Duration and Timing for the Elderly

- **Duration**: A **short nap** of **20 to 30 minutes** is optimal for most elderly individuals. This duration is enough to improve alertness and energy without entering deep sleep, which could lead to grogginess.
- **Timing**: It's best to nap **early in the afternoon**, around **1:00 PM to 3:00 PM**, when the body naturally experiences a dip in energy. Napping too late in the day can interfere with falling asleep at night.

Conclusion:

For elderly individuals and retirees, a **short, well-timed nap** can be beneficial, improving cognitive function, mood, and energy levels. However, **napping too long or too late** in the day can disrupt nighttime sleep and reduce overall sleep quality. Keeping naps under 30 minutes and avoiding them in the late afternoon is key to reaping the benefits while minimizing any negative effects.

12.3 Say No to Smoking

ALARMING FACTS

1. Smoking is the number one preventable cause of death in the U.S., killing over 480,000 people per year.
2. Secondhand smoke causes more than 41,000 deaths in the U.S. each year.
3. According to the World Health Organization (WHO), tobacco use kills more than 8 million people every year

4. Tobacco is the world's leading preventable cause of death and illness. It's a major risk factor for many health conditions, including cardiovascular and respiratory diseases, and over 20 types of cancer.

History of Smoking

The practice of smoking dates back thousands of years, with evidence suggesting that people in the Americas used tobacco for ceremonial and medicinal purposes as early as 5000 BC. The habit spread globally after European explorers, like Christopher Columbus, encountered tobacco during their travels to the New World in the late 15th century.

By the 16th and 17th centuries, smoking had become widespread, with pipes and cigars being the most common methods. The invention of the cigarette-making machine in the late 19th century significantly boosted cigarette production, making smoking more accessible and affordable.

In the mid-20th century, the health risks of smoking began to emerge through scientific studies, linking it to lung cancer, heart disease, and other illnesses. This led to public health campaigns, regulations, and smoking bans in many countries. Despite these efforts, smoking remains a significant global health issue today.

Smoking releases a wide range of harmful chemicals-many of which are toxic or carcinogenic (cancer-causing). Here are some of the most dangerous chemicals produced during smoking:

1. Nicotine

- **Effect**: An addictive substance that stimulates the nervous system and raises heart rate and blood pressure.
- **Harm**: Contributes to addiction and can lead to cardiovascular problems.

2. Tar

- **Effect**: A sticky substance that coats the lungs.
- **Harm**: Causes lung damage, contributes to lung cancer, emphysema, and bronchitis.

3. Carbon Monoxide (CO)

- **Effect**: A colorless, odorless gas that reduces oxygen in the blood.
- **Harm**: Interferes with the heart's ability to pump oxygen, leading to heart disease and other cardiovascular problems.

4. Formaldehyde

- **Effect**: A chemical used to preserve dead bodies.
- **Harm**: Known carcinogen that can cause nose and throat cancer and lung irritation.

5. Benzene

- **Effect**: A solvent used in the manufacture of chemicals.
- **Harm**: Linked to leukemia and other blood disorders.

6. Hydrogen Cyanide

- **Effect**: A poisonous gas used in chemical weapons.
- **Harm**: Affects the body's ability to use oxygen, damaging the lungs and heart.

7. Ammonia

- **Effect**: A chemical used in household cleaners.
- **Harm**: Added to cigarettes to enhance nicotine absorption, leading to increased addiction.

8. Arsenic

- **Effect**: A toxic chemical used in pesticides.
- **Harm**: Linked to lung, skin, and bladder cancer.

9. Lead and Cadmium

- **Effect**: Heavy metals found in batteries.
- **Harm**: Can damage the kidneys, lungs, and bones, and contribute to cancer risk.

10. Polycyclic Aromatic Hydrocarbons (PAHs)

- **Effect**: Found in tobacco smoke as a result of incomplete combustion.
- **Harm**: Known carcinogens that damage DNA and lead to cancer.

11. Acetone

- **Effect**: Used in nail polish remover.
- **Harm**: Can irritate the eyes and lungs, contributing to respiratory diseases.

12. Acrolein

- **Effect**: A chemical used in herbicides.
- **Harm**: Irritates the lungs and reduces the body's ability to clear out mucus, leading to respiratory issues.

13. Nitrosamines

- **Effect**: Potent carcinogens formed during the curing of tobacco.
- **Harm**: One of the primary cancer-causing agents in tobacco.

14. Phenol

- **Effect**: Used in plastics and disinfectants.
- **Harm**: Can cause irritation to the respiratory tract and damage the skin and lungs.

15. Chromium

- **Effect**: A metal used in steel (Stainless Steel & Hardened Steel) production.
- **Harm**: Linked to lung cancer and other respiratory diseases.

Caution:

Smoking in elderly individuals and retirees can have severe negative side effects on both physical and mental health. As people age, the body becomes more vulnerable to the harmful effects of tobacco. Here are the key risks:

1. Respiratory Issues

- Smoking damages the lungs, leading to conditions like chronic bronchitis, emphysema, and chronic obstructive pulmonary disease (COPD).
- It increases the risk of lung infections such as pneumonia, which can be more severe in older adults.

2. Increased Risk of Heart Disease and Stroke

- Smoking accelerates atherosclerosis (hardening of the arteries), increasing the risk of heart attacks, stroke, and other cardiovascular diseases.
- It raises blood pressure and heart rate, putting extra strain on the heart.

3. Weakened Immune System

- Smoking weakens the immune system, making retirees more susceptible to infections and slowing down healing from injuries or surgeries.

4. Higher Cancer Risk

- Smoking is a leading cause of many types of cancer, including lung, throat, mouth, esophagus, and bladder cancer, which remains a significant concern even in older age.

5. Cognitive Decline

- Smoking increases the risk of dementia, Alzheimer's disease, and other cognitive impairments due to reduced blood flow to the brain.

6. Bone Health Issues

- Smoking leads to bone density loss, increasing the risk of osteoporosis and fractures, which are more dangerous in the elderly due to slower recovery.

7. Vision Problems

- Smoking raises the risk of cataracts and macular degeneration, both of which can lead to vision loss in older adults.

8. Worsened Circulation

- It impairs circulation, leading to poor wound healing, cold hands and feet, and an increased risk of peripheral artery disease (PAD).

9. Reduced Quality of Life

- Smoking can decrease overall mobility and physical fitness, making it harder for retirees to stay active and independent.
- It also affects social life and emotional well-being by contributing to isolation and increased stress or anxiety.

10. Passive Smoking

Caution: also known as **secondhand smoke** or **involuntary smoking**, occurs when non-smokers inhale smoke from burning tobacco products, such as cigarettes, cigars, or pipes, or from the exhaled smoke of smokers. This smoke contains harmful chemicals and toxins similar to those inhaled by smokers themselves.

There are two types of smoke involved in passive smoking:

1. **Mainstream smoke**: The smoke exhaled by the smoker.
2. **Sidestream smoke**: The smoke emitted directly from the burning end of a cigarette or other tobacco products.

Passive smoking can pose serious health risks to non-smokers, including respiratory issues, heart disease, and an increased risk of lung cancer.

Conclusion

Smoking introduces more than 7,000 chemicals into the body, hundreds of which are toxic, and at least 70 are known to cause cancer. These chemicals have devastating effects on the body, leading to respiratory problems, cardiovascular diseases, and various cancers.

For the elderly and retirees, smoking drastically increases the risk of serious health conditions, worsens quality of life, and speeds up physical decline. Quitting smoking at any age significantly improves health outcomes and overall well-being.

Here are some engaging and impactful sayings about smoking:

1. A cigarette is a thief that steals your breath and your future
2. Every cigarette shortens your life but lengthens your regrets
3. Smoking is the one thing you pay for to harm yourself and others
4. A smoker doesn’t light a cigarette; they ignite their health
5. The real cost of smoking is measured in years, not dollars
6. Quitting smoking doesn’t add days to your life—it adds life to your days
7. A cigarette today is a hospital bed tomorrow
8. Smoke signals aren’t calls for help; they’re cries for health
9. Cigarettes: The fire that burns your wallet, health, and dreams
10. Throw away your cigarettes before they throw away your life
11. Smoking is a slow poison
12. A cigarette is a burning stick that lights the way to the grave
13. Every puff is a step closer to your last breath
14. smoking doesn't just kill you—it kills everyone around you
15. Cigarettes are the perfect product: They kill the customer
16. Quit smoking, or smoking will quit you
17. A smoker’s life burns out faster than the cigarette

12.4 Say No to Alcohol

Before diving into the topic, let's take a moment to reflect on a heartfelt and wise piece of advice President Donald John Trump shared with his then-four-year-old son, Barron, back in 2010—a lesson that carries timeless value.

"I want all A's. And when you get older, no drugs, no alcohol, no cigarettes. And, you know what else? No tattoos. I don't ever want to see tattoos on you."

When did alcoholic consumption start in human history?

Alcohol consumption has deep historical roots, dating back to prehistoric times. Here's an overview of its origins:

Early Beginnings

- **10,000–7,000 BCE**: Archaeological evidence suggests that early humans in the Neolithic period consumed fermented beverages. Traces of fermented drinks made from rice, honey, and fruit have been found in pottery from Jiahu, China, around this time.
- **7,000–5,000 BCE**: Evidence of wine production has been discovered in the Zagros Mountains of Iran. Early winemaking likely involved the natural fermentation of wild grapes.
- **3,000 BCE**: The Sumerians of Mesopotamia are among the first recorded civilizations to consume beer. They even wrote hymns to Ninkasi, the goddess of beer, detailing brewing processes.

Alcohol in Ancient Civilizations

- **Egyptians (3,000 BCE)**: Beer and wine were central to Egyptian culture, used in religious ceremonies and as offerings to the gods. Beer was also a staple drink for workers building the pyramids.
- **Greeks and Romans (1,500 BCE–500 CE)**: The Greeks refined winemaking techniques, and wine became a symbol of sophistication and religious rituals. Romans adapted and expanded this culture, even establishing vineyards across their empire.

Medieval Period

- **Monasteries and Distillation (500–1500 CE)**: In medieval Europe, monks played a vital role in preserving and advancing brewing and winemaking techniques. The invention of distillation during this period led to the production of spirits like brandy.

Modern Alcohol Consumption

- **1500s–Present**: The colonization of the Americas introduced European alcoholic traditions to the New World, while indigenous practices influenced settlers. The Industrial Revolution later made alcohol production more efficient and widespread.

Throughout history, alcohol has been consumed for various purposes, including religious rituals, social bonding, medicinal uses, and recreation. However, its overuse has also been linked to societal and health issues.

ALARMING FACTS

In The US alone, more than half of all deaths attributed to alcohol are due to deteriorating health effects from drinking too much over time. This includes cancer, liver, and heart disease. Men also make up the bulk of alcohol-related deaths annually.

95,000 Americans die from alcohol-related causes annually; 68,000 of them are men.
27,000 of them are women.
47,500 deaths are attributable to the long term health consequences of drinking too much over time.
80% of alcohol-related deaths involved adults aged 35 or older.
22.1% of prescription opioid overdose deaths were related to alcohol consumption.
9,937 committed suicide annually while consuming alcohol beforehand.
1,043 Americans die annually from drowning while under the influence of alcohol.
2,015 Americans die annually from fall injuries while under the influence of alcohol.
Meanwhile, 129 people pass away annually due to firearm injuries while drinking.

- Meanwhile, 296 people pass away annually from Hypothermia while drinking.
- 126 people are killed annually from occupational and machine injuries when alcohol is involved.
- 2000–2020: The rate of alcohol-related deaths among adults 65 and older increased from 2.4 to 8.8 deaths per 100,000 people in The US.
- 2019–2020: The rate of alcohol-related deaths among adults 65 and older increased by more than 18%.(**United States**, based on data from the Centers for Disease Control and Prevention (CDC).
- 2020: More than 11,000 older adults died from alcohol-related causes in The US.

Note:- These figures underscore the pervasive and multifaceted dangers of excessive alcohol consumption across various demographics and situations in the U.S.

Alcohol-related deaths among the elderly and retirees have been on the rise, according to both global and U.S. data. **The World Health Organization (WHO) reports that globally**, alcohol consumption contributed to 2.6 million deaths in 2019. Among older adults, alcohol-related health risks include cardiovascular diseases, liver diseases, and cancers, which are particularly prevalent in this age group. Alcohol consumption is linked to over 230 diseases and health conditions

In the U.S, alcohol-induced deaths among people aged 65 and over have significantly increased, rising by 18% from 2019 to 2020. Alcohol-related death rates are higher among men in this age group, especially those aged 75 and older. Ethnic disparities also exist, with American Indian and Alaskan Native individuals having particularly high rates of alcohol-related deaths.

Against Alcohol Consumption for Elderly & Retirees Considering Major Religions - Facts

Across **Islam**, **Judaism**, **Christianity**, **Hinduism**, **Buddhism** & **Sikhism** there is a shared ethical and spiritual discouragement of alcohol consumption, particularly for elderly individuals and retirees. As people age and move into reflective stages of life, these religious philosophies emphasize purity, self-control, and spiritual growth. Alcohol, which impairs judgment, health, and mindfulness, is seen as incompatible with these values.

1. **Islam**: Complete prohibition
    - Alcohol is explicitly prohibited in the Qur'an due to its harmful effects on health and its ability to impair mental clarity and spiritual focus. For elderly and retirees, who are often engaged in prayer and spiritual reflection, avoiding alcohol is essential for maintaining a clear mind and body in preparation for the afterlife.
    - Quranic verses like Surah Al-Baqarah (2:219) and Surah Al-Ma'idah (5:90-91) highlight the harms of intoxicants, urging believers to avoid them.
2. **Judaism**: Warning
    - While wine is used in some religious ceremonies, excessive alcohol consumption is discouraged. The elderly, who are expected to lead with wisdom and self-discipline, are urged to avoid intoxication, which leads to a loss of dignity and moral integrity.
    - Verses like Proverbs 20:1 emphasize the dangers of alcohol, warning that it can mislead people and cloud their judgment.
3. **Christianity**: Warning
    - While moderate consumption of alcohol may be allowed in some Christian traditions, drunkenness is consistently condemned. For retirees and elderly, sobriety is linked to a life of wisdom, clarity, and spiritual focus.

- Ephesians 5:18 advises against drunkenness, urging believers to be filled with the Spirit, while 1 Timothy 3:2-3 emphasizes the importance of self-control, particularly for leaders and elders.

4. **Hinduism**: Warning
   - Vedic philosophy advises against alcohol, especially for elderly individuals who are in the *Vanaprastha* (retirement) and *Sannyasa* (renunciation) stages of life. Alcohol is seen as an indulgence that distracts from spiritual growth and meditation.
   - Texts like the *Manusmriti* warn that alcohol leads to degradation, which conflicts with the dharmic responsibility of maintaining purity and wisdom, especially in later life.
5. **Buddhism**: Abstention
   - Buddhism emphasizes abstention from intoxicants as part of the Fifth Precept. Alcohol clouds the mind and hinders the path to enlightenment, particularly for elderly individuals who are focused on deepening their mindfulness and preparing for the end of life.
   - The emphasis on *Right Mindfulness* and ethical living in Buddhism makes avoiding alcohol crucial for maintaining spiritual progress and avoiding negative karma.

6. Sikhism: Complete Prohibition

Sikhism strictly prohibits the consumption of alcohol. The **Guru Granth Sahib**, the Sikh holy scripture, advises against intoxicants, as they cloud the mind and prevent spiritual awakening. Sikh teachings emphasize a clear and sober mind to connect with God.

For elderly Sikhs, who are often in the later stages of life focused on spiritual growth and legacy, abstinence from alcohol is integral to maintaining purity in thought and action.

Conclusion:

In all six major religious traditions, alcohol consumption is seen as detrimental to the physical health, mental clarity, and spiritual well-being of elderly individuals and retirees. These later stages of life are considered times for reflection, ethical leadership, and spiritual preparation, and alcohol consumption is viewed as an obstacle to achieving these goals.

The negative effects of alcohol use in elderly individuals and retirees can be particularly severe due to age-related physical and mental changes. Here's a breakdown of the specific risks:

1. Increased Risk of Falls and Injuries

- Alcohol impairs balance, coordination, and reaction time, which increases the likelihood of falls and accidents—a significant risk for older adults who are more prone to fractures and injuries.

2. Weakened Immune System

- Alcohol can further weaken the immune system, making elderly individuals more vulnerable to infections and illnesses, and slower to recover from injury or surgery.

3. Exacerbation of Chronic Conditions

- Alcohol can worsen existing health problems common in retirees, such as:
    - High blood pressure
    - Diabetes
    - Heart disease
- It can interfere with the management of these conditions and increase complications.

4. Medication Interactions

- Many elderly individuals take prescription medications. Alcohol can dangerously interact with drugs like:
  - Blood thinners (increasing the risk of bleeding)
  - Painkillers (increasing the risk of overdose or liver damage)
  - Sedatives or sleep medications (leading to dangerous drowsiness or breathing difficulties).

5. Cognitive Decline

- Alcohol accelerates cognitive decline, worsening conditions like dementia, Alzheimer's disease, and other age-related memory issues. It can also impair judgment and increase confusion.

6. Sleep Disruption

- While alcohol might initially induce sleep, it disrupts sleep cycles, leading to poor-quality sleep, insomnia, and daytime fatigue—issues already common in older adults.

7. Liver Damage

- The liver's ability to process alcohol diminishes with age, increasing the risk of liver diseases like cirrhosis and alcoholic hepatitis, even with smaller amounts of alcohol.

8. Dehydration and Malnutrition

- Alcohol can lead to dehydration and malnutrition in the elderly, as it suppresses appetite and interferes with the body's ability to absorb essential nutrients.

9. Cardiovascular Issues

- Alcohol raises blood pressure and can contribute to irregular heart rhythms (arrhythmias), heart attacks, and stroke, especially in individuals with pre-existing cardiovascular issues.

10. Increased Risk of Depression and Anxiety

- Retirees and elderly individuals often face social isolation and emotional stress. Alcohol, instead of relieving stress, can worsen depression and anxiety and contribute to feelings of loneliness.

11. Worsened Bone Health

- Alcohol can impair calcium absorption, leading to osteoporosis and weaker bones, which increases the risk of fractures—a serious concern in elderly individuals.

12. Impaired Judgment and Independence

- Alcohol can impair judgment and lead to poor decision-making, putting older adults at risk of accidents, financial problems, or other dangerous situations that threaten their independence.

Conclusion

For elderly individuals and retirees, alcohol is a hidden trap that can quietly erode health, steal mental clarity, and diminish the joys of a well-lived life. It doesn't just worsen existing health issues—it amplifies them, leaving the body and mind vulnerable. The danger of accidents, with consequences far more severe in later years, looms larger for those who indulge too freely. Choosing to limit or avoid alcohol entirely isn't just a precaution; it's a powerful step toward safeguarding independence and vitality.

But beware: there comes a moment when the balance shifts. What starts as a casual indulgence can spiral into a dependency so gripping that you lose control over yourself. In that state, it's no longer you holding the bottle;

it's the bottle holding you. Protect yourself from ever reaching that point—choose well-being over the fleeting comfort of the glass.

Let me put it this way: *enough is enough.* Whatever alcohol you've consumed in the past has already left its mark on your health—whether the damage is visible or hidden. At this stage of life, there's no room for patchwork solutions. Your body, much like an aging engine, requires the cleanest, purest fuel to keep running efficiently. Contaminants like alcohol only clog the system, putting unnecessary strain on your ability to move forward.

Now is the time to prioritize nourishing your body with the right kind of "fuel"—wholesome, nutritious foods that provide the energy and strength you need to live comfortably and safely. Treat your body with the care it deserves, ensuring it carries you forward with grace and stability. Remember, it's never too late to choose a better path for your health and happiness.

12.5 "Avoid Overexertion During Physical Activity"

For elderly individuals and retirees, it is important to seek medical advice before starting any new health regimen, as their bodies may have different needs or limitations due to age or medical conditions. A doctor can provide personalized recommendations based on their overall health, medications, and risk factors.

Excess physical exercise can be detrimental to both physical and mental health. While staying active is crucial for overall well-being, over-exercising can lead to various health issues, including:

1. Physical Impact

- Muscle Strain and Injuries: Excessive exercise can result in sprains, fractures, and chronic joint pain due to overuse.
- Weakened Immune System: Over-exercising increases cortisol levels, which can suppress immune function, making you more susceptible to infections.
- Cardiovascular Stress: Overtraining can strain the heart and lead to arrhythmias or other cardiovascular issues.
- Fatigue and Exhaustion: Excessive workouts can deplete energy levels, leading to chronic fatigue.

2. Mental and Emotional Impact

- Burnout: Over-exercising can lead to mental exhaustion and loss of motivation.
- Anxiety and Depression: A compulsive need to exercise can foster unhealthy mental patterns.
- Poor Sleep Quality: Excessive training can disrupt sleep, affecting overall recovery and mental clarity.

3. Negative Long-Term Effects

- Hormonal Imbalance: Over-exercising can disrupt hormone levels, causing issues such as irregular periods in women or decreased testosterone in men.
- Bone Density Issues: Excessive physical strain can lead to stress fractures and reduced bone density.
- Heart Health Risks: Persistent overexertion may lead to heart enlargement or other chronic cardiovascular conditions.

4. Balancing Exercise for Optimal Health

- Follow Guidelines: Moderate-intensity aerobic activity for 150 minutes per week, combined with strength training twice a week, is recommended for most adults.
- Listen to Your Body: Pay attention to signs of fatigue, pain, or burnout.
- Prioritize Recovery: Incorporate rest days and focus on sleep and nutrition for proper recovery.
- Diverse Workouts: Engage in varied activities to prevent overuse of specific muscles and joints.

Conclusion

Additionally, avoid excessive physical exercise. While regular physical activity is essential for maintaining strength, balance, and cardiovascular health, overexertion can lead to injury or strain. Gentle exercises like walking,Cycling on a stationary bike, Stretching routines focusing on the back, hips, shoulders, and legs, Standing on one leg, swimming, or yoga are usually recommended for retirees to stay active without overdoing it. Always prioritize safety and moderation in physical activities.

12.6 "Avoid the use of Tobacco

Avoid tobacco to protect your health, extend your life, and improve your quality of living. It may offer short-term relief, but brings long-term harm. Choosing to stay tobacco-free is a powerful step toward a healthier, stronger you.

"Puffs Through Time: The Long and Complicated Story of Tobacco in Human Life"

The history of tobacco use stretches back thousands of years and spans multiple cultures and continents. Here's a detailed look at its origins and evolution:

Early Origins (Pre-Columbian Era)

- **6,000 BCE**: Tobacco plants are believed to have first grown in the Americas, likely in the Andean regions of South America.
- **3,000 BCE**: Evidence suggests that indigenous peoples in the Americas began cultivating tobacco. It was used in religious ceremonies, as medicine, and for social rituals.

Indigenous Use

- Indigenous groups in Central and South America smoked tobacco in pipes, cigars, or rolled leaves.
- The Mayans and Aztecs used tobacco for religious rituals, offering it to gods or burning it as incense. Shamans used it for spiritual guidance and healing.
- Native North American tribes often smoked tobacco in peace pipes during negotiations and ceremonies, symbolizing respect and unity.

Introduction to Europe (15th–16th Century)

- **1492**: Christopher Columbus encountered tobacco when he arrived in the Americas. Indigenous people shared their tobacco practices with European explorers.
- **1500s**: Spanish and Portuguese explorers brought tobacco back to Europe, where it was initially used for medicinal purposes, believed to cure ailments like headaches and respiratory issues.
- **1560**: French diplomat Jean Nicot (from whom nicotine derives its name) popularized tobacco in France, claiming it had therapeutic properties.

Global Spread (16th–18th Century)

- Tobacco quickly spread to other parts of Europe and Asia, becoming a symbol of wealth and sophistication.
- The Portuguese introduced tobacco to Africa, India, and Japan through trade routes.
- The British established large-scale tobacco plantations in North America during the 17th century, driven by high demand in Europe.

Tobacco as a Commercial Commodity

- By the 17th century, tobacco became one of the most valuable cash crops globally.
- It was a key driver of the transatlantic slave trade, as enslaved people were forced to work on tobacco plantations in the Americas.
- Cigarettes were invented in the 19th century, making tobacco more accessible and popular.

Health Awareness and Modern Challenges (20th–21st Century)

- **Mid-20th Century**: Research linked tobacco use to lung cancer, heart disease, and other health problems.

- Governments began imposing regulations, such as warning labels on tobacco products and restrictions on advertising.
- Public health campaigns have worked to reduce smoking rates worldwide, though tobacco use remains a significant global health challenge.

Cultural and Economic Impact

Tobacco has influenced economies, societies, and cultures across the globe. It has been a symbol of status, a source of income, and a cause of addiction and disease. Efforts continue to reduce its negative health impacts while acknowledging its historical and cultural significance.

Different types of Tobacco

Gul powder, raw tobacco, gutka, paan, paan bahar, khaini, and other raw powdered tobacco products commonly used in Southeast Asian countries

The use of **Gul powder (Teeth cleaning powder- contains- pyrolysed powdered tobacco product with ash of tendu leaves)**, **Raw tobacco**, **Paan (** Pan or "paan" is a traditional preparation that involves wrapping a combination of areca nut (betel nut) and other ingredients such as slaked lime, catechu, sweeteners, and sometimes tobacco, in a betel leaf. It is chewed for its stimulant effects, and the user typically spits out the residual red juice after chewing). **Pan Bahar**, **Khaini**, and other raw powdered tobaccos in Southeast Asian countries has several serious health risks not only for elderly & Retirees but in all ages of individuals.

Simultaneously, users of these types of tobacco often chew them incessantly and spit in public places, creating an unhealthy environment that is both unsanitary and visually unpleasant. This behavior not only poses health risks but also tarnishes the cleanliness and aesthetic appeal of shared spaces.

1. **Oral Cancer**: These products contain carcinogens that significantly increase the risk of mouth, throat, and esophageal cancers.
2. **Gum and Tooth Damage**: They cause gum erosion, tooth decay, and loss due to their abrasive nature and tobacco content.
3. **Nicotine Addiction**: Prolonged use leads to nicotine dependence, which increases risks for heart disease, stroke, and high blood pressure.
4. **Respiratory Issues**: Inhaling powdered forms can irritate the lungs, leading to respiratory diseases like COPD.
5. **Digestive Problems**: Swallowing tobacco can cause ulcers, stomach cancer, and acid reflux.
6. **Infections and Poor Oral Health**: Continuous use leads to oral infections, ulcers, and delayed healing.
7. **Cognitive Decline**: Tobacco use contributes to memory problems and increases the risk of dementia.

Conclusion

- Tobacco: A thief that steals your health, wealth, and life.
- Tobacco is a silent killer with a loud impact.
- Tobacco: The ash that ruins lives.

12.7 "Daily Routines and Activities for Seniors and Retirees"

"A moment of caution can save a lifetime of regret."

Accidents can occur in many everyday activities for the elderly and retirees, especially during tasks that may seem routine but carry hidden risks. As we age, our reflexes slow down, balance can become more fragile, and strength may decrease, making these activities potentially hazardous without proper care. Here are detailed considerations and tips to help ensure safety while enjoying these everyday tasks:

1. Traveling

- **Accident Risks**: Elderly individuals are more prone to slips and falls, especially in unfamiliar environments like airports, train stations, or new destinations.
- **Precautionary Tips**:
  - **Plan Ahead**: Book assistance services like wheelchairs or airport shuttles if necessary to minimize the physical strain of walking long distances.
  - **Pack Light**: Use lightweight, easy-to-carry luggage to avoid strain when lifting or pulling bags.
  - **Stay Hydrated**: Dehydration can lead to dizziness, so always have water handy, especially on long trips.
  - **Wear Comfortable Footwear**: Non-slip shoes with good support can reduce the risk of falls during travel.
  - **Cabin Baggage-** Handle carefully in the overhead bin. If you can not handle it, seek help from co-passengers or cabin staff.
  - Avoid consuming **chilled water or cold drinks**.

2. Maintaining and Cleaning Housing

- **Accident Risks**: Climbing ladders, handling cleaning chemicals, and using household tools can be hazardous due to decreased agility and strength.
- **Precautionary Tips**:
    - **Use Proper Equipment**: Opt for lightweight tools with ergonomic grips to avoid hand and wrist strain. For ladders, make sure they are sturdy, and always have someone to assist.
    - **Avoid Overreaching**: When dusting or cleaning high surfaces (ceiling fans, central air conditioning ducts & flappers, wall paintings, hanging windows or doors etc) use extension tools instead of stretching or climbing.
    - **Wear Protective Gear**: Use gloves & mask when handling cleaning chemicals and non-slip shoes to avoid falls on slippery floors.

3. Cleaning House Floors and Washrooms

- **Accident Risks**: Wet or freshly cleaned floors pose a serious fall hazard. Cleaning washrooms, which often have slippery surfaces, can lead to dangerous falls.
- **Precautionary Tips**:
    - **Use Non-Slip Mats**: Place these in bathrooms and kitchens, and make sure wet areas are dried quickly.
    - **Grab Bars in Bathrooms**: Installing grab bars near toilets and showers can provide extra support.
    - **Safe Cleaning Products**: Use mild, non-toxic cleaning agents that are less likely to cause dizziness or irritation.

4. Car Maintenance

- **Accident Risks**: Bending down, lifting heavy car parts, or working in awkward positions or postures can cause strain and injury.

- **Precautionary Tips**:
    - **Seek Professional Help**: Instead of tackling complex maintenance tasks, consider taking the car to a mechanic.
    - **Light Cleaning Only**: Focus on simple tasks like vacuuming or wiping down surfaces and leave heavy-duty cleaning or repairs to experts.

5. Gardening

- **Accident Risks**: Bending, kneeling for long periods, handling sharp tools, or lifting heavy objects can lead to back pain, joint issues, or cuts.
- **Precautionary Tips**:
    - **Use Knee Pads or Garden Stools**: These reduce pressure on the knees and make gardening more comfortable.
    - **Light Tools**: Use ergonomically designed, lightweight tools to reduce strain on hands and wrists.
    - **Stay Hydrated and Avoid Sunburn**: Wear a hat, apply sunscreen, and take regular breaks, especially in hot weather.
    - **Use of Hadgloves:** Protect your hands, fingers, and nails from unexpected cuts and injuries while gardening with this essential safety kit. Designed to shield you from mishaps caused by slips or sharp tools, it's your ultimate companion for safe and enjoyable gardening. Don't let a simple mistake spoil your green thumb—gear up and garden confidently.
    - **Use of Masks & Eye glasses:** Always ensure to wear a suitable mask and protective eye glasses while gardening. These essential precautions shield you from airborne particles, pollen, and insects that could irritate your respiratory system or cause eye infections. Stay safe and enjoy your gardening without worries.

6. Working in Front & Back Yards

- **Accident Risks**: Outdoor work like mowing the lawn or trimming bushes can lead to falls, cuts, or strains.
- **Precautionary Tips**:
    - **Use Electric Tools Over Manual Ones**: Electric lawnmowers or trimmers are easier to handle and require less physical effort.
    - **Avoid Overexertion**: Take breaks to avoid overexertion and never try to finish tasks quickly, which increases the risk of accidents.

7. Picking Fruits in Yards

- **Accident Risks**: Climbing ladders to pick fruit can lead to falls, while handling sharp tools like pruning shears can cause cuts.
- **Precautionary Tips**:
    - **Use a Long-Handled Fruit Picker**: This tool allows you to reach higher branches without the need for climbing.
    - **Stable Ladder**: If a ladder is necessary, make sure it's stable and that someone is nearby to assist if needed.
    - **Wear Gloves and Eye glasses**: Always wear gloves and protective eye glasses while working in yards. Gloves safeguard your hands from thorns, sharp branches, and pesky insects, while eye glasses keep your eyes safe from infections and unexpected insect encounters.

8. Playing Light Games with Grandchildren

- **Accident Risks**: While fun and a great way to stay active, playing games like badminton or table tennis may strain muscles or lead to trips and falls and limit your duration till you feel not much tired & exhausted.
- **Precautionary Tips**:
    - **Start Slowly**: Warm up before starting to play. Light stretching can prevent muscle strains.

    - **Play in Safe Areas**: Ensure the playing area is free of obstacles, uneven surfaces, or items that could cause tripping.
    - **Use Lighter Equipment**: Opt for lightweight rackets and soft shuttlecocks or balls to reduce strain and prevent injury.

9. Weekend Barbecue Outings

- **Accidental Risks**: Handling hot grills, sharp utensils, and slippery outdoor surfaces could result in burns or cuts.
- **Precautionary Tips**:
    - **Use Grill Safety Measures**: Always use long-handled tools to keep a safe distance from the flames and wear heat-resistant gloves.
    - **Check for Fire Hazards**: Keep a fire extinguisher nearby and avoid wearing loose clothing that could catch fire.
    - **Ensure Stable Seating**: Provide stable chairs and tables to avoid tipping or falling while enjoying the meal.

10. General Accident Prevention for the Elderly

- **Stay Physically Active**: Regular light exercise can improve balance, flexibility, and strength, reducing the risk of falls.
- **Vision Check-ups**: Poor vision can increase the risk of accidents. Regular eye check-ups can help maintain good eyesight.
- **Keep Surroundings Tidy**: Avoid clutter that can lead to tripping, especially in frequently used areas like hallways and kitchens.
- **Emergency Preparedness**: Carry a mobile phone or medical alert device while engaging in any activity, whether indoors or outdoors, so you can quickly summon help if needed.
- **Always avoid lifting heavy objects** that exceed your strength during household tasks. If you must lift something, be sure to maintain proper posture to protect your back and hips from strain or injury.

Note: Accidents may not be completely avoidable, but with the right precautions and proactive measures, their likelihood can be significantly reduced, ensuring greater safety and peace of mind. By taking these precautions, elderly individuals and retirees can continue to enjoy all the joys of daily living, from gardening to spending time with grandchildren, while significantly reducing the likelihood of accidents.

12.8 "Try to avoid exposure to common allergens to reduce the risk of allergic reactions."

As individuals age, they may become more susceptible to certain allergies or experience heightened sensitivity to allergens that they didn't have earlier in life. For elderly individuals and retirees, managing allergies effectively is important to maintain a high quality of life. Here are precautions to take for various types of allergies:

1. Seasonal Allergies (Hay Fever)

- **Common Allergens**: Pollen from trees, grass, weeds, and mold.
- **Precautionary Tips**:
    - **Monitor Air Quality**: Check daily pollen forecasts, especially during high-pollen seasons (spring and fall), and try to stay indoors when pollen counts are high.
    - **Keep Windows Closed**: To prevent pollen from entering the home, especially on windy days, keep windows closed and use air conditioning with a clean filter.
    - **Shower After Outdoor Activities**: Pollen can stick to hair, clothes, and skin. After spending time outside, it's a good idea to shower and change into clean clothes to avoid spreading pollen indoors.
    - **Use an Air Purifier**: Installing an air purifier with a Nanoprotect HEPA filter can help reduce airborne allergens inside the home.
    - **Use of N95 respiratory masks** when going outside during high levels of contamination in the atmosphere.

2. Food Allergies

- **Common Allergens**: Nuts, dairy, shellfish, gluten, eggs, and certain fruits or vegetables.
- **Precautionary Tips**:

  - **Read Food Labels Carefully**: As we age, our sensitivity to certain foods may increase, so it's important to read food labels to avoid accidental exposure to allergens.
  - **Carry Antihistamines**: Keep over-the-counter antihistamines on hand to manage mild allergic reactions.
  - **Consider an Allergy Test**: If a retiree experiences new or worsening food sensitivities, seeing an allergist for testing can help identify the exact triggers.
  - **Dining Out Precautions**: When eating at restaurants, inform the staff about any known food allergies and ask about how meals are prepared to avoid cross-contamination.

3. Dust, Mold, and Indoor Allergens

- **Common Allergens**: Dust mites, mold spores, pet dander, and indoor plants.
- **Precautionary Tips**:
  - **Regular Cleaning**: Dust frequently and vacuum with a vacuum cleaner that has a HEPA filter. Pay special attention to areas where dust accumulates, such as curtains, carpets, and furniture.
  - **Control Humidity Levels**: Mold thrives in damp environments. Use a dehumidifier to keep indoor humidity below 50% and ensure proper ventilation in bathrooms and kitchens.
  - **Wash Bedding Regularly**: Dust mites often live in bedding, so wash sheets, pillowcases, and blankets weekly in hot water to kill dust mites.
  - **Avoid Wall-to-Wall Carpeting**: Hardwood, tile, or vinyl floors are easier to clean and don't trap allergens like carpets do.

4. Pet Allergies

- **Common Allergens**: Dander from cats, dogs, or other pets, as well as saliva and urine.
- **Precautionary Tips**:
    - **Regular Grooming**: If you have pets, bathe and groom them regularly to reduce the amount of dander they shed.
    - **Create Pet-Free Zones**: Keep certain rooms, such as bedrooms, pet-free to minimize exposure to allergens where you sleep and rest.
    - **Wash Hands After Petting**: Always wash your hands after handling pets to reduce the risk of spreading allergens to other parts of the home or your body.
    - **Consider Hypoallergenic Breeds**: If considering a new pet, hypoallergenic breeds may produce less dander and be less likely to trigger allergic reactions.

5. Medication Allergies

- **Common Allergens**: Penicillin, antibiotics, aspirin, NSAIDs (nonsteroidal anti-inflammatory drugs), and certain heart medications.
- **Precautionary Tips**:
    - **Inform Healthcare Providers**: Always inform doctors, pharmacists, and healthcare providers about any known medication allergies to avoid accidental prescriptions of harmful drugs.
    - **Read Labels**: Many over-the-counter medications contain ingredients that may cause allergies, so always read labels carefully and consult a healthcare provider if unsure.
    - **Keep an Updated List**: Maintain a current list of medications you're taking, along with any allergic reactions you've had in the past, so that healthcare providers are aware of your sensitivities.

6. Skin Allergies (Contact Dermatitis)

- **Common Allergens**: Certain soaps, detergents, perfumes, fabrics, or metals like nickel in jewelry.
- **Precautionary Tips**:
    - **Choose Hypoallergenic Products**: Opt for unscented, hypoallergenic soaps, lotions, and detergents to avoid skin irritation.
    - **Wear Protective Gloves**: When cleaning, gardening, or handling harsh chemicals, wear rubber gloves to prevent direct skin contact with potential irritants.
    - **Patch Testing**: If you're unsure about a new skincare product or fabric, apply a small amount to a patch of skin to see if it causes a reaction before using it extensively.

7. Insect Sting Allergies

- **Common Allergens**: Bee, wasp, hornet, and ant stings.
- **Precautionary Tips**:
    - **Wear Protective Clothing**: When gardening or spending time outdoors, wear long sleeves, pants, and closed-toe shoes to minimize skin exposure.
    - **Avoid Scented Products**: Insects are attracted to scented lotions, perfumes, and shampoos. Avoid using these products when spending time outside.
    - **Keep EpiPen Accessible**: If allergic to insect stings, always carry an epinephrine auto-injector (EpiPen) in case of a severe allergic reaction.
    - **Remove Nesting Areas**: Keep the yard and garden free of insect nests, and avoid areas where bees or wasps are known to gather.

8. Cold-Induced Allergies

- **Common Allergens**: Exposure to cold air or cold water can trigger allergic reactions in some individuals, especially as they age.
- **Precautionary Tips**:
  - **Wear Layers in Cold Weather**: Dress warmly and in layers when going outside during colder months. Cover exposed skin with hats, scarves, and gloves.
  - **Warm up Before Exercise**: If exercising outdoors in cold weather, warm up indoors first to prepare the body for temperature changes.
  - **Avoid Cold Water Exposure**: When swimming, opt for warmer pools and avoid sudden dips in cold water.

9. Latex Allergy

- **Common Allergens**: Latex gloves, balloons, or medical devices made with latex.
- **Precautionary Tips**:
  - **Use Latex-Free Products**: If allergic to latex, ensure all gloves, bandages, and other household or medical items are labeled "latex-free."
  - **Inform Medical Providers**: Always inform doctors and dentists about your latex allergy to ensure latex-free alternatives are used during medical exams or treatments.

By following these precautions, elderly individuals and retirees can manage allergies effectively and continue to live comfortably. Regular communication with healthcare providers is key to staying updated on potential allergens and treatment options.

12.9 Avoid Lending or Borrowing Money

Financial Caution for Elderly & Retirees

In retirement, financial stability is essential. Retirees often live on a fixed income, such as pensions or savings, with limited opportunities to generate new income. This makes it critical to manage money wisely. One important aspect of this is avoiding the risks associated with lending and borrowing money.

1. **Why You Shouldn't Lend Money:** Lending money, even to close friends or family, can be risky. As a retiree, you may not have a steady flow of income to recover any money lent, and repayment from others can be delayed or never happen at all. Lending can also strain relationships, leading to uncomfortable situations if the borrower is unable to repay you.
2. **The Emotional and Financial Strain:** The emotional toll of lending is another factor. When a borrower cannot repay, you might feel pressured to forgive the debt, which can put you under financial stress. Additionally, lending often places you in a situation where you prioritize someone else's needs over your own, potentially jeopardizing your own security in later life.
3. **Why Borrowing Should Be Avoided:** On the other hand, borrowing money as an elderly person or retiree can lead to a cycle of debt. With fixed incomes and increasing healthcare and living costs, it may be challenging to repay borrowed money. High interest rates, especially with credit cards or personal loans, can lead to mounting debt that diminishes your savings.
4. **Avoid Borrowing to Sustain a Failing Business:** Borrowing money to maintain a sinking business can deepen financial troubles. It often leads to accumulating debt without solving the root issues causing the business to fail. Instead of taking on more loans, it's wiser to evaluate the business's viability, cut losses, and explore other strategies, such as restructuring or selling assets. Protecting your financial stability, especially in retirement,

is crucial—borrowing for a failing venture may jeopardize your savings and future security.

5. **Impact on Retirement Savings:** Both lending and borrowing can deplete your hard-earned retirement savings, leaving you vulnerable to financial emergencies. Unforeseen health expenses, home repairs, or other unexpected costs may arise, and you'll need to have enough reserves to cover these without relying on others.
6. **Focus on Financial Stability:** As a retiree, your priority should be maintaining your financial independence and stability. It's vital to protect your nest egg and ensure that your savings last through your retirement years. Instead of lending or borrowing, consider helping in non-financial ways, like offering advice or emotional support to those in need.

Summary: to safeguard your financial well-being, avoid both lending and borrowing money. Staying financially secure in your retirement years will allow you to enjoy peace of mind and focus on what truly matters—your health, happiness, and spending quality time with loved ones.

12.10 Choose your friends wisely

Bad company can lead to poor decisions

That's a very wise piece of advice. For elderly individuals and retirees, choosing good company and friendships is essential to maintaining emotional well-being, mental clarity, and even physical health. Bad company or toxic friendships can lead to unnecessary stress, negative influences, and even financial or emotional exploitation. Here are a few reasons why avoiding bad company is important during retirement:

1. Emotional Well-being

- Retirement is a phase to enjoy life with peace and contentment. Surrounding yourself with positive, uplifting people helps enhance emotional health, while toxic or negative individuals can drain your energy and disrupt your peace.
- Good friendships provide support, love, and care, which are essential for maintaining happiness in later years.

2. Avoiding Stress and Anxiety

- Bad company often brings drama, gossip, or conflicts that can lead to unnecessary stress. At an older age, it's important to minimize sources of stress, as it can have a direct impact on physical and mental health.
- Choose friendships that are peaceful, honest, and supportive instead of those filled with tension or manipulation.

3. Protecting Your Finances

- Retirees can be vulnerable to financial exploitation, especially by so-called "friends" who might take advantage of trust. It's essential to keep a distance from people who may have selfish motives.
- Focus on people who value your well-being over material gain or exploitation.

4. Maintaining Good Habits

- Being around people with bad habits (such as excessive drinking, gambling, or other negative behaviors) can lead to poor decisions. It's better to surround yourself with friends who encourage healthy habits, both mentally and physically.
- Good company will motivate you to stay active, engage in meaningful hobbies, and maintain a healthy lifestyle.

5. Positive Influence on Family Life

- Maintaining good, trustworthy friendships has a ripple effect on family life as well. Your family will feel at ease knowing you're surrounded by people who care for you genuinely, which strengthens family bonds.
- Good friends can enhance your family life by offering support in times of need, while bad friends might cause unnecessary conflicts or misunderstandings.

6. Spiritual and Personal Growth

- Retirement is also a time for reflection and spiritual growth. Being in the company of like-minded, spiritual, or morally upright individuals can help you deepen your connection with your faith and life goals.
- Avoid friendships that steer you away from your values, faith, or personal growth.

Final Thoughts

Choose friends who bring joy, peace, and positivity into your life—those whose presence feels like a breath of fresh air. In your retirement years, time becomes more precious, and the company you keep can deeply influence your emotional and spiritual well-being.

Surround yourself with people who uplift your spirit, respect your journey, and share the values that matter most to you. Whether it's laughter over tea, thoughtful conversations, or silent companionship, the right friends add richness to your days and comfort to your soul.

Avoid toxic relationships that drain your energy or stir unnecessary stress. At this stage of life, harmony is more valuable than drama, and genuine connections far outweigh shallow ties.

True friendship in later life is not about numbers—it's about warmth, trust, and the shared joy of simply being together.

12.11 Avoid Neck Crackling

Neck cracking, or "neck manipulation," is a common practice in barber shops, especially in some third-world countries, where barbers may perform quick twists or pressure movements on the neck to produce a cracking sound. While some people find this relieving or relaxing, it can pose serious risks, particularly for elderly or retired individuals. Here's why:

1. **Fragile Bones and Joints**: In older adults, bones and joints, including those in the neck, become more fragile due to age-related conditions like osteoporosis or arthritis. Sudden, forceful movements can cause injury to the spine, vertebrae, or neck muscles.
2. **Risk of Stroke**: Neck manipulation has been associated with a small risk of arterial dissection (a tear in the artery wall), which can lead to stroke, especially in individuals with pre-existing vascular conditions or weakened arteries.
3. **Increased Vulnerability**: The elderly often have reduced flexibility and stability in the cervical spine, making them more vulnerable to injury from these techniques.
4. **Lack of Professional Training**: In many barber shops in third-world countries, barbers may not have formal medical training. While they may perform this practice based on tradition, it lacks the precision or safety considerations seen in professional chiropractic care.

For elderly or retirees, it's advisable to avoid neck cracking at barber shops and instead seek care from trained professionals if neck discomfort or stiffness is an issue.

12.12 Avoid Eating Alone while watching TV or using Tablets

For elderly or retirees, it's important to avoid eating alone while watching TV or using tablets.

1. **Mindful Eating**

Eating in front of the TV or while using a tablet can lead to **mindless eating**, where you might consume more food without realizing it. This can lead to overeating and potential weight gain, which can be harmful, especially for seniors.

2. **Improved Digestion**

When you're focused on your food and enjoying the process, digestion improves. **Distractions like TV or tablets** may lead to eating too quickly, which can cause indigestion, bloating, or discomfort—common issues for older adults.

3. **Better Food Choices**

Without the distraction of the media, retirees can focus on choosing **healthier, balanced meals**. Watching TV or using a tablet can lead to unhealthy snacking or poor dietary habits.

4. **Mindful Solo Dining:**

   If eating alone is unavoidable, turn off screens, set the table nicely, and savor each bite.

12.13 Be careful & safe

Retirees must take proactive steps to safeguard their health, as many illnesses in later life can be not only painful but, at times, life-threatening. With age comes wisdom—and the opportunity to prioritize well-being through mindful choices, regular check-ups, and a balanced lifestyle.

Prevention is far better than cure. Simple habits like eating healthy, staying active, managing stress, and avoiding harmful substances can go a long way in keeping diseases at bay.

Your golden years should be a time of peace, not pain—of joyful living, not frequent hospital visits. By staying informed and vigilant, retirees can enjoy a fuller, healthier, and more vibrant life, free from the shadows of avoidable health risks.

From Malaria, jaundice, dengue, TB, variants of COVID-19, insomnia, Asthma, pneumonia to other pulmonary embolisms.

For elderly and retirees, it's crucial to take extra precautions to avoid serious illnesses such as malaria, jaundice, dengue, tuberculosis (TB), variants of COVID-19, insomnia, asthma, pneumonia, and pulmonary embolisms (especially those who are suffering from Diabetes & Blood Pressure and cardiac issues). Here's why and how they can stay safe:

1. Malaria

- **Risk**: Malaria is transmitted by mosquito bites, which can cause severe fever, chills, and other complications, especially for older adults.
- **Prevention**:

- **Eliminate Standing Water:** Regularly check your garden for stagnant water in pots, drains, or containers where mosquitoes may breed.
    - **Protective Clothing:** Wear long-sleeved shirts, full-length pants, gloves, and socks to minimize skin exposure.
    - **Use Mosquito Repellent:** Apply a reliable insect repellent on exposed skin before stepping out.
    - **Gardening at Safe Times:** Avoid gardening during dawn and dusk when mosquitoes are most active.
    - **Install Mosquito Traps:** Set up mosquito-repelling plants like citronella or install traps to reduce their presence.

2. Jaundice

- **Risk**: Jaundice in elderly people can be a sign of liver dysfunction or infections like hepatitis.
- **Prevention Tips:**

1. **Maintain Good Hygiene:** Wash your hands thoroughly with soap and water, especially before eating and after using the restroom.
2. **Drink Safe Water:** Stick to clean, filtered, or boiled water to avoid waterborne infections like Hepatitis A and E, which can cause jaundice.
3. **Eat Fresh Food:** Consume well-cooked meals and avoid street food or unwashed fruits and vegetables.
4. **Vaccinate:** Get vaccinated for Hepatitis A and B to reduce the risk of liver infections.
5. **Limit Alcohol Consumption:** Avoid excessive alcohol, as it can harm your liver over time. Better to avoid consuming alcohol.
6. **Stay Clear of Contaminated Areas:** Be cautious in regions with poor sanitation, as infections are more likely to spread there.

3. Dengue

- **Risk**: Dengue is another mosquito-borne illness that can be dangerous for the elderly due to the risk of severe dehydration and internal bleeding.

- **Prevention**:
    - Dengue Alert: When gardening, it's crucial to protect yourself from mosquito bites, especially in areas where dengue fever is prevalent. Wear long-sleeved clothing, gloves, and use a mosquito repellent. Dengue-carrying mosquitoes thrive in stagnant water, so regularly check and remove any standing water around your garden to keep these pests at bay. Stay safe and enjoy gardening without the risk.

4. Tuberculosis (TB)

- **Risk**: TB spreads through the air and can be particularly serious for older adults with weakened immune systems.
- **Tuberculosis (TB) Prevention Tips:**
    - **Get Vaccinated:** Ensure you receive the Bacille Calmette-Guérin (BCG) vaccine, especially if you're at risk or live in an area where TB is common.
    - **Practice Good Hygiene:** Cover your mouth and nose with a tissue or your elbow when coughing or sneezing to prevent the spread of germs.
    - **Improve Ventilation:** TB spreads through the air, so keep your living and working spaces well-ventilated.
    - **Avoid Crowded Spaces:** Limit exposure to crowded, poorly ventilated places where TB bacteria can spread easily.
    - **Strengthen Immunity:** Eat a balanced diet, exercise, and get adequate sleep to keep your immune system strong.
    - **Regular Health Checkups:** If you're at risk or have been in contact with someone with TB, get tested regularly for early detection.
    - **Complete Treatment:** If diagnosed, follow the full course of TB treatment as prescribed to prevent the spread and recurrence.

5. COVID-19 Variants

- **Risk**: COVID-19 variants continue to pose a risk, especially to elderly people who may experience more severe symptoms or complications.
- **COVID-19 Variant Prevention Tips**:
    - **Stay Up-to-Date with Vaccines:** Get the latest vaccinations and booster doses recommended for emerging variants to maintain immunity.
    - **Wear High-Quality Masks:** Use N95, KN95, or equivalent masks, especially in crowded, enclosed spaces or areas with high transmission rates.
    - **Enhance Indoor Ventilation:** Improve airflow in your home or workplace using air purifiers, exhaust fans, or by opening windows.
    - **Practice Good Hygiene:** Wash hands frequently with soap and water or use hand sanitizer with at least 60% alcohol.
    - **Monitor Symptoms Closely:** Watch for new or variant-specific symptoms, even if mild, and test promptly if unwell.
    - **Avoid Crowded and Poorly Ventilated Areas:** Social distancing and good air circulation reduce the risk of transmission.
    - **Follow Travel Advisories:** Be cautious when traveling and check for health and safety guidelines in affected areas.
    - **Stay Informed:** Keep track of health updates and recommendations from reliable sources like WHO, CDC, or your local health authority.
    - **Limit Close Contact:** Avoid unnecessary physical contact and gatherings during periods of high variant transmission.
    - **Encourage Community Awareness:** Support preventive measures in your community, such as promoting mask-wearing and vaccination campaigns.

6. Insomnia

- **Risk**: Chronic insomnia can weaken the immune system, lead to cognitive decline, and cause other health issues like high blood pressure.

Insomnia Prevention Tips:

1. **Maintain a Sleep Schedule:** Go to bed and wake up at the same time every day, even on weekends, to regulate your body clock.
2. **Create a Relaxing Bedtime Routine:** Engage in calming activities before bed, such as reading, meditating, or taking a warm bath.
3. **Limit Screen Time:** Avoid electronic devices like phones, tablets, and TVs at least 1-2 hours before bedtime, as blue light can interfere with sleep.
4. **Avoid Stimulants:** Limit caffeine, nicotine, and alcohol intake, especially in the evening.
5. **Optimize Your Sleep Environment:** Keep your bedroom cool, quiet, and dark. Invest in a comfortable mattress and pillows.
6. **Limit Daytime Naps:** If you nap, keep it short (20-30 minutes) and avoid napping late in the day.
7. **Exercise Regularly:** Engage in physical activity during the day to improve sleep quality, but avoid vigorous exercise close to bedtime.
8. **Watch Your Diet:** Avoid heavy meals, spicy foods, or sugary snacks before bed. Opt for light, sleep-friendly snacks if needed.
9. **Manage Stress:** Practice relaxation techniques like deep breathing, yoga, or mindfulness to calm your mind.
10. **Seek Natural Light Exposure:** Spend time in natural sunlight during the day to help regulate your sleep-wake cycle.

If insomnia persists, consult a healthcare professional to address underlying causes or explore further treatments. A good night's sleep is key to a healthy and balanced life.

7. Asthma

- **Risk**: Asthma can worsen with age, and elderly individuals are more vulnerable to respiratory infections, which can trigger asthma attacks.

Asthma Prevention Tips:

1. **Identify and Avoid Triggers:** Stay away from allergens like pollen, dust mites, mold, pet dander, and smoke, which can worsen asthma symptoms.
2. **Maintain a Clean Environment:** Regularly clean your home, use air purifiers, and wash bedding in hot water to minimize allergens.
3. **Avoid Smoking and Secondhand Smoke:** Smoking and exposure to secondhand smoke can severely aggravate asthma.
4. **Manage Stress:** Practice relaxation techniques like deep breathing, meditation, or yoga to prevent stress-induced asthma attacks.
5. **Stay Active Safely:** Engage in regular exercise, but consult your doctor about activities and precautions if exercise triggers asthma.
6. **Be Cautious with Weather Changes:** Protect yourself from cold air, humidity, or extreme temperature changes by dressing appropriately or using a scarf over your mouth.
7. **Follow Your Treatment Plan:** Take prescribed medications, such as inhalers, as directed by your healthcare provider.
8. **Avoid Strong Odors and Chemicals:** Steer clear of perfumes, cleaning products, or paints that can irritate airways.
9. **Stay Up-to-Date with Vaccines:** Get flu and pneumonia vaccinations to prevent respiratory infections that can worsen asthma.
10. **Monitor Air Quality:** Check daily air pollution levels and avoid outdoor activities on days with high pollution or pollen counts.
11. **Eat a Healthy Diet:** Consume anti-inflammatory foods like fruits and vegetables to support lung health.

12. **Have an Asthma Action Plan:** Work with your doctor to create a plan for managing symptoms and knowing when to seek emergency care.

8. Pneumonia

- **Risk**: Pneumonia can be life-threatening in elderly individuals, particularly those with weakened immune systems or pre-existing lung conditions.

Pneumonia Prevention Tips:

1. **Get Vaccinated:** Stay updated with pneumococcal and flu vaccines to protect against common causes of pneumonia.
2. **Practice Good Hygiene:** Wash your hands frequently with soap and water, especially after coughing, sneezing, or using the restroom.
3. **Avoid Smoking:** Smoking damages your lungs and weakens their defense against infections.
4. **Maintain a Healthy Lifestyle:** Eat a balanced diet, exercise regularly, and get enough sleep to strengthen your immune system.
5. **Stay Hydrated:** Drink plenty of fluids to keep your respiratory tract moist and reduce the risk of infection.
6. **Avoid Close Contact with Sick People:** Minimize exposure to individuals with respiratory illnesses, especially during flu season.
7. **Cough and Sneeze Etiquette:** Cover your mouth and nose with a tissue to prevent spreading or contracting infections.
8. **Manage Chronic Conditions:** Keep illnesses like diabetes, asthma, and heart disease well-controlled, as they increase pneumonia risk.
9. **Monitor Air Quality:** Avoid exposure to air pollution and allergens that can irritate your lungs.
10. **Be Cautious with Infants and Elderly:** Take extra precautions for high-risk groups like young children, seniors, and those with weakened immunity.

11. **Use Proper Ventilation:** Ensure good airflow in your living spaces to reduce the risk of airborne infections.
12. **Stay Informed:** Follow health advisories, especially during outbreaks of respiratory illnesses.

9. Pulmonary Embolisms

- **Risk**: Pulmonary embolisms (blood clots in the lungs) are dangerous for elderly individuals, especially those with reduced mobility or cardiovascular conditions.

Pulmonary Embolism (PE) Prevention Tips:

1. **Stay Active:** Engage in regular physical activity to improve blood circulation and reduce the risk of blood clots.
2. **Avoid Prolonged Sitting:** If traveling or sitting for long periods, stand up, stretch, and walk around every 1-2 hours.
3. **Wear Compression Stockings:** Use these to improve blood flow in your legs, especially if you're at risk or have a history of blood clots.
4. **Stay Hydrated:** Drink plenty of water to prevent dehydration, which can increase the risk of clot formation.
5. **Maintain a Healthy Weight:** Obesity increases the risk of blood clots, so work towards a healthy weight through diet and exercise.
6. **Avoid Smoking:** Smoking damages blood vessels and increases the likelihood of clotting.
7. **Know Your Medications:** If prescribed blood thinners (anticoagulants), take them as directed to reduce clot risks.
8. **Elevate Your Legs:** When sitting or lying down for long periods, elevate your legs to promote circulation.
9. **Manage Chronic Conditions:** Control underlying health issues like diabetes, hypertension, and heart disease.
10. **Recognize Symptoms Early:** Be alert for symptoms of deep vein thrombosis (DVT), such as swelling, pain, or redness in the legs, and seek medical attention promptly.

11. **Post-Surgery Care:** Follow your doctor's instructions carefully after surgery, as immobility increases the risk of clots. Early ambulation is key.
12. **Avoid Tight Clothing:** Wear loose, comfortable clothing to ensure proper blood flow in your legs and abdomen.

General Tips for Elderly & Retirees:

- **Stay Hydrated**: Drink plenty of water to avoid dehydration and keep the body functioning well.
- **Regular Check-ups**: Routine medical check-ups can help catch illnesses early and manage chronic conditions effectively.
- **Healthy Diet**: A balanced diet with nutrients, vitamins, and minerals strengthens the immune system.
- **Exercise**: Engage in light exercise like walking, which promotes overall health and helps prevent conditions **like pulmonary embolism and pneumonia.**

Note - Taking above precautions can help elderly individuals avoid these serious diseases and maintain their overall health and well-being.

12.14 Prostate Gland

CAUTION

- A large percentage of elderly men are affected by prostate issues, particularly benign prostatic hyperplasia (BPH).
- By age 60, about half of men have signs of BPH, and by age 85, about 90% do. BPH is the most common prostate problem in men over 50.

Prostate health becomes a significant concern for elderly men, especially retirees, due to the higher risk of prostate-related conditions that often emerge with age. The prostate gland, a small walnut shaped organ located just below the bladder, plays a key role in male reproductive health, but it tends to enlarge and become problematic as men grow older.

Common Prostate Conditions in Elderly Men

1. **Benign Prostatic Hyperplasia (BPH)**:
    - **BPH** is the non-cancerous enlargement of the prostate, which is very common in men over the age of 50. By the time men reach their 60s, about 50% of them will have some signs of BPH, and this rises to about 80% by the age of 80.
    - **Symptoms of BPH** include:
        - Frequent urination, especially at night.
        - Difficulty starting urination or weak urine flow.
        - Incomplete emptying of the bladder.
    - Though BPH is not life-threatening, it can significantly impact the quality of life for elderly men by causing discomfort and sleep disturbances.
2. **Prostatitis**:
    - **Prostatitis** is inflammation of the prostate, which can occur at any age but is more common in older men. It can be caused by bacterial infection or other factors like stress or injury.

- **Symptoms** include:
    - Pain in the pelvic area or lower back.
    - Painful urination.
    - Fever (in cases of bacterial infection).
- Prostatitis can often be treated with antibiotics (if bacterial) or other medications to manage symptoms.

3. **Prostate Cancer**:
    - **Prostate cancer** is one of the most common cancers in older men, with risk increasing significantly after age 50. It is especially prevalent in men over the age of 65.
    - **Risk factors** include:
        - **Age**: Prostate cancer is rare before the age of 50, but the risk increases significantly with age.
        - **Family history**: Men with a family history of prostate cancer are at higher risk.
        - **Diet and lifestyle**: A diet high in red meat and processed foods, along with low physical activity, may increase the risk.
    - **Symptoms** of prostate cancer may be similar to BPH but can also include:
        - Blood in the urine or semen.
        - Erectile dysfunction.
        - Bone pain (in advanced stages).
    - Early detection through **prostate-specific antigen (PSA) testing** and **digital rectal exams (DRE)** can help in timely diagnosis and treatment, which may include surgery, radiation therapy, hormone therapy, or active surveillance.

Impact on Elderly and Retirees

1. **Quality of Life**:
    - Prostate conditions like BPH and prostate cancer can affect **quality of life**, leading to urinary difficulties, sleep disturbances, discomfort, and anxiety.

- Men with these conditions may experience limitations in daily activities, affecting their ability to travel or participate in physical hobbies often associated with retirement.

2. **Mental Health**:
   - Prostate health concerns can cause **emotional distress**, particularly if symptoms are severe or cancer is diagnosed. Fear of cancer progression or invasive treatments may increase anxiety or depression in elderly men.
3. **Financial Burden**:
   - The cost of treatment for prostate conditions, especially prostate cancer, can impose a significant **financial burden** on retirees, particularly those without sufficient healthcare coverage or savings.
4. **Impact on Relationships**:
   - Prostate issues can affect **intimacy and sexual health**. Conditions like BPH and prostate cancer treatments can lead to erectile dysfunction (ED), impacting sexual relationships. Open communication with partners and seeking medical advice can help address these challenges.

Management and Preventive Strategies

1. **Regular Check-ups**:
   - Elderly men, especially retirees, should have **regular prostate screenings**, including PSA tests and digital rectal exams, to detect any abnormalities early.
2. **Diet and Lifestyle**:
   - A **healthy diet** rich in fruits, vegetables, and whole grains, along with **regular physical activity**, can reduce the risk of prostate problems.
   - Reducing the intake of red meat, processed foods, and maintaining a healthy weight are also recommended for prostate health.
3. **Medications**:

   - For men with BPH or prostatitis, medications like alpha-blockers or antibiotics can help manage symptoms effectively.
4. **Prostate Cancer Screening**:
   - **PSA testing** is a common screening tool for prostate cancer, though the decision to screen should be based on individual risk factors and discussed with a healthcare provider. Early detection is key for better outcomes.
5. **Minimally Invasive Treatments**:
   - For BPH, minimally invasive treatments, such as **laser therapy** or **transurethral resection of the prostate (TURP)**, can help alleviate symptoms without major surgery.
6. **Coping with Prostate Cancer**:
   - Men diagnosed with prostate cancer have a variety of treatment options depending on the stage of the disease, including **active surveillance**, **radiation therapy**, **surgery**, and **hormonal therapy**. Support from healthcare professionals, family, and cancer support groups is crucial for mental and emotional well-being during treatment.

Importance of Proper Hydration

Proper hydration is essential for everyone, but it holds particular significance for elderly individuals, especially those dealing with prostate-related conditions such as Benign Prostatic Hyperplasia (BPH), prostatitis, or prostate cancer. Adequate water intake can help manage symptoms, improve overall urinary health, and enhance quality of life. However, it's important to balance hydration to avoid exacerbating certain prostate issues, such as frequent nighttime urination (nocturia). Below is a comprehensive overview of the role of water for elderly persons with prostate conditions:

1. Importance of Hydration for Prostatic Health

a. Promotes Urinary Function

- Flushing the System: Adequate water intake helps flush out the urinary system, reducing the concentration of substances that can irritate the bladder and prostate.
- Prevents Urinary Tract Infections (UTIs): Staying well-hydrated dilutes urine, making it harder for bacteria to thrive and reducing the risk of UTIs, which can be particularly problematic for those with prostate enlargement.

b. Alleviates BPH Symptoms

- Reduces Urinary Tract Strain: Proper hydration ensures smooth urine flow, potentially minimizing the strain on the bladder and prostate.
- Prevents Kidney Stones: Adequate water intake reduces the risk of kidney stones, which can complicate BPH symptoms.

c. Enhances Kidney Function

- Detoxification: The kidneys rely on water to filter waste products from the blood effectively, supporting overall health and reducing the burden on the prostate.

2. Balancing Water Intake for Prostatic Conditions

While hydration is crucial, it's equally important to manage water consumption to avoid worsening certain symptoms associated with prostate issues.

a. Managing Nocturia

- Limit Evening Fluids: To reduce nighttime trips to the bathroom, elderly individuals with prostate conditions may benefit from limiting fluid intake in the late afternoon and evening.

- Monitor Caffeine and Alcohol: Both caffeine and alcohol can increase urine production and should be consumed in moderation, especially in the hours leading up to bedtime.

b. Timing of Fluid Intake

- Distribute Throughout the Day: Encourage consistent hydration by spreading water consumption evenly throughout the day rather than consuming large amounts at once.
- Before and After Meals: Drinking water before meals can aid digestion, while drinking after meals helps in nutrient absorption and waste elimination.

3. Recommended Water Intake

a. General Guidelines

- Elderly Hydration Needs: Older adults often require more attention to their hydration status due to factors like decreased thirst sensation and potential mobility issues. A common recommendation is to aim for 6-8 glasses (about 1.5 to 2 liters) of water per day, but individual needs may vary.

b. Personalized Hydration Plans

- Consult Healthcare Providers: It's essential to tailor water intake based on individual health conditions, medications, and lifestyle. Healthcare providers can offer personalized recommendations.

4. Signs of Dehydration to Watch For

Elderly individuals are at higher risk of dehydration, which can exacerbate prostate symptoms and lead to other health complications.

a. Common Symptoms

- Dark Urine: Indicates concentrated urine, a sign of dehydration.

- Dry Mouth and Thirst: Persistent dry mouth despite adequate fluid intake.
- Fatigue and Weakness: Dehydration can cause overall tiredness and muscle weakness.
- Dizziness or Confusion: Severe dehydration may lead to cognitive impairments.

b. Preventive Measures

- Regular Fluid Checks: Encourage regular monitoring of urine color and frequency.
- Accessible Fluids: Keep water and other hydrating beverages within easy reach to promote frequent intake.

5. Best Practices for Hydration Management

a. Incorporate Hydrating Foods

- Fruits and Vegetables: Foods like cucumbers, watermelon, oranges, and strawberries have high water content and contribute to overall hydration.

b. Use Reminders and Tools

- Scheduled Drinking: Set reminders to drink water at regular intervals throughout the day.
- Hydration Apps: Utilize smartphone apps designed to track and remind users to hydrate.

c. Choose the Right Beverages

- Water: The best choice for hydration without added calories or sugars.
- Herbal Teas: Can be a good alternative, but avoid those with caffeine.
- Broths and Soups: Provide hydration along with essential nutrients.

6. Special Considerations for Prostate Cancer Patients

a. During Treatment

- Radiation and Chemotherapy: Treatments may cause side effects like nausea and vomiting, increasing the risk of dehydration. Adequate hydration helps manage these side effects and supports kidney function during treatment.

b. After Surgery

- Recovery Support: Proper hydration aids in recovery by promoting healing and reducing the risk of infections.

7. Potential Risks of Excessive Water Intake

While adequate hydration is beneficial, excessive water consumption can lead to:

a. Hyponatremia

- Definition: A condition where sodium levels in the blood become dangerously low.
- Symptoms: Nausea, headache, confusion, and in severe cases, seizures.
- Overhydration, or drinking too much water, can dilute the sodium in your bloodstream, creating a dangerous imbalance that causes your body's cells to swell. This cellular swelling can trigger a range of health issues, from mild discomfort to life-threatening complications.

b. Increased Urinary Frequency

- Impact on BPH Symptoms: Overhydration can exacerbate urinary frequency and urgency, worsening the symptoms of BPH.

8. Practical Tips for Maintaining Optimal Hydration

a. Set Daily Goals

- Track Intake: Use a journal or an app to monitor daily water consumption.

b. Make It Enjoyable

- Flavor Enhancements: Add natural flavors like lemon, lime, or cucumber slices to make drinking water more appealing.

c. Use Appropriate Containers

- Accessible Bottles: Carry a water bottle to encourage frequent sipping throughout the day.

Note: An optimal daily hydration goal is about 2.7 liters (11.5 cups) for women and 3.7 liters (15.5 cups) for men, including all fluids from both beverages and food. This balance supports bodily functions without risking overhydration.

Here are a few tips to maintain healthy hydration:

1. Listen to Your Body: Thirst is a natural indicator; drink when you feel thirsty and aim to spread water intake throughout the day.
2. Adjust for Activity Level: Increase hydration on hot days or during exercise, as your body loses more water through sweat.
3. Monitor Hydration with Urine Color: Pale yellow is a good sign; dark yellow can indicate dehydration, while completely clear urine may mean you're drinking too much.
4. Use Reminders: Try a water-tracking app or set reminders if you often forget to drink enough water.

This flexible approach keeps hydration balanced and healthy.

9. When to Seek Medical Advice?

If an elderly person with prostate issues experiences symptoms that may be related to hydration levels, such as persistent dizziness, confusion, or significant changes in urinary patterns, it's important to consult a healthcare professional promptly.

Conclusion

Water plays a vital role in managing prostate health for elderly individuals. By maintaining adequate hydration, managing fluid intake timing, and being mindful of the balance between too little and too much water, retirees and older adults can better manage prostate-related conditions and enhance their overall well-being. Always consult with healthcare providers to create a personalized hydration plan that considers individual health needs and prostate health status.

For retirees and elderly men, maintaining prostate health is essential to ensuring a good quality of life. Regular medical check-ups, a healthy lifestyle, and timely treatment of prostate conditions can help manage symptoms and prevent complications. As life expectancy increases, proactive management of prostate health is more important than ever for aging men.

12.15 Anger and Temper

Anger, in elderly persons, is an intense emotional response often triggered by frustration, helplessness, or unmet expectations, influenced by physical decline, emotional struggles, or social challenges, and can manifest as irritability, outbursts, or passive-aggressive behavior.

Temper, refers to a person's emotional state or mood, particularly their capacity to remain calm or become easily angered. It reflects how an individual manages frustration or stress, with expressions ranging from mild irritability to intense outbursts of anger.

CAUTION: Anger and temper are particularly dangerous for elderly individuals as they can lead to heightened stress levels, increased blood pressure, and a higher risk of heart attacks or strokes. Emotional outbursts may strain relationships, lead to isolation, and exacerbate existing mental health issues like anxiety or depression. Additionally, unmanaged anger can impair decision-making, disrupt daily routines, and diminish overall quality of life.

Triggers of Anger in the Elderly

- Loss of Purpose: After retirement, some individuals struggle to redefine their identity and purpose, leading to frustration and irritability.
- Health Issues: Chronic pain, mobility problems, or cognitive decline can make them feel helpless, contributing to outbursts of anger.
- Financial Stress: Worry about limited income or unexpected expenses can be a source of anxiety and frustration.
- Loss of Loved Ones: Grief over losing friends, family, or a spouse may cause underlying sadness that manifests as anger.

- Lack of Control: Dependence on others for daily activities can lead to feelings of powerlessness and resentment.
- Social Isolation: Loneliness and lack of social engagement can increase irritability and a sense of being overlooked or forgotten.
- Intergenerational Conflicts: Differences in values or habits between them and younger family members can cause friction.
- Perceived Disrespect: Feeling ignored or undervalued by family or society can provoke anger.

Negative Effects of Anger in Elderly Persons

Anger in elderly individuals can have significant physical, emotional, and social consequences:

1. Physical Health Impacts

- **Heart Problems:** Chronic anger can increase blood pressure and strain the cardiovascular system, raising the risk of heart attacks and strokes.
- **Weakened Immunity:** Stress and anger can suppress the immune system, making them more vulnerable to infections and illnesses.
- **Chronic Pain:** Anger can exacerbate conditions like arthritis, back pain, and migraines due to muscle tension.
- **Sleep Disturbances:** Persistent anger may lead to insomnia or poor-quality sleep, further affecting overall health.
- **Digestive Issues:** Stress-related anger can lead to problems like acid reflux, ulcers, and irritable bowel syndrome.

2. Emotional and Psychological Effects

- **Increased Stress and Anxiety:** Constant anger creates a cycle of emotional distress, leading to chronic stress and heightened anxiety.

- **Depression:** Feelings of frustration and unresolved anger can evolve into long-term sadness and depression.
- **Cognitive Decline:** Prolonged emotional strain may contribute to memory problems and slower cognitive functioning.

3. Social Consequences

- **Strained Relationships:** Frequent outbursts or irritability can alienate family members, friends, and caregivers.
- **Isolation:** Fear of conflict or misunderstanding can lead to withdrawal from social interactions.
- **Loss of Respect:** Persistent anger can make it difficult for others to empathize, leading to decreased support and understanding.

How to Control Anger in Elderly Persons

1. Self-Awareness

- **Identify Triggers:** Encourage them to recognize situations or behaviors that provoke anger.
- **Reflect on Feelings:** Help them understand the root causes of their emotions, such as fear, frustration, or grief.

2. Emotional Regulation Techniques

- **Deep Breathing:** Practicing slow, deep breaths can help calm the mind and reduce physical symptoms of anger.
- **Mindfulness Meditation:** Regular mindfulness exercises can help them stay present and detach from reactive emotions.
- **Count to Ten:** Pausing before responding allows them to think rationally instead of acting impulsively.

3. Healthy Lifestyle Choices

- **Regular Exercise:** Physical activity, such as walking, swimming, or yoga, can release endorphins and reduce stress.

- **Balanced Diet:** Avoiding excessive caffeine and sugar can prevent mood swings and irritability.
- **Adequate Sleep:** Good sleep hygiene can improve emotional resilience.

4. Social Engagement

- **Family Support:** Spending quality time with loved ones can provide emotional comfort.
- **Community Groups:** Joining clubs or social organizations can help them form meaningful connections and reduce loneliness.

5. Channeling Energy Positively

- **Hobbies and Interests:** Encourage creative outlets like painting, gardening, or writing to redirect energy constructively.
- **Volunteer Work:** Helping others can foster a sense of purpose and fulfillment.

6. Professional Help

- **Therapy or Counseling:** A therapist can help them process unresolved anger and learn coping mechanisms.
- **Anger Management Classes:** Structured programs can teach practical strategies to manage emotions.
- **Medical Consultation:** If anger stems from a medical condition, addressing the root cause can alleviate symptoms.

7. Spiritual and Religious Practices

- **Faith-Based Activities:** Prayer, religious gatherings, or reading scripture can provide peace and perspective for those inclined.
- **Gratitude Practice:** Reflecting on blessings can shift focus from negativity to positivity.

By addressing anger with empathy and practical solutions, elderly individuals can lead healthier, happier lives while improving their relationships with others.

13.0 Starting a business after retirement

A brilliant opportunity or a risky gamble?

Starting a business after retirement can be both a good or bad idea, depending on various factors such as personal goals, financial situation, health, and risk tolerance. Here's a breakdown of the pros and cons to help evaluate whether it's a good or bad idea for you:

Why Is It a Brilliant Idea?

1. Purpose and Fulfillment:
    - Retirement can sometimes lead to a lack of daily structure or purpose. Starting a business provides retirees with a meaningful way to stay productive, follow a passion, and gain a sense of achievement.
2. Income Generation:
    - A business can supplement your pension or retirement savings, providing additional financial security. This can be especially helpful if healthcare costs or living expenses rise.
3. Leveraging Experience:
    - After years of working, retirees possess valuable skills, knowledge, and networks. These assets can be effectively applied to a new business, reducing the steep learning curve many new entrepreneurs face.
4. Flexibility:
    - Being your own boss means you can set your own hours and pace, which is ideal during retirement. A small, part-time venture might suit your lifestyle without overwhelming you.
5. Mental and Social Engagement:
    - Running a business can keep retirees mentally sharp and socially engaged. It provides opportunities to interact with

customers, employees, or other entrepreneurs, which can help combat loneliness and isolation.

Why It Could Be a Bad Idea?

1. Financial Risk:
    - Starting a business can require significant upfront costs, and there is no guarantee of success. If a business venture fails, it could jeopardize retirement savings or create financial strain at a time when many retirees rely on fixed incomes.
2. Health and Energy Concerns:
    - Running a business can be physically and mentally demanding. If your health is declining or you want a more relaxed retirement, managing a business might become a burden rather than a source of joy.
3. Market Uncertainty:
    - Business ventures inherently involve risk due to unpredictable market conditions, competition, and other economic factors. A failed business could lead to stress and potential financial losses.
4. Time Commitment:
    - Even small businesses require a time commitment, which could interfere with the freedom retirees desire to travel, spend time with family, or enjoy hobbies.
5. Potential Strain on Relationships:
    - Running a business could take time away from family and social activities, which are often priorities for retirees. It could also add stress that impacts your relationships.

Conclusion:

- Good Idea: If you're passionate about a particular field, have the financial stability to take some risk, and are looking for purpose and income post-retirement, starting a business can be an exciting and fulfilling way to spend your retirement years.

- Bad Idea: If you are primarily seeking a relaxed, stress-free retirement or don't want to put your retirement savings at risk, the pressures of running a business may not be worth it.

The key is to assess your personal goals, health, financial situation, and risk tolerance before making a decision. A well-thought-out plan can make the difference between a rewarding venture and a risky gamble.

Basic principle of starting business after retirement

Starting a business after retirement can be a fulfilling and exciting venture, providing purpose, income, and the opportunity to pursue passions. However, it's important to approach it carefully to ensure success and financial security. Here are some basic principles to consider:

1. Leverage Experience and Skills

- Utilize your strengths: Start a business related to your previous career or a long-time passion. Your experience, network, and skills are valuable assets that can provide a competitive edge.
- Keep it manageable: Choose a business model that doesn't demand excessive physical or mental stress, as retirement is also a time to enjoy life.

2. Start Small and Scale Gradually

- Minimize financial risk: Start small with a low investment to test the market. This reduces financial strain and allows for flexibility if things don't go as planned.
- Learn the ropes: Even if you're experienced in your field, starting a business can have new challenges. Begin modestly and scale

the business as you gain more confidence and understand the market.

3. Choose a Business You Enjoy

- Pursue your passion: Retirement offers the freedom to engage in what you enjoy. This makes running the business more enjoyable and sustainable in the long run.
- Balance work and life: Choose a business that allows for flexibility, so you can still enjoy your retirement years and spend quality time with loved ones.

4. Do Market Research

- Know your customer: Identify a clear target market for your product or service. Conduct research to understand their needs and preferences.
- Analyze competition: Understand the competitive landscape to position your business effectively.

5. Create a Solid Financial Plan

- Set a budget: Be realistic about how much capital you're willing to invest without risking your retirement savings. Use personal savings wisely or consider small business loans if necessary ("Exercise exceptional caution when handling loans; even a small financial misstep can ripple into significant stress during retirement. Always prioritize financial security over risky borrowing, ensuring that every decision keeps your long-term peace of mind intact.").
- Plan for profitability: Ensure your business can generate a profit within a reasonable timeframe, or you may need to rethink your strategy.

6. Seek Professional Advice

- Consult experts: Work with financial planners, accountants, or business consultants to ensure your plan is viable and aligns with your retirement goals.
- Legal structure: Decide on the right legal structure for your business (e.g., sole proprietorship, LLC- Limited Liability Company), which can have tax and liability implications.

7. Stay Adaptable

- Embrace technology: Even if you're not tech-savvy, incorporating modern tools can improve efficiency and help reach more customers.
- Adjust based on feedback: Be open to refining your business model as you receive feedback and adapt to changing market conditions.

8. Ensure Work-Life Balance

- Avoid burnout: While starting a business is exciting, it should not take away from your personal life. Structure your time to enjoy retirement, travel, hobbies, and family.

By keeping these principles in mind, retirees can create businesses that bring joy, fulfillment, and financial stability in their post-retirement life.

14.0 Sincere and thoughtful guidance for retirees

Gentle and noble wisdom

Life is a magnificent gift from the Creator, a journey full of mystery and wonder. It's a path leading to an unknown destination, marked by highs and lows, triumphs and setbacks, joy and sorrow, and countless hidden challenges. The beauty—and the challenge—lies in the fact that none of us truly knows what lies ahead. Not even the most skilled astrologer can unveil the secrets the Creator has woven into the fabric of our lives.

Every twist and turn, every moment of uncertainty, is part of a grand design. Yet, despite the unknowns, one truth remains: it is your mission to move forward with resilience and a positive mindset. This journey isn't a simple, straight road—it's a winding path, taking you through various stages of life, each with its own lessons and experiences.

The key is to embrace the unpredictability, to keep striving, and to trust that every step—no matter how difficult—has its purpose. Life may not always be easy, but it is undeniably profound, offering countless opportunities to grow, learn, and leave your mark on the world.

Life is a journey through distinct phases, each marked by its own milestones and experiences. We have already traversed the earlier stations of this journey—childhood, youth, adulthood, and maturity—and now approach the final phase: retirement. Imagine your life as a train ride, stopping at various stations. Finally, the train reaches its last stop—retirement—where the journey slows, and the steam engine begins to lose its power. The engine, once vibrant and robust, is now exhausted, unable to generate the steam needed to keep pulling the train forward. At this point, the train halts, and it's time for you to step down and walk on your own.

This phase of life is not an end but a profound transition—an opportunity to embrace a deeper purpose. Life, a remarkable gift from the Creator, is to be cherished in every stage. As circumstances evolve, adapt with grace, learning to navigate new paths while finding joy in the journey. Surround yourself with positivity, nurture healthy relationships, and spread happiness to those around you. Be content with what you have, yet strive for more if you believe it's within your reach—always staying within the bounds of integrity and harmony.

Though your physical strength may wane, take pride in the pinnacle of your wisdom and the richness of your experiences—priceless treasures that no passage of time can diminish. Use them to inspire, guide, and leave a meaningful impact. This is your moment to reflect, contribute, and embrace life with unwavering positivity.

Remember, you are approaching the culmination of your earthly journey, where your Creator, the Sustainer of all, will eventually call you back. While your physical form may return to dust, your deeds, love, and legacy will live on, shaping the lives of others and echoing in eternity.

Life is a precious, one-time gift from the Creator—an unchanging truth of our existence with no second chances. It's a fleeting journey: vibrant and fulfilling when you embrace its joys, yet tinged with regret or despair if you dwell too long on past failures or successes. But remember, the past is a closed chapter. The only way forward is to move ahead with purpose and hope.

Cherish every moment. Live with happiness in your heart, positivity in your mind, and meaning in your actions. Life's final chapters, as Shakespeare eloquently captured in his 'Seven Ages of Man,' may find you stepping into the role of the aged—'sans teeth, sans eyes, sans taste, sans everything.' Like a child once more, you might become reliant on others.

Even in this vulnerable stage, there is beauty to be found. It is a time to reflect on a life well-lived, to find peace in simple joys, and to prepare for the ultimate journey—returning to the loving embrace of your Creator. So, make your days count, for every moment is a step closer to the eternal.

This life is but a fleeting moment in the grand design of the universe. Make it count. Be alive, be content, and leave a legacy of love, wisdom, and fulfillment as you approach the final destination of this extraordinary journey.

Here are **detailed tips** under the theme of **Sincere and Thoughtful Guidance for Retirees & elderly**:

1. Embrace a New Purpose

- **Stay Active Mentally and Physically:** Retirement often feels like the end of a productive phase, but it can be the beginning of self-discovery. Engage in activities that stimulate the mind, like learning a new skill or language, and adopt a daily exercise routine to maintain physical health.
- **Set New Goals:** Define what you want to achieve post-retirement. This could range from writing a book - like I am doing, to traveling, mentoring, or pursuing hobbies.
- **Stay Active**, Stay Alive: Life is too precious to spend in idleness. Keep your body moving, your mind sharp, and your spirit energized with purposeful activity. Whether it's pursuing hobbies, engaging in meaningful conversations, or simply taking a walk in nature, every moment of activity adds value to your life. However, when it's time to relax, do it wholeheartedly—allow yourself to unwind completely. True relaxation isn't laziness; it's a gift that rejuvenates your mind, body, and soul, preparing you to embrace life's next challenge with renewed energy and focus.

2. Financial Planning and Stability

- **Reassess Your Finances:** Review your financial portfolio to ensure it aligns with your current and future needs. Consult a financial planner if needed.
- **Live Within Your Means:** Retirement brings a new rhythm to life—and often, a fixed income. This makes it essential to spend wisely and prioritize what truly matters. Start by drawing a clear line between necessities and desires. Necessities are the

essentials—food, shelter, healthcare—that sustain your well-being. Needs, on the other hand, are the extras that add comfort or pleasure but may not always be affordable. If your financial resources are limited, embrace simplicity by focusing on necessities alone. Living within your means isn't a compromise; it's a mindful choice that ensures financial stability and peace of mind in this rewarding phase of life.

- **Invest Wisely:** If investing, opt for low-risk options **-** i.e MF, Fixed Deposits (FDs),Government Bonds, Post Office Saving Schemes, Debt/equity Mutual Funds, Public Provident Fund (PPF), Certificate of Deposits (CDs), Low-Risk Exchange-Traded Funds (ETFs), Islamic Shariah-Compliant Investments- For Muslim Retirees, (Which includes - **Sukuk Bonds:** Islamic equivalent of bonds, offering returns compliant with Islamic law & **Halal Real Estate Investments:** Investments in rental properties that comply with Shariah guidelines.

3. Health is Wealth

- **Prioritize Preventive Healthcare:** Regular check-ups and a healthy diet are vital to avoiding potential health issues. Adopt habits like **meditation**, **yoga** and Five times prayer-**Salah** (for Muslim Retirees), prayers for christians & Judaism to improve mental and physical health.
- **Stay Informed:** Learn about common health issues for retirees, such as arthritis, diabetes, or heart conditions, and take proactive measures.
- **Adequate Rest and Sleep:** Ensure a proper sleep routine, as quality sleep rejuvenates both body and mind.

4. Build,Maintain and enrich Relationships with spouse

A spouse is more than just a partner; it is a divine connection, often believed to be forged in the heavens—a bond predestined by fate. This sacred relationship represents a social and emotional union between a man and a woman, sealed by an agreement rooted in mutual respect, trust, and shared values. Whether it begins as a love marriage, love after marriage, an arranged union, or a chance encounter that blossoms into a lifelong commitment, the essence remains the same: two individuals choosing to walk the path of life together.

This bond transcends societal norms, embracing cultures and traditions universally. It is a partnership not just of living together but of growing together, supporting each other through life's joys and challenges. Spouses are companions in every sense, balancing each other's strengths and weaknesses, celebrating achievements, and weathering hardships.

Ultimately, the beauty of this relationship lies in its versatility—love that may precede, follow, or evolve over time. It is the cornerstone of family, the essence of companionship, and a testament to the strength of human connection.

The true essence of companionship reaches its most profound and beautiful bloom in the twilight years of life. At this stage, it transforms into a bond enriched with tender romance, enduring love, and unwavering care. It becomes a relationship where each partner is not just a support system but a mirror reflecting shared memories, mutual understanding, and the resilience built over a lifetime.

In these later years, when physical strength may wane and the world slows down, the companionship of a spouse often becomes the most reliable source of comfort and strength. For many, there is no better option for navigating this stage of life than leaning on the love and presence of their partner. Together, they find joy in simple moments, courage in shared struggles, and purpose in being there for each other. This unique interdependence, born out of decades of togetherness, is a testament to the enduring beauty of their bond—a love story that grows deeper and more meaningful with time.

Maintaining a strong relationship with your spouse during retirement requires intentional effort, mutual understanding, and a shared sense of purpose. Here are thoughtful tips to nurture your bond in this new phase of life -

- **Rediscover Each Other:** Retirement offers a chance to reconnect, Spend time learning about your spouse's current interests, goals, and dreams.
- **Strengthen Family Bonds:** Spend quality time with family, especially grandchildren, as these relationships bring joy and a sense of purpose. Make it a cherished tradition to share at least one meal together with your children and grandchildren each day, if residing under the same roof. This simple act of togetherness fosters deeper bonds, creates joyful memories, and provides an opportunity to share stories, laughter, and love. A family meal isn't just about food; it's a time to connect, nurture relationships, and strengthen the fabric of your family with warmth and unity.
- **Create Shared Rituals:** Start new traditions, like morning walks, having tea together, or enjoying a weekly movie night.
- **Share Your Feelings:** Retirement can bring both joy and challenges. Be open about your emotions and listen to your spouse's concerns without judgment.
- **Avoid Misunderstandings:** Spending more time together often brings minor issues to the surface, which can quickly escalate if not handled thoughtfully. To maintain harmony, approach concerns with calmness, respect, and an open mind. It's natural not to align on every aspect of life, but finding common ground and meeting halfway can strengthen your bond. A healthy relationship thrives on compromise—it's not about winning an argument but preserving the connection. Remember, life becomes richer when mutual understanding and flexibility are prioritized. By nurturing your relationship with care and smart choices, you can create a foundation of trust and enduring happiness.
- **Explore New Hobbies:** Learn a skill or start a hobby that both of you can enjoy, such as cooking, gardening, or painting.
- **Travel as a Team:** Discover new places together, even if it's just exploring local attractions.
- **Volunteer Together:** Engage in community service or charitable activities, fostering teamwork and a sense of accomplishment.

- **Pursue Individual Interests:** While spending time together is important, allow each other space to follow personal passions.
- **Encourage Growth:** Support each other's endeavors, whether it's learning a new skill or pursuing a long-held dream.
- **Surprise Each Other:** Small gestures, like leaving a heartfelt note or planning a special dinner, can reignite the spark.
- **Go on Dates:** Retirement doesn't mean the end of romance. Plan outings, whether simple or extravagant, to keep the relationship exciting.
- **Pray Together:** For Muslim couples, performing Salah side by side or reading the Quran together can strengthen not only their spiritual bond but also their emotional connection, creating a shared journey toward inner peace and faith. Couples of other faiths can embrace the power of shared meditation, finding harmony in their collective energy. Meditating together amplifies the experience, fostering deeper mental clarity, emotional intimacy, and physical relaxation. These shared spiritual practices nurture both the soul and the relationship, creating a profound sense of unity and fulfillment.
- **Reflect on Shared Values:** Discuss and reinforce the principles that have guided your relationship over the years.
- **Encourage Healthy Habits:** Exercise together, prepare nutritious meals, and remind each other of medical check-ups.
- **Be a Caregiver and Partner:** Offer emotional and practical support if health challenges arise.
- **Collaborate on Budgeting:** Plan finances together to ensure mutual understanding of income, expenses, and savings.
- **Discuss Future Plans:** Talk about travel, gifts for grandchildren, or any big decisions that may impact both of you.
- **Relive Memories:** Take a walk down memory lane together—flip through old photos, read cherished letters, or watch videos that capture the journey of your life. Let nostalgia bring laughter and joy as you talk about your first meeting or that unforgettable date when you were just two innocent, young lovers, brimming with excitement and dreams. Share stories of how your love grew,

reaching the heights of passion and affection, like scaling the peaks of a majestic mountain together.

Revisit those magical early days of romance, when the world felt like it revolved around your love for each other, and every moment was filled with wonder and delight. Laugh at the silly things you did in the name of love and bask in the warmth of those beautiful memories. This is your treasure chest of moments—open it often, for it holds the essence of your bond, reminding you of the love that continues to thrive.

➢ **Celebrate Milestones:** Celebrate milestones with love and gratitude—be it anniversaries, achievements, or other cherished moments. These occasions are not just a reflection of your journey but a beautiful opportunity to bring the family together. Invite your children and grandchildren to join in the joy, turning these celebrations into treasured family memories.

Share stories from your past, laugh over fond recollections, and let the younger generations see the beauty of a life well-lived. Their presence will not only amplify the happiness but also create a sense of continuity and belonging that binds everyone closer. Every special occasion becomes richer when shared with those you love, making it a joyous tapestry of togetherness and gratitude.

➢ **Attend Counseling:** If challenges arise, don't hesitate to seek advice from a counselor or trusted advisor.
➢ **Join Support Groups:** Engaging with others in similar situations can offer new perspectives and solutions.

5. Find Joy in Giving Back

- **Volunteer Work:** Engage in community service or charitable activities. This helps you remain connected and gives a sense of accomplishment.

- **Teach and Share Knowledge:** Conducting workshops or writing articles allows you to share your expertise in areas like engineering, management, or poetry, creating meaningful connections with your past, present, and future. Imagine inspiring a new generation of engineers by unraveling the intricacies of power systems or guiding budding managers on leadership principles rooted in real-world experience.

  For poetry, your words can transcend time, weaving stories that reflect the wisdom of the past, the challenges of the present, and the hopes for the future. Workshops could bring like-minded individuals together, sparking creativity and fostering a sense of community, while articles serve as timeless beacons of knowledge and inspiration for readers across the globe.

  By combining your professional insights with your artistic soul, you create a bridge that not only shares knowledge but also leaves an enduring legacy.

6. Emotional and Spiritual Well-being

- **Stay Positive:** Retirement may come with challenges, but adopting a positive outlook helps navigate them with grace.
- **Seek Spiritual Growth:** Deepen your spiritual practices, whether through prayer, meditation, or reading religious authentic texts, as these can provide peace and direction.
- **Express Gratitude:** Maintain a journal to note down things you're thankful for. Gratitude can transform your perspective on life.

7. Cultivate New Interests

- **Explore Hobbies:** Now is the time to revive old passions or discover new ones, whether it's cooking, gardening, painting, or storytelling.
- **Travel:** Explore places you've always wanted to visit, keeping in mind your health and budget.

- **Join Groups:** Participate in clubs or societies focused on your interests, such as book clubs, art workshops, or nature walks.

8. Learn and Grow

- **Keep Educating Yourself:** Attend seminars, online courses, or community education programs to stay updated and engaged. As someone enriched with decades of wisdom, you may find yourself less acquainted with the marvels of new technology—be it the intricate realm of computer science or the awe-inspiring discoveries about space and galaxies that deepen our understanding of the Creator of the universe. Embrace these advancements as opportunities to broaden your horizons, modernize your thinking, and transform the way you perceive and engage with the world.

  Remember, life is an endless journey of learning, and every day is an invitation to upgrade your knowledge and perspective. By staying curious and open to new ideas, you not only bridge the gap between tradition and innovation but also enrich your soul with the wonder of discovery. After all, a true seeker never ceases to learn and evolve.

  Discover the boundless potential of digital tools and platforms to transform how you communicate, learn, and find joy in creativity. Imagine embracing digital painting—an art form that demands no costly supplies or messy setups, just a simple tablet. With a swipe of your finger or a stylus, you can craft breathtaking landscapes, capture the beauty of nature, and express your innermost imagination.

  Dive into the world of digital technology to unlock new dimensions of learning and entertainment, where the only limit is your curiosity. Let these tools become your gateway to skills and passions that bring fulfillment and connect you with a vibrant, creative community.

9. Prepare for Aging Gracefully

- **Plan for End-of-Life Matters:** Have your legal documents in order, such as wills and healthcare directives. It's a responsible step for your peace of mind and your loved ones.
- **Discuss with Family:** Communicate your preferences about future care openly with your family members.

10. Enjoy the Present Moment

- **Live Mindfully:** Embrace the beauty of the present moment, letting go of worries about the past or anxieties about the future. Practicing meditation and offering heartfelt prayers can help nurture this mindset of gratitude and presence.Take a moment to reflect on the grace of the Creator, who crafted us with care and guided us through life's unpredictable seas—sometimes navigating stormy oceans, other times wading through murky waters—until we finally anchored in a haven of safety and peace.This moment, right now, is a treasure. It brings the serenity of being surrounded by your spouse, the joy of your children's love, and the unparalleled delight of your grandchildren, whose presence you may have once only dreamed of. These blessings are gifts, a divine boon from the Mighty Creator, who has showered us with favor and mercy. Pause to thank Him, not just for the past and the future, but for the miracle of this very moment.
- **Celebrate Small Joys:** Take pleasure in daily routines, like having tea in the garden, reading a favorite book, or playing with your grandchildren.
- **Soft Music & Ghazals** (a deeply emotional theme, fits beautifully into the contemplative and melancholic tone of an Urdu **ghazal**. It often reflects feelings of missed opportunities, unfulfilled desires, or the bittersweet pain of the past)**:** Immerse yourself in the soothing embrace of soft music or the enchanting melodies of Urdu Ghazals if you belong to subcontinents—a timeless form of poetry that originated from Arabic traditions, blending deep

emotion with artistic expression. Set the mood in your bedroom, where the gentle rhythms and poetic verses can calm your mind and rejuvenate your soul.

Ghazals, with their soulful words and tender tunes, have a way of touching the heart, evoking love, longing, and reflection. Allow their beauty to transport you to a place of serenity and introspection, where worries fade, and peace takes over. This simple yet profound ritual can be your haven of tranquility, a gift of poetry and music to yourself.

11. Build a Routine

- Develop a daily schedule that balances activities, hobbies, family time, and relaxation. A routine gives structure and purpose to your day while avoiding the feeling of aimlessness.

12. Downsize Wisely

- Downsize Wisely: Embrace simplicity to better manage financial challenges. Consider moving to a smaller, more manageable home that aligns with your needs and reduces expenses. Let go of possessions that no longer serve a purpose, keeping only those that hold sentimental or practical value.
- Downsizing doesn't mean sacrificing comfort or joy; it's about prioritizing what truly matters and creating a more sustainable lifestyle. Think of it as a fresh start—less clutter, fewer financial burdens, and more room to focus on experiences that bring you happiness. Make thoughtful choices, and see this as an opportunity to turn challenges into a pathway to freedom and peace of mind.

13. Explore Your Spiritual Side

- Spend time reflecting on life's purpose and deepening your connection with your faith or personal beliefs. Meditation, prayer, or attending community religious events can be enriching.

14. Stay Connected Digitally

- Learn to use technology to stay in touch with loved ones and access resources. Video calls, social media, and messaging apps can help you remain connected, especially with distant family members.

15. Pursue Lifelong Learning

- Sign up for online courses, attend workshops, or join local classes to continue growing intellectually. Subjects like history, art, or technology could spark a new passion.

16. Maintain a Healthy Diet

- Fuel Your Body Right: Focus on balanced, nutritious meals to support your health and vitality. Think of your body as a finely tuned diesel engine—it thrives only when its fuel tank is filled with pure, high-quality input. Just as a diesel engine demands clean, unadulterated fuel for optimal performance, your body requires wholesome, natural foods free from harmful additives or chemicals. When the wrong 'fuel' is introduced, the effects are evident in sluggishness, fatigue, or even illness.

  Make healthy eating a delightful part of your life by learning new recipes or joining a cooking class. Imagine the joy of creating delicious, nutritious meals while connecting with others who share your enthusiasm. Turn your kitchen into a space of discovery and creativity, where each meal becomes an act of care for your body—a testament to living well and staying vibrant. Here are some essential and practical tips for maintaining a well-balanced diet, especially tailored to support your health and vitality in your golden years.

  - ➢ Fruits, Vegetables, Whole grain, Lean proteins, and healthy fats

- ➢ Stay hydrated- Plenty of luke warm water, Cucumber, Watermelon & soup
- ➢ Minimize processed & packaged food and artificially additives to enhance the test
- ➢ Cut back sugar & salt to flavor your meals
- ➢ Eat in moderation - Avoid overeating
- ➢ Include Omega-3 fatty acids (Salmon, Walnuts, or flaxseeds, and cold compressed oil of Olive, or Avocado)
- ➢ Consume plenty of fibre (beans, lentils, oats) to support digestion
- ➢ Calcium & Vitamin-D (milk, cheese, yogurt, spinach, orange juice, salmon, nuts & seeds, white beans, chickpeas, lentils, figs, tuna, mushrooms, fortified dairy products etc)
- ➢ Replace chips and sugary snacks with nuts, seeds, yogurt, or fresh fruits.
- ➢ Choose snacks that are as close to their natural state as possible.
- ➢ Eat slowly and stop when you feel satisfied—not overly full.
- ➢ Notice how different foods affect your energy and digestion, and adjust accordingly..

Note: "Food is not just sustenance; it's your ally in living a vibrant and healthy life. By making mindful choices and enjoying what you eat, you'll not only nourish your body but also fuel your happiness and longevity."

17. Plan for Social Engagements

- Make it a priority to nurture your social connections—regularly meet with friends, join local groups, or participate in community events that bring joy and a sense of belonging. Social interaction is a cornerstone of emotional well-being, keeping your spirits high and your mind engaged.

- Stay connected with old friends, even if they live far away. A heartfelt phone call can rekindle cherished memories, while planning occasional meetups adds a spark to life. Consider gathering with friends at an affordable restaurant for a cozy lunch or dinner, or opt for a serene natural spot where you can relax, laugh, and reminisce with your spouses by your side.
- These moments of togetherness not only strengthen bonds but also bring a renewed zest for life, reminding you that companionship is one of life's greatest treasures.

18. Create a Legacy

- Write a memoir. Document your family's journey. Create keepsakes your grandchildren will cherish long after you're gone. These are more than just words on paper — they are gifts of love, windows into your soul, and bridges that connect generations.
- By sharing your stories, values, and life lessons, you don't just preserve memories — you leave behind a legacy.
- That's exactly what inspired me to write my book, ***"Conversations with My Great Grandchildren: Wisdom Across Generations."***
  It's a heartfelt dialogue between curious young minds and a loving great-grandfather — filled with innocent, thought-provoking questions and answers grounded in experience, compassion, and wisdom.
- May it inspire you to begin your own journey of storytelling — because somewhere down the line, a grandchild will be grateful you did.

19. Be Flexible with Plans

- Life in retirement can be unpredictable. Stay open to adapting your plans and embracing new opportunities, even if they are outside your comfort zone.

20. Adopt a Pet

- If circumstances allow, consider welcoming a pet into your life—a dog, cat, bird, or any animal that resonates with you and is safe for your health. Pets are more than just companions; they bring warmth, reduce stress, encourage physical activity, and offer unwavering loyalty, often becoming an integral part of the family. As George Eliot aptly said, "Animals are such agreeable friends. They ask no questions; they pass no criticisms.

  To illustrate the depth of a pet's loyalty, let me share the timeless story of Hachiko, a dog from Japan whose devotion to his master became legendary. Every day, Hachiko accompanied his owner to Shibuya Station and returned in the evening to welcome him home. Tragically, one day his master passed away unexpectedly in his office & did not return back home, but Hachiko continued to wait for him at the station every single day for nearly 10 years until his own death.

  This heartwarming tale of Hachiko is a testament to the profound connection and loyalty pets can offer. Bringing a pet into your life could mean not just gaining a companion but also experiencing the joy of a bond that is pure, selfless, and deeply enriching.

- Another story I want to share is about my beloved pet parrot, Mango. This tale unfolds during my final years in Saudi Arabia, five years before my retirement and eventual return to India. Mango, a vibrant yellow and red parrot, wasn't much of a talker, but his actions spoke volumes. He was incredibly friendly, forming a unique bond with me that left an indelible mark on my heart.

  Mango quickly became a part of my daily life. Every meal I had at home, he would join me, observing intently from his cage. It was as if he was trying to learn my ways, and understand my habits. In the early mornings, as I woke up to offer my prayers, Mango would wake too, imitating my movements and capturing my routine in his curious way. After my prayers, as I prepared breakfast, he would eagerly participate, sharing the moment in his silent yet expressive manner. His actions were not just endearing; they were deeply moving and inspiring.

Mango's attachment to me was evident in his behavior. Whenever I left home, he would become visibly sad, and upon my return, his exuberant actions would unmistakably convey his happiness. His joy was contagious, filling the house with warmth and love.

But then came the difficult day—I had to prepare for my departure. Retirement loomed, and I had to sell my household belongings and leave the home I had known for years. The realization that I couldn't take Mango with me was heart-wrenching. He was more than a pet; he was family.

One day, as buyers came to remove the furniture and items from my house, Mango's demeanor changed drastically. He couldn't understand what was happening, and his distress was palpable. From within his cage, he grew aggressive, squawking loudly and flapping his wings with desperation. He was trying, in his way, to stop the dismantling of our home. Despite my efforts to calm him, Mango became inconsolable, breaking feathers and exhausting himself. His rapid breathing and erratic movements spoke of his confusion and anguish.

When the house was finally emptied, save for Mango and me, I sat on the bare floor, watching him. He, too, seemed to be watching me, his eyes filled with sorrow. I tried to cheer him up by offering snacks, as I often did, hoping he would join me for breakfast. But this time, he refused, his sadness overpowering his usual enthusiasm. It felt as though he longed to escape the cage, not to fly away but to embrace me, to cry with me in shared grief.

As I prepared to leave my rented home, I took Mango and his cage with me to my daughter's house in the same city. Once there, I placed his cage in the sitting room and tried to make him comfortable with fresh water and food. But Mango was dejected. He wouldn't eat or drink, his spirit seemingly crushed. For the first time, I felt helpless, unable to console my little friend.

It was only the next day that Mango began to nibble at his food and sip water. Slowly, he adjusted to his new surroundings, growing fond of my grandchildren and finding joy in their company. With time, he started to forget the painful upheaval and found happiness again.

When the time came for me to return to India, I stood before Mango to say a sorrowful goodbye. He seemed to understand the gravity of the moment, watching me with those soulful eyes, as I, too, gazed back at him. It was a moment of profound sadness, a goodbye that words couldn't convey.

Four years later, I revisited Saudi Arabia and stayed with my daughter. Mango was still there. At first, he wasn't as responsive to me, as if he had forgotten our bond. But as the days passed, his memories seemed to return. He began to mimic his old habits, joining me during meals and expressing his love in the unique way only he could.

Mango's story is a testament to the love and affection a pet can bring into one's life. Their companionship can brighten even the twilight years, filling them with moments of joy, connection, and purpose. For me, Mango was not just a pet; he was a friend, a confidant, and a cherished part of my life's journey.

21. Manage Stress Proactively

- Learn techniques like deep breathing, yoga, or tai chi or Salah (for Muslims) to handle stress and stay calm during challenging situations.

22. Take Safety Precautions at Home

- Make your living space more senior-friendly by adding grab bars, ensuring good lighting, and eliminating tripping hazards (a condition that could cause someone to lose their balance & fall).

23. Prepare for Emergencies

- Keep a list of emergency contacts, medical records, and financial documents in an easily accessible place.

24. Celebrate Small Wins

- Acknowledge and celebrate small accomplishments, whether it's completing a book, fixing something at home, or mastering a new skill.

25. Explore Nature

- Immerse yourself in the wonders of nature—it could be tending to your garden, taking a peaceful hike through a forest trail, or bask in the breathtaking beauty of a sunrise, where vibrant clouds paint the sky, and the night's darkness gracefully retreats, surrendering to the gentle embrace of daylight.. Relish the sound of raindrops as you watch from the comfort of your living room or bedroom window, or marvel at the delicate dance of snowflakes falling outside while a cool breeze whispers through your home. Each of these moments connects you to the natural world, offering a sense of calm and renewal. Nature, with its serene beauty and rhythmic cycles, is a powerful healer for both the mind and body, inviting you to pause, breathe, and rejuvenate your spirit.
- Witness the enchanting charm of the sunset as the sky transforms into a mesmerizing canvas of pink, orange, and crimson hues. Darkness gently embraces the fading daylight, while a cool breeze caresses your ears, carrying whispers of soothing melodies that bring peace to your heart and calmness to your soul. Look above, where the sky is alive with the vibrant flight of birds, gracefully

returning to their nests—a symbol of serenity and harmony, Vibrant butterflies flutter gracefully, their delicate wings painting the air with hues of enchantment as they dance joyfully in harmonious groups. Around them, fireflies weave a magical tapestry of twinkling light, their golden glow adding a celestial charm that transforms the scene into a breathtaking wonderland of beauty and serenity. The entire atmosphere seems to pause, exuding a tranquil energy that wraps you in its embrace. As the last traces of daylight give way to the quiet of the night, the world slips into a serene rhythm, inviting you to do the same. It's a gentle call to retreat, to rest, and to let the tranquility of the evening guide you into a night of relaxation and sweet dreams

- Take a gentle stroll through your garden and immerse yourself in the serene embrace of nature. Observe the vibrant blooms swaying gracefully, as if performing a joyous dance and singing in harmony to welcome your presence. Each colorful petal radiates beauty and whispers peace to your soul, offering a symphony of tranquility. Feel your worries melt away as the soothing sights and scents uplift your mind and spirit, washing away the stress and strain of a restless night. Nature, with its boundless charm, is a silent healer—a balm for the ailments of the soul and body, offering what no medicine can truly replicate. Let this moment of connection refresh you, bringing balance and serenity to your day.

26. Avoid Negative Influences

- Protect your well-being by steering clear of toxic relationships and unhealthy habits that can harm your body or mind. Avoid alcohol, drugs, smoking, and tobacco in any form, and resist the temptation of excessive daytime sleep that can disrupt your energy flow. Prioritize staying hydrated and make it a routine to monitor your health through regular checkups for blood pressure and sugar levels. Above all, distance yourself from activities or influences that drain your energy or disturb your inner peace. Embrace habits and relationships that nurture your body, mind, and soul, allowing you to live a more vibrant and harmonious life.

- Stay vigilant and protect yourself from harmful social media groups that spread negativity, misinformation, or divisive content. These platforms can influence individuals and society in destructive ways, eroding trust and harmony. Choose to engage with uplifting, truthful, and constructive content that fosters positivity and unity, both online and in the real world.

27. Leave a Positive Impact

- Make a difference by helping others, sharing wisdom, or supporting causes close to your heart. Retirement is an opportunity to create a meaningful legacy.

28. Shield from invisible threats

- **Shield yourself of pollution in all its forms**—be it the harsh effects of weather, harmful solar radiation, relentless noise, or the toxic grip of unhealthy air filled with solid particles and dangerous emissions like CO, CO_2, SOx, and NOx. and other chemical fumes. Prioritize your well-being by staying vigilant and taking proactive steps to guard against these silent intruders that jeopardize your health and quality of life.
- **Stay safe during spring if you're allergic to pollen**! Spring is a season of renewal and vibrant beauty, marked by blooming flowers, budding trees, and warmer days. Nature awakens as animals emerge, birds sing melodious tunes, and landscapes transform into colorful tapestries. It's a time of growth, fresh beginnings, and a gentle reminder of life's enduring cycle.

  As nature bursts into bloom, the air may carry allergens that trigger discomfort. Protect yourself by keeping windows closed during peak pollen hours, wearing sunglasses & mask outdoors, and rinsing off after returning home. Equip yourself with medications or remedies recommended by your doctor, and stay one step ahead of allergies to fully enjoy the season's beauty without worry

- **Technology Misinformation:** Believing false information about health remedies or online scams can lead to harmful choices, such as ineffective treatments or financial losses. Staying informed through credible sources and exercising caution online is essential to avoid these pitfalls.
- **Environmental Risks:** Indoor pollutants such as mold, dust, room refresher sprays, and poor air circulation can significantly impact respiratory health. Prolonged exposure may lead to allergies, asthma, or other respiratory conditions, often going unnoticed until symptoms worsen. Ensuring proper ventilation and regular cleaning is essential for a healthier living environment.
- **Chronic Stress:** Financial concerns, adapting to a new lifestyle, or caring for others can silently build stress, which contributes to hypertension, diabetes, and other health problems.

29. Embrace the beauty of prayers from diverse faiths, honoring each belief system to foster peace of mind, nurture the soul, and discover profound inner harmony and fulfillment.

The Gift of Salah for Muslims: Five daily prayers, performed with proper ablution and in the correct manner, are not just acts of worship—they are the ultimate exercise for the soul and body. For Muslims, Salah offers a profound connection with the Creator, a moment of peace amidst life's chaos, and a way to maintain spiritual and physical discipline. The movements of prayer—standing, bowing, prostrating, and sitting—are a complete workout, promoting flexibility, circulation, and mindfulness. With every prostration, feel the burden of stress lift, and with every recitation, let your heart find tranquility. Truly, Salah is the best regimen for a balanced life.

Prayers from Christianity: The Lord,s Prayer, Hail Mary (Catholic Tradition), Serenity Prayer, Psalm

Prayers from Judaism: Shema Yisrael, Amidah,, Kaddish, Modeh Ani (Morning prayer)

Meditation among Hinduism, Buddhism, Jainism & Sikhism: Meditation across these traditions nurtures mental clarity, emotional balance, and spiritual fulfillment. Regular practice helps individuals rise above worldly distractions and align with their higher purpose.

30. Travel wisely and with care — especially in your golden years. Whenever possible, travel with your spouse or a trusted companion. Shared journeys aren't just safer — they're also more joyful.

Avoid venturing out alone, particularly to unfamiliar places. And try to steer clear of peak hours, when crowds, traffic, and stress levels are at their highest. A little planning goes a long way in making your outings smoother, safer, and more enjoyable.

15.0 A Writer's Journey: Behind the Making of This Book

Writing this book was not an easy task. **The journey of writing this book was both meaningful and demanding.** In fact, it became one of the most emotionally challenging and mentally demanding experiences of my retired life. It wasn't just about putting words on paper — it was about pouring decades of thoughts, observations, hopes, and life lessons into a form that others could understand, relate to, and hopefully benefit from.

There were moments when self-doubt crept in like a quiet shadow. I often asked myself: *Will anyone take the time to read this — especially in today's TikTok age, where people seek instant laughs and even quicker forgetfulness?* I wondered if my words were reaching the heart... *Am I expressing myself clearly? Am I being too personal? Too practical? Or perhaps too philosophical for the times we live in?*

These questions circled my mind endlessly, especially during those long, silent hours — when the house was still, and I sat staring at a blank screen, waiting for my thoughts to breathe life into words. It felt like standing at the edge of a deep well, lowering my bucket slowly, unsure whether I'd draw up clarity... or just more questions.

And yet, I kept writing — because some truths are worth the wait.

I was not a trained writer. I am a retired mechanical engineer who spent nearly four decades working in power generation. But the transition into retirement stirred something new in me — a need to share, to reflect, and to contribute in a different way. I realized that retirement is not the end of the road — it's a beautiful new chapter waiting to be written, lived, and shared.

This book was born out of that realization — and from countless cups of tea, late-night revisions, and the patient support of my family, especially my grandchildren, whose innocent questions and bright smiles gave me hope and inspiration.

There were technical challenges too — and they were no less daunting than any engineering task I'd faced in my career. Formatting, editing, navigating writing software — all of it felt like stepping into a new world. After spending decades with torque wrenches and slugging tools in my hands, fine-tuning the control of voltage and frequency in complex electrical systems, or managing gas turbines running under high vibration and high temperature spread stress — this was unfamiliar terrain. I was used to safeguarding machines, ensuring their reliability and availability under extreme conditions, not wrestling with page layouts and grammar tools.

Yet, with every step forward, I discovered a quiet joy in the process. Each learning curve reminded me of something I had almost forgotten — the thrill of being a student again. I was curious, hopeful, and above all, fueled by a renewed sense of purpose.

If you're holding this book now, I thank you from the depths of my heart. It means that my journey -with all its struggles and stories-has found its way into your hands. And if my reflections and experiences help even one person embrace retirement with more peace, clarity, and enthusiasm, then every challenge I faced in writing this book will have been more than worth it.

Warmly,
M.N. Ashraf

16.0 Final Reflections from the Author

As I close this book, I do so not with a full stop, but with a heartfelt pause.

Retirement is not the fading of life's light—it is the golden hour when we finally slow down to enjoy what truly matters: our faith, our family, our health, our time, and above all, the joy of giving back.

In these precious years, we are gifted with a new role—not just as retirees, but as mentors, storytellers, grandparents, and torchbearers of values. Our wisdom becomes a guide, our silence a comfort, our presence a gift.

To my fellow retirees: *you may no longer wear a uniform or clock into an office, but you now wear something far more meaningful—the legacy of your life. Wear it with pride, live it with grace.*

To our beloved grandchildren and younger generations: *remember, the retired ones around you are not simply resting—they are* ***rooted****. In their company lie the answers to many of life's questions. Sit with them, listen, laugh, learn, and carry forward their light.*

And to the readers of this book, I say with love and sincerity:

> **The sun has set on your working years, but a new sunrise awaits—filled with purpose, peace, and the power to inspire those who come after you.**

May your retirement be not an ending, but a beautiful beginning.

With humble gratitude,
M.N. Ashraf

www.ingramcontent.com/pod-product-compliance
Lightning Source LLC
Chambersburg PA
CBHW041301210926
51847CB00010B/101
* 9 7 8 9 3 3 4 3 9 2 7 2 2 *